LAW AND PRACTICE OF INTERNATIONAL FINANCE

TITLE FINANCE, DERIVATIVES, SECURITISATIONS, SET-OFF AND NETTING

AUSTRALIA
The Law Book Company
Brisbane * Sydney * Melbourne * Perth

CANADA
Carswell
Ottawa * Toronto * Calgary * Montreal * Vancouver

AGENTS:
Steimatzky's Agency Ltd., Tel Aviv;
N.M. Tripathi (Private) Ltd., Bombay;
Eastern Law House (Private) Ltd., Calcutta;
M.P.P. House, Bangalore;
Universal Book Traders, Delhi;
Aditya Books, Delhi;
MacMillan Shuppan KK, Tokyo;
Pakistan Law House, Karachi, Lahore.

TITLE FINANCE, DERIVATIVES, SECURITISATIONS,
SET-OFF AND NETTING

QUICK REFERENCE GUIDE

LAW AND PRACTICE OF INTERNATIONAL FINANCE

TITLE FINANCE, DERIVATIVES, SECURITISATIONS, SET-OFF AND NETTING

By

Philip R Wood

BA (Cape Town), MA (Oxon)

Solicitor of the Supreme Court

Visiting Professor, Queen Mary
& Westfield College,
University of London

LONDON
SWEET & MAXWELL
1995

Published in 1995 by
Sweet and Maxwell Limited of
South Quay Plaza, 183 Marsh Wall,
London E14 9FT
Computerset by Interactive Sciences, Gloucester
Printed in Great Britain by
Butler & Tanner, Frome and London

No natural forests were destroyed to make this product:
only farmed timber was used and re-planted

**A CIP catalogue record for this book is
available from the British Library**

ISBN 0 421 54270 5

To my wife Marie-elisabeth, my twin sons
John Barnaby and Richard,
my daughter Sophie and my son Timothy

PREFACE

This book is one in a series of six works on international financial law which, taken together, are the successor to my *Law and Practice of International Finance* which was published in 1980 and which was reprinted eight times.

The works now cover a much broader range of subjects, with substantial additions in the fields of comparative law, insolvency, security, set-off, netting payments, and title finance, as well as specialist subjects like securitisations and swaps and derivatives. But the works have the same objectives as the original book. However great a gap there may be between the aim and the actuality, the objectives I have sought to achieve are to be practical as well as academic, to provide both a theoretical guide and legal source-book as well as a practitioner's manual, to be international, to provide serious comparative law information, to get to the point as quickly as possible, to simplify the difficulties, to find the principles underlying the particularity, to inform, and, most of all, to be useful.

The six works are separate but they are nevertheless related. Together the books are intended to form a complete library for the international banking and financial lawyer, as well as for specialists in related areas such as insolvency, leasing, and ship and aircraft finance. The topics covered by each volume are summarised on the inside of the front cover.

These books offer what I hope is a fundamentally new approach to comparative law in this area and, for the first time perhaps, provide the essential keys to an understanding of the world's jurisdictions, the keys to unlock the dark cupboard of financial law so that the light may shine in. These keys are not merely functional; they are also ethical and they are driven by history. The ideas are really quite simple, once discovered, but this should not obscure the difficulty of their application to the variety of circumstances. The core of the first book, entitled *Comparative Financial Law*, is a classification and snap-shot of virtually all the jurisdictions in the world – more than 300 of them – according to various financial law criteria. These criteria are developed in succeeding books in the series and applied to particular transactions. I believe that this also is the first time that a classification of this type has been done in this detail; but it has to be done because comparative law is no longer an academic luxury: it is a practical necessity if we are to have an orderly international legal regime.

My hope is that my voyage of discovery into what is really going on in world financial law will help to mitigate international legal surprises and legal risks and, in the wider context, that jurisdictions will be better equipped to make essential choices as to what their legal systems should achieve. This is particularly important in view of the fact that at least 30 per cent of the world's population live under legal systems which are still emerging and that the remainder live in jurisdictions divided into camps which often do not agree on basic policies. There is no reason why we should not agree on the basic policies: we do not have to have a muddle. The law is our servant, not our master. It must set us free, not tie us down. It must satisfy our sense of justice.

This book contains a discussion of a miscellany of topics – title finance, securitisations, set-off, netting and derivatives – which are mainly applied law. Much more international research needs to be done on the comparative reception of title finance and I have therefore confined myself to stating what the main aspects are as a framework. The approach to derivatives is similar. The chapter on securitisations is largely practical. I hope that the shorter treatment of these topics will be useful in providing a bird's eye view and will alert the practitioner to the points which require legal investigation. Set-off and netting are crucial topics in international finance and therefore merit an extended treatment.

The books also contain lists of about 250 research topics in total which might be appropriate for further research and which I hope will be useful to prospective writers.

I am acutely conscious of the fact that, in writing about legal systems other than my own (which is England), I will often have committed some real howlers and I hope that my foreign colleagues will be tolerant of my ignorance. Obviously one must always confirm the position with competent local lawyers.

As regards style, I have endeavoured to be as economical as possible in these works. The citation is selective: there are now millions of cases and it is hopeless to try and list even a proportion of them. I am easily terrorised by footnotes and therefore, if material is good enough to go in the footnotes, it is good enough to go in the text: as a result there are no footnotes in these works. At least one does not have to read the text in two places at once. Tables of cases and statutes seemed less sensible in a work endeavouring to cover hundreds of jurisdictions where there is an avalanche of names and numbers and dates and acts and statutes and decrees, and, in view of this, I decided to omit them.

I have endeavoured to reflect the law round about the middle of 1994 based on the international materials then available to me, although some subsequent changes were introduced in the course of publication.

Philip R Wood
One New Change
London

Request for Information

Works on the law in the jurisdictions of the world must rely heavily on information from private sources. With a view to improving the information in any subsequent editions there may be, I would be very pleased to receive papers of all kinds on subjects covered by this and other works in this series — seminar papers, essays, articles, client briefings by law firms, memoranda, notices of book publications, and the like. Material should be sent to me at the following address:

Philip R Wood
Allen & Overy
One New Change
London EC4M 9QQ

Fax: 0171 330 9999

ACKNOWLEDGEMENTS

I owe to many a debt of gratitude in the help they gave me in preparing this work.

I am grateful to many partners and colleagues at Allen & Overy and to secondees from foreign firms for their advice and assistance. Sections in chapter 11 on netting legislation in various countries were based on materials provided by Marc Taeymans (Belgium), Pierre Gissinger of Gide Loyrette Nouel (France), Dr Uwe Jahn (Germany) and Edward H Murray (United States). Paul Bedford read and corrected the chapters on securitisation. Julia Salt and Alex Pease advised me on the financial leasing of aircraft. Parts of the chapters on swaps and derivatives are based on drafts prepared by my partner Edward H Murray. I owe a particular debt to the authors of the works listed in the bibliography and of a very large number of articles and books not listed in this book or in the bibliography without which it would not have been possible to write this book: if I have used their words, as I believe I often have, this is because they said it much better than I ever could. There are many others – practitioners, students, academics, bankers and others – who have contributed to this work in one way or another: it would be impossible for me to thank them all individually.

None of the above is of course responsible for the defects in this work.

I am most grateful to my secretary Sue Wisbey and to the Allen & Overy word processing department and checkers who laboured so magnificently to produce this work.

I am thankful to my publishers for their hard work and patience in bringing this work, and the other books in this series, to fruition and also for their support through all the years.

My brother John, my sister Melanie and my mother all encouraged me and were tolerant of my efforts.

My late father Leslie Wood, who was also a lawyer, first inculcated in me a fascination for the law while I was a boy in Northern Rhodesia, now Zambia.

Finally, I owe an enormous debt to my wife and children and can only express my affection for them by the token of dedicating this book to them.

CONTENTS

PART II: SECURITISATIONS

PART III: SET-OFF AND NETTING

PART IV: SWAPS AND DERIVATIVES

ABBREVIATIONS

ABGB	Austrian General Civil Code
Art	Article
BA	Bankruptcy Act
BC	Bankruptcy Code
BGB	German Civil Code
BL	Bankruptcy Law
c	chapter (of laws)
CC	Civil Code
CCP	Code of Civil Procedure
CO	Code of Obligations
ComC	Commercial Code
Conflicts Restatement	Restatement of the Law, Conflict of Laws 2d, by the American Law Institute
Dicey	Lawrence Collins (general editor), *Dicey and Morris on the Conflict of Laws* (12th ed 1993) Sweet & Maxwell
EISO	Philip Wood, *English and International Set-off* (1989) Sweet & Maxwell
IA	Insolvency Act
ICSID	International Centre for the Settlement of Investment Disputes
IR	Insolvency Rules (England)
Mann, Money	FA Mann, *The Legal Aspect of Money* (5th ed 1992) Clarendon Press, Oxford
Ord	Order
PILA	Private International Law Act 1987 (Switzerland)
Restatement	Restatement of the Law by the American Law Institute
RSC	Rules of the Supreme Court (England)
s	section
Sched	Schedule
UCC	Uniform Commercial Code (United States)
ZPO	Code of Civil Procedure (*Zivilprozessordnung*)
Zweigert/Kötz	K Zweigert and H Kötz, *An Introduction to Comparative Law* (2nd ed 1987)

PART I

TITLE FINANCE

CHAPTER 1

TITLE FINANCE: GENERAL PRINCIPLES

Introduction

Generally

These chapters briefly review transactions which are (mainly) in the form of a sale or a lease but in substance are a financial transaction which could equally well have been framed as a mortgage. Most of them are of great commercial importance and large amounts of capital may be ventured on the faith of their validity. The chief question is whether a jurisdiction upholds the transaction, in which event the vendor or lessor is a super-priority creditor, on insolvency in the same class (or even better) than a secured creditor or will recharacterise these transactions as in substance mortgages for the purposes of insolvency laws, notably the prohibition on non-possessory mortgages or mortgages without registration so as to observe the false wealth objection. Aside from that question, the transactions primarily involve the ordinary law of sale and leasing and it is not proposed to add to the already abundant literature on those topics. Hence these chapters aim at no more than framework and concept.

The growth of these transactions, their immense importance in international finance and their popularity raises the question of the desirability of recharacterisation. Their frequent objective is to avoid rules which are inimical to the freedom of transactions, particularly mortgage laws, many of which (some would allege) are seriously out of date. Hence the attempts by courts in some countries to uphold the form rather than the substance is to be regarded not as a curious blindness to commercial realities, but rather a covert means of avoiding obsolete laws which are out of touch with the needs of modern societies. Conversely, those jurisdictions which do recharacterise take the view that the mortgage laws are justifiable, and therefore that it should not be possible to escape them by the form of transaction. The dispute therefore is not about whether a title finance transaction is logically a mortgage, but rather about whether the restrictions of mortgage laws are appropriate to finance outside the consumer context.

1–1

Main forms of title finance

1–2   The main transactions are:

Vendor-security

1.   Retention of title to goods (conditional sales)

2.   Factoring and discounting of receivables and forfaiting

3.   Sale and repurchase (all assets)

Lessor-security

4.   Finance leasing

5.   Hire purchase

6.   Sale and leaseback

   The transactions are variously described as "vendor/lessor security" or as "asset-based finance" or as "title financing". The term "title financing" will be used here since in each case the financier has title to or ownership of the asset as opposed to a mortgage of the asset.

   Set-off has the commercial effect of security and is reviewed in subsequent chapters.

One may now briefly summarise these transactions:

Title retention

1–3   This transaction, known as conditional sale in many jurisdictions, involves the sale of an asset to a debtor on terms that the debtor is not to acquire title to the asset until the asset has been paid for. The seller transfers possession immediately. If the buyer becomes insolvent without having paid, the seller retakes possession. In ordinary sale of goods transactions (as opposed to conditional sales of large equipment) forms of retention clauses may include a "current account" clause which extends the retention of title until all indebtedness of the buyer to the seller is paid, including the unpaid price on other supplies, a "resale proceeds" clause which extends the seller's rights to the proceeds of resale by the buyer to his sub-buyer, a "continued retention" clause which seeks to continue the seller's title against sub-purchasers from the buyer, and an "aggregation clause" which extends the seller's title to products in which the goods are incorporated during manufacture. These extensions meet with much reduced success everywhere.

   The object of the transaction is to enable the buyer to acquire the goods on credit so that he pays for them when he re-sells them, but at the same time to give the seller "security" for the unpaid purchase price, thereby protecting the seller against the insolvency of the buyer.

The original seller could instead have transferred the ownership of the goods to the buyer immediately on sale and the buyer could have granted the seller a mortgage on the goods (and their proceeds) to secure the price plus interest. This would have constituted a non-possessory chattel mortgage and a security assignment of the re-sale proceeds, both of which present problems in some jurisdictions.

Factoring and forfaiting

Factoring is a term used to describe a method of receivables financing   **1—4** whereby a company sells its receivables to a finance house for a discounted lump sum or for a periodic commission representing interest. If the seller becomes insolvent, the buyer is the owner of them and is a super-priority creditor. The sale may be with recourse, with limited recourse (e.g. as to the amount or the period within which claims must be made) or without recourse. Recourse means that the seller guarantees that the receivables will be paid. The sale may be with warranties (e.g. as to the legal enforceability of the claim assigned and its freedom from set-offs and other defences) or without warranties (a "quit-claim" assignment). Often the sale is not notified to the debtors and the seller is appointed as the buyer's agent to collect the receivables. The receivables may be represented by negotiable instruments when the transaction is often referred to as forfaiting.

The seller could instead have charged the receivables to the financier in return for a loan. This would have had a similar economic effect to a sale of the receivables to the financier with recourse to the seller if they were not paid.

The transaction is used for (a) short-term trade finance, (b) medium-term secured finance and (c) securitisations: see chapters 4 and 5.

As mentioned, forfaiting is the sale by a seller to a financier of negotiable bills of exchange or promissory notes given to the seller by the buyer of goods to represent the unpaid purchase price. The instrument may bear the "aval" or guarantee of the seller (with recourse) or (more usually) be unavalised. The advantage of negotiable instruments is that everywhere they avoid obstacles to the assignment of ordinary debts. But often the formalities applying to the instruments are restrictive.

Securitisations are an advanced form of factoring and many of the principles discussed in chapters 4 and 5 in relation to securitisations will also apply to factoring.

Sale and repurchase

1–5   The debtor sells the asset to a finance house on terms that the finance house will resell the asset to the debtor after a specified period at a price which reflects the original sale price plus a margin equal to the buyer's rate of interest on the original sale price until resale. Commonly the resale obligation is a call option by the original seller and a put option by the original buyer. If the original seller becomes insolvent, the original buyer can call the original seller's call option, resell as owner and claim any shortfall between the resale price and the option repurchase price as damages from the original seller.

The original buyer is a super-priority creditor as if he were secured. The debtor could equally well have mortgaged the asset to the financier in return for a loan.

Repos are widely used in relation to bullion and securities, instead of charging the bullion or securities to the financier.

Stock lending

1–6   Repos are also used in relation to stock-lending but in adapted form. In swiftly-moving stock markets, sellers of stock may find that they do not have sufficient stock to deliver to their buyers on the settlement day, either because they sold "short" (i.e. sold without having previously bought the stock) or because of delays in delivery by sellers to them because of hold-ups in stock exchange settlement procedures. So the seller "borrows" equivalent stock from somebody else. But this is not a bailment of the stock, because the "borrower" agrees not to return the same stock (he has delivered it to his buyer) but rather to re-deliver equivalent stock or pay the market value of the stock in cash on the redelivery date. To "secure" the lender, the borrower transfers other securities of equivalent value to the lender on terms that the lender must redeliver equivalent stock or cash on the redelivery date. Each transaction is a full transfer of ownership of the relevant stock and the transferee can use the stock transferred to him as he pleases, e.g. by selling it on. If the borrower defaults, the lender sets off the reciprocal obligations to pay cash and is thereby protected (assuming the jurisdiction of the borrower allows insolvency set-off), just as if each party owed the other a bank deposit as a debt.

Alternatively, if each transfer is drafted as a sale and repurchase, then, on default by one, the counterparty cancels both contracts (his obligation to repurchase and his obligation to resell), calculates the loss or gain on each contract compared to prevailing market prices and sets off any loss payable to him against any gain payable by him to the other. To close out in this way, the insolvency laws of the jurisdiction of the defaulter must allow close-out netting, i.e. the right to cancel contracts on insolvency and the right of insolvency set-off. See chapter 10.

The borrower could equally well have borrowed the stock and in return mortgaged other stock to the lender to secure the borrower's obligations to redeliver. But a mortgage of stock may have been registrable, e.g. in England either as a floating charge (if the borrower has rights of substitution) or as a charge on "book debts" (unlikely).

Finance leasing

Instead of purchasing an asset on deferred credit terms and then mortgaging   1–7
it back to the seller in order to secure the credit instalments, the seller leases the equipment to a buyer on terms that the title to the equipment remains with the seller but the buyer is to have the possession of the equipment under a lease whereby hire is calculated to include the capital cost and the finance charge. Alternatively and more commonly the seller could sell the equipment to a finance house and thereby receive immediate payment of the purchase price and the finance house would then lease the equipment to the buyer. In each case the primary term of the lease is sufficient to allow recovery of the capital plus an amount equal to interest (often over the useful life of the asset) and thereafter the lessee may retain possession at a nominal rent. On the insolvency of the lessee, the lessor is required by the terms of the lease to sell the equipment and account to the lessee for any excess of the sale proceeds over the accelerated rental payments due to the lessor. This is treated as a rebate of rental so that effectively the lessee receives the excess residual value as he would in the case of a mortgage. Again, the lessor is a super-priority creditor as if he had security over the equipment and could foreclose and keep it or its proceeds as owner.

These financial leases are to be distinguished from "operating" or "true" leases. In a finance lease, the lessee has substantially all the risks and rewards of ownership. As to risks, he takes the asset "as is" without warranties as to condition or fitness from the financier, he must maintain the asset, insure it and must continue to pay the lessor the full rentals, even if the asset is lost or damaged or requisitioned, subject to a right to terminate on payment of all the unrecovered capital, usually out of insurance or requisition proceeds payable to the lessee. As to rewards, he has full possession and use of the asset over its useful life and, if it is sold on his default, he receives any surplus by way of a rebate of rentals. In an operating lease, the main risks and rewards remain with the lessor. Typically he warrants the condition and fitness of the asset, and he maintains and insures it. If the asset is lost, rentals cease and the lessor is paid the insurance under his policies. As to rewards, the lease is not normally for the full useful life of the asset so that the lessor gets it back after the short term of the lease and can re-lease it. Plainly, there can be many gradations between finance and operating leases according to how the lease distributes risks and rewards.

A variation originally developed in the United States in order to finance rolling stock and other items of expensive equipment was the equipment trust. The equipment is purchased by a trustee who is financed by the sale of equipment trust certificates issued to a syndicate of banks or other financial institutions. The trustee then leases the equipment to the buyer and holds the benefit of the lease and the equipment itself on trust for the holders of the equipment trust certificates.

Finance leasing is used primarily to finance large chattels, such as aircraft, and also land, buildings and industrial plant. The motive is usually to secure tax advantages: see para 1–22.

Hire purchase

1–8   A lease may be coupled with an option which entitles the buyer to purchase the asset at the end of the lease period for a nominal sum or earlier upon payment of the unpaid instalments. In that way the hirer acquires the residual value of the equipment as if he were a mortgagee redeeming the security on payment of the secured debt. This is the classic hire purchase agreement.

Sale and leaseback

1–9   The debtor sells an asset to a finance house which leases it back to the debtor for a period equivalent to the useful life of the asset. The lease instalments comprise amounts equal to principal and interest. If the lessee becomes insolvent, the lessor forfeits the lease with the same consequences as a finance lease described above. The debtor could have instead mortgaged the asset to the financier in return for a loan. Sale and leasebacks are commonly used in relation to land, buildings and industrial plant, and to large chattels, like aircraft or rolling stock.

Objectives of title finance

1–10   The main objectives sought to be achieved by these transactions vary but may include those set out below. Many of the transactions exploit the distinction between absolute ownership and a mortgage, and seek to escape the inconveniences of mortgage law.

Capital-raising

The usual main objective of these transactions is to raise capital or credit which is effectively "secured" on assets. Because it is commercially "secured", the finance may be cheaper. In some cases, the transaction may be the only way of obtaining credit. The transaction may also give access to non-bank sources of finance, e.g. from equipment lessors or discount houses, and thereby enable the debtor to diversify his sources of funding, so that he is less reliant on bank borrowings. The objective of the title financier is to be secured.

Objections to non-possessory chattel mortgages

In many jurisdictions non-possessory chattel mortgages are impossible or **1—11** impracticable unless the mortgagee takes actual or constructive possession of the goods. This is unrealistic where the borrower wishes to use the goods for the purposes of his operations. The conferring of possession without title avoids the difficulty if the jurisdiction does not recharacterise the transaction as security. See chapter 2.

In England the hire-purchase technique was developed, mainly for consumer finance, as a direct result of nineteenth century bills of sale legislation inhibiting chattel mortgages by individuals.

No registration

The transaction may not be publicly registrable as a security interest. Thus **1—12** in England none of the above transactions would be registrable if properly structured (except for certain retention of title clauses) unless it were struck out as a sham and converted into a secured loan. But some states require registration of certain of the transactions, i.e. for this purpose they recharacterise the transaction as security. Registration would be inconvenient in relation to small transactions (retention of title, consumer conditional sales or hire purchase), or short-term transactions (retention of title, forfaiting, stock-lending, securities repos – often overnight) or swiftly-moving transactions (stock-lending, repos of bullion or securities). Registration and public filing of security interests are reviewed elsewhere in this series of works.

Enforcement remedies

It is often easier for the owner of leased assets to retake possession if he is **1—13** the owner than if he were a mortgagee. In the case of a mortgage, he may, for example, have to go through tiresome and expensive public auction procedures which would be necessary in the case of a mortgage. He may be subject to delays where an insolvency administrator has a right to sell security. American equipment trusts were developed partly in response to enforcement problems in respect of chattels, notably railway rolling stock.

Negative pledges

1–14   The transaction may enable a negative pledge to be avoided. This is a contractual clause found in many unsecured credit agreements whereby the borrower is prohibited from creating security. However these clauses may expressly extend to transactions "which have the effect of security". Hence unsecured loan creditors have their remedy in appropriate drafting if they wish to protect themselves against loss of priority as a result of these transactions. Anti-disposal clauses may prohibit some title financings where an existing asset of the debtor is financed, e.g. a repo or sale and leaseback since these involve a disposal by the debtor.

Residual value

1–15   A hirer or buyer under a conditional sale agreement or a finance lease has no claim to a surplus on resale if there is a default unless otherwise provided (which it commonly is). In leasing transactions, it is usually provided that the lessee is entitled to any surplus on sale by the lessor as a rebate of rentals, usually after deduction by the lessor of a percentage commission. In hire purchase, the lessee gets the residual value by exercising his option to purchase. In retention of title clauses extending to the proceeds of resale by the buyer, the seller is entitled only to a proportion of the sub-sale proceeds equal to the original sale price plus interest. In factoring transactions, the seller may have a right of repurchase, but often the factor keeps any residual value if he takes the risk of non-payment of the receivables he has bought. Alternatively the factor may repay surpluses by way of rebate of the original purchase price. In repos, the original seller has a right of repurchase; if he defaults, the contract may credit him with any gains on a sale of the asset to third parties by his counterparty.

But in the case of a mortgage, the lender has to hand back any surplus on the sale, after applying the proceeds of realisations to the secured debt. Success fees, large premiums and the like may be suspect.

Priority against floating charges

1–16   In those jurisdictions where floating charges are traditionally required by banks (e.g. mainly English-based states), retention of title or the vesting of title in the finance house can in effect confer "security" upon the finance house without the finance house running the risk of being postponed to the prior floating charge. Because the title to the asset is not vested in the company creating the floating charge, the floating charge does not grip on to it. The holder of the floating charge has a remedy in that he can protect himself by prohibitions on title financings in his floating charge and rely on compliance by the chargor company. In practice, extra protection in favour of the floating charge holder is conferred by the fact that the vendor/lessor is likely to check the terms of the floating charge in the case of a large-scale transaction in order to protect himself, e.g. against liability for the tort of inducing a breach of contract by the debtor.

Schemes whereby a company sells goods to a financier on terms that the company will retain possession and sell them as agent for the financier and account for the sale proceeds which belong to the financier are very common in England and, if properly structured, are upheld as true sales escaping the floating charge, as in *Welsh Development Agency v Export Finance Co Ltd* [1992] BCC 270, CA. For example, a motor manufacturer may sell vehicles to a financier which sells them subject to retention of title terms to a motor dealer who takes possession and on-sells to customers as agent for the financiers.

In the case of the Germanic fiduciary transfer in Germany, the Netherlands, Switzerland, Japan, South Korea and Luxembourg, the retention of title supplier usually ranks ahead of the fiduciary transferee because the debtor cannot transfer what he does not own. The priority position with regard to retention of title clauses which extend to the proceeds of sub-sale by the buyer is more complex in these countries.

In the United States, under Art 9 of the Uniform Commercial Code, a special priority is given to the "purchase money security interest" which would normally include retention of title and some other forms of title financing. The theory is that the debtor shall be able to finance new assets without losing priority to any existing floating lien over inventory and receivables because the new asset is an addition to the collateral of the existing financier.

Other priorities

Title financing may confer on the financier a better priority against sub- 1–17
sequent purchasers and mortgagees from the debtor.

In the English-based group, the general rule for goods is that a person cannot confer title on a purchaser or mortgagee, of assets which he does not own — *nemo dat quod non habet*. Hence if the owner gives possession to the debtor under a lease of the goods or equipment or on terms that the debtor has an option (not the right) to purchase — as in the case of a conventional hire purchase contract or repo with a cash option – then the debtor has no title which he can pass on and the financier is protected. Thus hire purchase escapes the rule that buyers or sellers in possession can pass good title to good faith purchasers under the Factors Act 1889 s 9 or the Sale of Goods Act 1979 s 25(2) (see *Helby v Matthews* [1895] AC 471), although this has been altered in relation to consumer credit transactions. This just leaves the risk that a "mercantile agent" in possession can pass title to a good faith purchaser or pledgee under the Factors Act 1889 s 2 – debtors will not usually be mercantile agents. Hence leasing is protected but not retention of title. However a sale and lease back may give a purchaser from the seller priority over the lessor because here the original seller is left in possession.

However in many civil code countries, particularly those basing themselves on the French Civil Code, *"possession vaut titre"* and the person in possession of goods can pass title to a good faith purchaser. The result is that in these countries, priority protection is less of a benefit. The financier must rely on fixing plates or decals to the goods recording his ownership, e.g. on an aircraft, in the hope that buyers from the debtor will be put on notice and therefore not be able to get good title.

If the transaction were a registered mortgage, then registration may protect the financier against loss of priority, so that title financing may be less safe than a conventional mortgage from this point of view. In American UCC states, title financings which are intended to create security are subject to the filing requirements of Art 9 of the UCC, e.g. public filing, and so may benefit from the Art 9 priority protection against subsequent purchasers and mortgagees, although there are exceptions to this in the case of goods in the possession of the debtor. English-based corporate registration systems are not primarily priority systems.

Priorities in relation to land depend on the registration system. Priorities in relation to ordinary receivables and securities are complex, but in the case of these assets, as well as land, there is perhaps not a substantial difference in priority protection as between title and mortgage financings – at least in England.

Bankruptcy freezes

1–18   Some rehabilitative insolvency proceedings impose freezes on the enforcement of security in the interests of the rescue, e.g. the UK administration order, the Irish examinership, the US Chapter 11 and the French *redressement judiciaire*. Typically these also extend to repossessions under retention of title clauses, finance leases and the like, either because of specific provisions (as in the case of the UK administration) or because of a wide automatic stay on contract cancellations by reason of the insolvency, as in

France and the United States. All that can be said is that title financing may fare marginally better internationally than security. Rehabilitation proceedings are reviewed in another work (on insolvency) in this series on international financial law.

Other advantages of title security

Other miscellaneous advantages of title over secured finance may include: 1–19

— lesser formalities for sales and leases than mortgages, e.g. notarisation, public deed in Franco-Latin countries, but not relevant in common law countries;

— ability to "secure" foreign currency debt, which may not be possible for mortgages, and an escape from "maximum amount" mortgages;

— improved recognition on bankruptcy internationally since it is possibly true that better recognition is accorded to title financings than, say, non-possessory chattel mortgages which are not permitted in many countries;

— ability to grant "security" to an unapproved financier in those countries which allow certain types of security only to be granted to locally authorised banks;

— ability to access sources of finance from institutions which are not regulated credit institutions and do not require a licence to provide title finance but would for loan finance;

— regulatory power of a debtor to enter into title financing when the grant of security would be prohibited, especially banks and insurance companies;

— no limitations on events of default applicable to security;

— ability to escape legal prohibitions on clauses restricting or postponing a borrower's right to prepay and redeem the security.

Some of these matters are dealt with in a book on the comparative law of security which is one of the works in this series.

Moneylending and usury laws

If the transaction is not treated as a loan, it may avoid local moneylending   1–20 and usury legislation. Some of these transactions are the foundation of Islamic banking where the financing bank wishes to make a "secured" loan, but is prohibited by Shariah law from charging interest.

Borrowing limits

1–21   If the transaction is not treated as a loan, it may escape being counted towards borrowing limits binding on a borrower, e.g. financial limits and ratios in credit agreements. The remedy of the creditors concerned is to bring these transactions within the scope of the definition of borrowing for the purpose of their ratios. Freedom of contract resolves the problem for them.

Taxation

1–22   The transaction may have tax advantages. Under local taxation laws the debtor may be able to deduct lease payments for the purposes of calculating its liability to tax but not interest payments. The finance house which has title to leased equipment may be able to claim capital allowances which allow it to shelter taxable income and pass the benefit on in reducing the rentals and hence the cost of financing. The benefit may be a "double-dip", i.e. the lessor can set capital allowances against his taxable income from the lease in his jurisdiction and the lessee can also claim capital allowances in his jurisdiction so that the tax benefit is doubled.

The transaction may avoid stamp duties or other documentary taxes on mortgages which are not chargeable on sales or leases (but documentary taxes on sale transfers of land, receivables and securities are common).

The transaction may avoid withholding taxes on interest (if the sale price or rentals are not also subject to withholding taxes).

But value added taxes are more likely on sales and leasing than on loans and interest.

In sale transactions, the tax treatment of losses and gains, as compared to mortgage loans, will be relevant.

Accounting treatment

1–23   The transaction may allow a prettier balance sheet, e.g. where local accounting rules do not require capitalisation of financial lease commitments, so that only current rentals are recorded on the balance sheet, not the whole amount of future discounted rentals representing the amount of the finance. This is now less likely internationally.

Commercial disadvantages of title financing

1–24   Where the jurisdiction honours the legal form of the transaction, the treatment may attract commercial disadvantages for the financier when compared to mortgages. These risks tend to show that the legal form is not just a paper-thin veneer or mark: the legal form does result in a different distribution of risks. The risks may be summed up as follows:

— warranty liability for the asset;

— restrictions on default remedies and repossessions;

— frustration of contract;

— owner's liabilities.

Each is discussed below.

Warranty liability

The seller or lessor of an asset may have imposed on him certain implied   1–25
warranties on the sale or lease to which a mortgagee would not be subject.
Examples in the case of English leases of goods are a condition as to title
(*Karflex v Poole* [1933] 2 KB 251), a term that the goods correspond with
their description (*Astley Industrial Trust Ltd v Grimley* [1963] 2 All ER 33),
and a term that the goods are fit for the purpose. The Supply of Goods
(Implied Terms) Act 1973 (hire purchase agreements) and Supply of Goods
and Services Act 1982 (contracts for the hire of goods) introduced (or codified) implied terms as to quality, fitness for purpose and correspondence
with description. These can only be excluded where permitted under the
Unfair Contract Terms Act 1977, usually, in the case of business users, if the
exclusion is reasonable (except for death or personal injury). An exclusion
in a business finance lease ought generally to be reasonable on the tests set
out in the Act, e.g. the bargaining position of the parties and whether the
goods were manufactured to the special order of the customer. Sale of goods
laws generally contain warranties as to title, merchantibility and fitness for
purpose.

While common practice in finance leases is to reduce the responsibilities
of the lessor to the minimum, there may be statutory restrictions, inspired
by consumerism and spilling over into business transactions, which limit the
exclusion of these implied terms. It may be impossible to exclude liability to
third persons who are not party to the exclusion clause. Further if the lessor
fails to comply with one of these implied terms or with the express provisions of the lease itself, the lessee may be able to claim damages for the
breach or, in the case of a serious default, to terminate the lease. The mortgage financier does not generally run these risks where they exist.

Remedies for default

A claim for a loan is simply a claim for a debt which is a liquidated amount.   1–26
The lender can accelerate a term loan. However, generally speaking, a claim

for default under another type of contract, such as a lease or a repurchase contract, is a claim for damages which are unascertained. Damages may be difficult to quantify, may be reduced by the lessor's or vendor's duty to mitigate losses or by foreseeability rules, and may take time and litigation to determine. Fortunately, it seems that most developed countries uphold clauses which endeavour to fix the damages in advance and which are a genuine pre-estimate of the damages likely to be suffered. But sometimes the position is not so clear. See *Campbell Discount Co Ltd v Bridge* [1962] AC 600. It follows that the amount claimable from a debtor, after taking into account the value of the returned asset, may be less than a claimable deficiency after realisation of a mortgaged asset.

In England it seems that a proper terminal payment payable on a voluntary termination by the lessee of a lease is not a penalty: *Associated Distributors Ltd v Hall* [1938] 1 All ER 511. Other terminal payments payable on terminating events which do not constitute a breach of contract, such as the liquidation of the lessee, may also be enforceable and are not penalties: *Granor Finance Ltd v Liquidator of Eastore Ltd* [1974] SLT 296. But in exceptional cases the courts have stopped a forfeiture: *Transag Haulage Ltd v Leyland Daf Finance plc*, January 13, 1994, Knox J (no repossession of hire purchase goods on appointment of receiver over lessee's assets). As to terminal payments on breach of contract by the lessee, the common practice in leases is to fix the liquidated damages as the arrears of rent plus costs of repossession, plus all future rentals (on a discounted basis to account for accelerated receipt) less the value of the repossessed equipment. There are many variations. In *IAC (Leasing) Ltd v Humphrey* (1972) 46 ALJR 106, the High Court of Australia upheld a terminal payment on a contractual default by a lessee which placed the risk on the lessee of a greater depreciation of equipment than had originally been anticipated.

Frustration of contract

1–27   Where a supervening event occurs which renders performance of the contract fundamentally different from that originally contemplated, the contract may terminate automatically under the doctrine of frustration. Typical events in the case of finance loans are requisition, expropriation and total loss. This is less likely to happen in the case of a loan secured by a mortgage on the asset than in the case of a commercial contract such as a lease because a contract merely to pay money is less likely to be frustrated than a commercial contract. Normally contractual provisions attempt to throw the frustration risk on to the debtor, but, although English case law tends not to apply the doctrine of frustration if the parties specifically contemplated the event and provided for it (since the contract is not then radically different from that originally contemplated), there are cases where the courts held that the clause was not wide enough to cover the events concerned. There sometimes is an all-embracing clause which specifically does not absolve the debtor from payment even though he is deprived of the possession or use of the asset. Wide clauses are typical of finance leases. Certain frustrating events giving rise to a total loss are commonly insured against and the proceeds payable to the lessor up to his interest under loss payable clauses.

Owner's liabilities

Where the finance house is the owner of the asset as lessor or seller rather **1–28** than as mortgagee, it may incur the liabilities of an owner, e.g. pollution liability (e.g. under s 1(1) of the British Merchant Shipping (Oil Pollution) Act 1971), other environmental liability and responsibility for death or personal injury to the debtor and third parties. Strict tort liability is common with dangerous equipment such as aircraft. As to product liability, the liability often applies to manufacturers but may be extended to other suppliers such as finance lessors. Thus the EC Directive 85/374 on product liability (implemented in the UK by the Consumer Protection Act 1987) applies strict product liability in certain cases to the producer and also to persons importing products into a member state from outside the European Union in order to supply it to a business user. These liabilities could be onerous and are usually insured against. Indemnities may be sought from the debtor.

Attempts to exclude the owner's liability may be restricted by statute; thus s 2 of the English Unfair Contract Terms Act 1977 provides that in certain cases a contracting party cannot exclude or restrict liability for death or personal injury resulting from his negligence. Exclusion of liability towards third parties may not be possible because they are not bound by the contractual exemption clause. These responsibilities can, depending on the type of asset, substantially increase the credit risk over and above the face amount of the credit.

These liabilities are extremely rare in the case of mortgages: the main exceptions are US environment liability and the potential exposure of mortgagees who take possession on a default, either directly or through a receiver.

CHAPTER 2

TITLE FINANCE: RECHARACTERISATION

Generally

2–1   The principal legal risk with title financings is that they may be recharacterised as a mortgage or other security. If this is so, the effect is that the financing is treated as a loan secured on the asset. Thus retention of title is a
non-possessory chattel mortgage, factoring or forfaiting is a charge on the
receivables or instruments, a repo is a mortgage of the assets (bullion,
securities, goods, land) to secure loans to the seller, a finance lease is a loan
secured on the leased asset, and similarly for hire purchase and sale and
leaseback.

   If the transaction is a mortgage, then it may be void as a prohibited non-
possessory chattel mortgage or for lack of registration (the principal risk); it
may be subject to onerous enforcement remedies; it may conflict with negative pledges; it may lose priority to a prior floating charge or lose the priority benefits of title ownership; the owner loses the right to the residual value;
it may be subject to bankruptcy freezes and the special rules relating to
mortgages where applicable, e.g. formalities, maximum amount, no secured
amount in foreign currency, no unapproved financiers, and limitations on
default clauses; it may conflict with moneylender and usury laws; and it
may violate a contractual borrowing limit. The result would usually be a
disaster for the financier. It may also be treated as a mortgage loan for taxation purposes or be treated as on-balance sheet and lose its accounting
advantages.

   Whether a transaction is characterised as a true sale or true lease or as a
mortgage loan in disguise depends upon the topic, so that the rules differ for
the purposes of:

— false wealth and secret security;

— accounting;

— capital adequacy of regulated institutions;

— tax;

— moneylending and usury laws;

— contractual restrictions, e.g. negative pledges, borrowing limits and anti-disposal clauses;

— other miscellaneous rules.

Recharacterisation: false wealth and secret security

In many countries, security must be published in order to avoid false wealth   **2–2** (the debtor has many possessions but no assets) and secret security which allegedly induces creditors to give false credit. If an asset can be snatched away on insolvency by a mortgagee, then this fact, so the theory goes, ought to be publicised. The publicity is achieved either by the creditor having possession of the asset (e.g. a possessory pledge of goods) or by registration or filing in a public register. It is plain that the title financier's ability to snatch away an asset on the insolvency of the debtor, e.g. to repossess leased equipment, is equivalent to the ability to take mortgaged property to repay the loan.

Publicity also serves another function, i.e. priorities. The argument goes that, if ownership or security interests are secret, the safety and predictability of transactions might be threatened by these hidden interests: purchasers and mortgagees of the asset may be prejudiced and the safety of commerce brought into question.

Whether the protection of commerce and the protection of creditors merits the stupendous weight given to the false wealth doctrine in many legal systems is a question which should be constantly reviewed.

The essence of a mortgage is two-fold. First, the creditor can realise the asset to pay the debt, as can the title financier since the asset belongs to him. Secondly, the debtor is entitled to the return of the asset once the debt is paid. So can the debtor under a title financing when the agreement enables him to recover any residual value, e.g. by a right to repurchase factored receivables, by a right to surplus proceeds on a sale of leased equipment by way of rebate of rental, by an option to purchase for a nominal sum under a hire purchase agreement, and by a right to terminate a repo or sale and leaseback. Hence title finance has the commercial effect of security.

Jurisdictions appear to have three solutions to this.

Form, not substance In the first group, form prevails over substance. The   **2–3** transaction is not set aside notwithstanding that it is similar in commercial effect to a mortgage provided that the form of the transaction is adhered to. The parties must use language appropriate to a sale or lease, and not, for example, refer to rentals as interest (since interest connotes a loan) or to a resale price as capital plus interest. They must also in subsequent dealings use the appropriate terms so that the transaction is not a sham. Whether openly expressed or not, the objective of this approach may be: to recognise that an owner is in a different legal position to a mortgagee, e.g. as regards ownership liabilities such as environmental liabilities; to facilitate credit in a jurisdiction hostile to security, e.g. Austria and Italy; to avoid registration which may be seen as conferring only marginal benefits; and to preserve bona fide transactions which might otherwise be struck down for non-registration or lose priority to a prior floating charge even though the transaction adds a new asset to the chargee's collateral.

This group comprises the English-based jurisdictions, apparently the Germanic and Scandinavian jurisdictions, as well as some Napoleonic jurisdictions, such as Austria and Italy, and Roman jurisdictions, such as Scotland.

In England the following have been upheld as not being mortgages requiring registration if properly structured:

Sale and repurchase: *Yorkshire Ry Wagon Co v Maclure* (1882) 21 Ch D 309, CA

Title retention: *Aluminium Industrie Vaassen BV v Romalpa Aluminium Ltd* [1976] 1 WLR 676, CA. There are numerous cases on the subject, sometimes striking them down, particularly clauses extending title to re-sale proceeds and to assets incorporated into other assets (glue in chipboard).

Factoring and block discounting, even if with recourse: *Olds Discount Co Ltd v John Playfair Ltd* [1938] 3 All ER 275; *Re George Inglefield Ltd* [1933] Ch 1, CA; *Lloyds & Scottish Finance Ltd Prentice* (1977) 121 Sol Jo 847, affirmed HL, *The Times*, March 29, 1979. Forfaiting by the purchase of negotiable bills is not a loan secured by a pledge on the bills: see, e.g. *Transport & Gnl Credit Corpn Ltd v Morgan* [1939] Ch 531.

Hire purchase: *Stoneleigh Finance Ltd v Phillips* [1965] 2 QB 537 and numerous other cases. But the transaction will be struck down as a sham if the parties implement the transaction as a secured loan, rather than as title financing in accordance with the documents, e.g. *Polsky v S&A Services* [1951] 1 All ER 1062, CA; *N Central Wagon Finance Co Ltd v Brailsford* [1962] 1 All ER 502.

2–4   **Substance not form: publicity required** In the second group, substance prevails over form but the transaction is allowed if it is publicised so as to deal with the false wealth and priority objections. American UCC states are in this group. Thus the UCC applies its perfection rules, e.g. filing, to all transactions intended to create security in personal property and fixtures, e.g.

reservation of title to goods, finance leases and hire purchase. The UCC also applies to the sale of certain receivables even if not intended to create a security interest. The problem with this test is that it is unpredictable, e.g. in relation to transactions which are borderline. An example is a lease of goods which bears some of the characteristics of an operating lease and some of the characteristics of a finance lease. The US case law is massive. The Personal Property Security Acts in some Canadian provinces are to similar effect.

Substance, not form: transaction prohibited In the final group, substance   2–5
prevails over form, but, since there is no adequate public registration system, the title financing cannot be achieved. This is particularly noticeable in relation to retention of title in many jurisdictions in the Franco-Latin group, but more research is required into the atttitude to other title finance transactions.

Recharacterisation: moneylending and usury laws

The purpose of moneylending and usury laws is mainly to protect impecu-   2–6
nious debtors from the allegedly rapacious moneylender or from the debtor's own imprudence or unsophistication. A debtor is as much exposed to loan finance as he is to title finance since in substance they are the same. The modern-day equivalents are consumer credit laws.

The treatment of title financing must depend upon the terms of the statute in question. Thus the British Consumer Credit Act 1974 applies the basic protections to any form of credit transaction with individuals within the financial limit of £15,000, regardless of form.

Recharacterisation: accounting

The purpose of financial statements is to show a true and fair view of the   2–7
financial condition of the company and therefore substance must prevail over form.

There is no reason why the accounting treatment should not be different from the legal treatment and it often is. For example, the consolidated accounts of a group comprising parent and subsidiaries ignore the separate veil of incorporation of the subsidiaries. Accounting is based on a going concern basis, the legal treatment on bankruptcy break-up. The usual accounting test is broadly to examine who has substantially all the risks and rewards of the asset, since these are the main incidents of ownership, regardless of who legally has the title.

In the case of factoring, the seller has the risks if he is liable to pay the buyer for defaulted receivables. He has the rewards if any surpluses are paid back to him or he has the option to repurchase the receivables so that he receives the residual value.

In the case of financial leasing, the lessee has the risk if he takes the asset "as is" without warranties and so is responsible for defects, if the duties to repair and insure are cast on him, if he must continue to pay rentals even if the asset is lost, and if he must pay the operating costs. He has the rewards if he can keep possession of the asset under the lease over substantially its full useful life and if he is entitled to any surplus by way of rebate of rental on a sale by the lessor. An operating lease would typically be short-term, not for the full life of the asset.

Although the test can be unpredictable, e.g. where a lease is mid-way between a finance lease and an operating lease, an incorrect characterisation of a borderline transaction for accounting purposes does not have the same fatal consequences as a recharacterisation for the purposes of security law. The accounts may not give a fair and true view but for the financier recharacterisation as a mortgage generally results in a total loss to him on the insolvency of the debtor because the asset protection is void and the financier is converted into a mere unsecured creditor who commonly receives little or nothing.

If the lease is recharacterised for accounting purposes, then the balance sheet must show the capitalised value of the rentals on one side and the value of the assets on the other. The lessee cannot merely record current rentals as a current liability, as would be the case with an operating lease.

See as to the UK, SSAP 21 and Financial Reporting Standard 5 of the Accounting Standards Board; as to the US, Financial Accounting Standards Board, "Accounting for leases" (FASB 13); and, internationally, International Accounting Standards Committee, "Accounting for leases" (IAS 17).

Recharacterisation: capital adequacy

2–8   Capital adequacy describes the rules imposed by regulators to supervise the solvency of institutions whose failure could seriously damage public confidence or cause great and unacceptable public losses, e.g. banks, insurance companies, and sometimes dealers in securities and investments. The rules typically require institutions to maintain adequate capital against exposures, e.g. against loan losses by banks and insurance pay-outs by insurance companies.

The emphasis of regulation is primarily upon risk of loss rather than rewards and in this they differ from the accounting approach. For example, it is likely to be more important whether or not a seller of receivables is liable to compensate the buyer for irrecoverable receivables – even morally – than on whether the seller keeps the rewards, e.g. by a rebate of sale price out of the surplus or by an option to repurchase.

The position is very detailed and fast-changing. See para 5–16 for an example in relation to securitisations.

Recharacterisation: tax

One of the main tax factors concerns capital allowances for capital expendi- 2–9 ture. Tax law may encourage capital expenditure by allowing the party incurring the expenditure to set the expenditure against its profits liable to tax, either all at once when the expenditure is incurred or in annual stages, with or without limits, so as to reduce the profits liable to tax. Thus if a lessor has taxable profits of 100 and buys an asset for 40 for onward leasing, then a full deduction reduces his taxable profits to 60 and this tax benefit can be passed on to the lessee by way of reduced rentals.

Jurisdictions differ as to whether capital allowances are permitted, as to whether these are claimable by the lessor or the lessee, and the rules for determining the transactions which qualify. The area is much too detailed and volatile for review.

A secondary tax factor is whether the financier, as lessor or vendor, is liable for taxes in his capacity as owner of the asset. A mortgagee is not liable for taxes on the mortgaged asset, but the title financier commonly is, unless altered by statute.

Recharacterisation: contractual restrictions

Whether or not a title financing is caught by a contractual restriction bind- 2–10 ing on the debtor, typically a negative pledge or borrowing limit in the debtor's bank loan agreements, depends entirely on the terms of the restriction. For example, a negative pledge may restrict only "mortgages, charges and other security" (which should not catch title financing) or it may go on to restrict "transactions having a similar effect to security" (which may catch title financings) which are not true sales or true lessees but substantially mortgages in disguise). The remedy of the parties is freedom of contract – to make their intentions clear.

Recharacterisation: miscellaneous

Recharacterisation may be relevant in various miscellaneous contexts. 2–11

One question relates to the question of the ability of the financier to cancel on insolvency. The usual rule is that, where a party becomes insolvent, the counterparty can cancel executory unperformed contracts (even if profitable to the estate) such as sale or foreign exchange contracts, but not divest the estate of a vested asset, such as the right to a deposit. The benefit of land and equipment leases may fall either side of the line, the object being to preserve the assets of the estate for unsecured creditors. Hence the right of repossession is stayed. In England, there is usually no bankruptcy bar to terminating an equipment lease on the insolvency of the lessee, notwithstanding a lower county court decision to the contrary. But there are exceptional cases (see para 1–26) and also special rules for real property leases. Some states specifically prohibit contract cancellation merely by reason of the insolvency, subject to exceptions e.g. Canada, France and the United States. These prevent repossessions specifically on formal rescue proceedings. The comparative law is reviewed in another work (on the principles of insolvency) in this series of works.

Other situations concern the treatment of title finance for stamp duties and tax purposes (e.g. withholding tax), the licensing of credit institutions, and rights of prepayment.

CHAPTER 3

ASPECTS OF FINANCE LEASES

Finance leases have already been briefly described at para 1–7 and other   3–1
aspects have already been alluded to in general terms, notably the lessor's
liability to the lessee for the equipment, the lessor's remedies on a default by
the lessee, exclusion of frustration doctrines which might cause the lease to
collapse and the lessor's liabilities as owner (para 1–24 *et seq*), as well as
recharacterisation: chapter 2. It is left to consider further selected aspects of
financial leasing.

A summary of the terms of a finance lease of an aircraft are set out later in
this chapter to illustrate the equipment lease.

Regulation of leasing businesses

Outside the Consumer Credit Act 1974, the operation of a leasing business   3–2
is not regulated in the United Kingdom and does not require an official authorisation. But if the lessor finances itself by "deposits" other than from an
authorised bank or its parent, it may require authorisation as a bank from
the Bank of England under the Banking Act 1987 and be subject to the
banking regulatory regime. Leasing subsidiaries of UK banks are subject to
the capital adequacy rules applicable to banks.

Manufacturers warranties

An important aspect of financial leasing is the method of conferring the   3–3
benefit of the manufacturers warranties regarding the equipment on the
lessee, e.g. warranties as to the condition and performance of the equipment. If the lessor purchases from the manufacturer, then the lessor will be
entitled to the warranties under the purchase agreement. But the lessor
excludes all liability for the equipment in the finance lease, so that it is the
lessee who needs the warranties. On the other hand, if the lease is prematurely determined, the lessor will need the warranties.

The lessor could assign the benefit of the warranties to the lessee, but the

---

lessee's rights could be no greater as assignee than that of the lessor-assignor. The fear is that the lessor's damages will be reduced by reason of the fact that the lessor suffers no loss: the lessee is liable to pay the rentals regardless of defects in the equipment – although there is an argument that damages should not be reduced merely because the innocent party has contracted for someone else to bear the loss (as in the case of insurance).

Alternatively, the manufacturer could give the warranties direct to both the lessee and to the lessor which the manufacturer may be unwilling to do.

Leveraged leases

3–4   A leveraged lease is a lease where the lessor is partly financed by a bank loan to buy the equipment and the bank takes the credit risk of the lessee. The basic structure is as follows:

- The lessor is a specially formed company which buys the equipment from the manufacturer and leases it to the lessee under a conventional finance lease.
- The banks make a loan to the lessor to finance the purchase of the equipment. This loan is secured by a mortgage on the equipment and an assignment of the finance lease, plus insurances, plus requisition compensation. The banks may agree to limit their recourse to the security.
- If the lessee sub-leases to an operating lessee, the lessee assigns the benefit of the operating lease, either to the banks as collateral security for the loan, or to the lessor as security for lessee's obligations under the head-lease. In the latter case, the head-lessee then assigns the operating lease to the banks by way of security for the loan.
- There may be a chain of leases and conditional sales agreements for tax purposes with an operating lease at the end. Leases may be "defeased", as where the lessee deposits cash with a bank which assumes the responsibility for paying the rentals to the extent of the cash. These defeasances are tax-driven and extremely odd.

Guarantees of financial leases

3–5   Where a lessor leases big-ticket equipment, such as an aircraft or ship, under a financial lease, it is relatively common for the obligations of the lessee to the lessor to be guaranteed by a bank guarantee. Thus, in project finance, part of the capital may be provided by bank loans and another part by a financial lease of heavy equipment or plant and the main lending banks then give a guarantee to the lessor.

The usual structure is that a bank or syndicate of banks gives a guarantee to the lessor of the obligations of the lessee to the lessor under the financial lease. The guarantee is usually of the "first demand bank guarantee" type or a standby letter of credit which is drawable on simple submission of a certificate that the lessee is in default and stating the amount payable, i.e. it is not an accessory guarantee. These guarantees are reviewed elsewhere in this series of works.

The lessee agrees in normal form to indemnify the bank guarantor in case the bank guarantor should be obliged to pay under the guarantee and, as security for its liability to reimburse the bank, assigns its rights under the lease to the bank. The lessee may also give other security, e.g. fixed and floating charges over all its other assets. The main right which the lessee has under the lease, apart from the right to use the equipment, is a right to any surplus of the proceeds of sale if the lessor should, on a default by the lessee, sell the equipment. Most financial leases provide that on such a sale the lessor must, after paying itself any outstanding rentals and the present value of future rentals, pay any surplus to the lessee by way of rebate of rental (less a commission) so that in effect the lessee gets back the surplus value of the equipment, just as he would if he actually owned the equipment and had mortgaged it to the lessor.

The guarantee agreement between the bank guarantor and the lessor will usually contain provisions as to the exercise of this right of sale on default by the lessee and sometimes give the guarantor a right to compel the lessor to exercise his rights on a default.

One possible weakness of this structure is that the bank guarantor takes   3–6
the risk of liens imposed on the equipment (flowing either from unpaid debts of the lessor or the lessee) which would dilute the proceeds of sale. The bank guarantor is also exposed to the bankruptcy of the lessor, in which event the enforcement of the duty to sell and account for proceeds may be somewhat complicated. These risks can be obviated if the lessor grants to the bank guarantor a mortgage over the equipment (which it owns) by way of collateral security, without personal liability, for the liabilities of the lessee to the bank under the reimbursement indemnity. But many financial lessors are not willing to grant security over their assets and furthermore they may argue that they require access to the unencumbered equipment which they own in order to have a fund out of which to recover any liabilities of the lessee which are not covered by the guarantee. For example, lease guarantees commonly cover only the fixed amount of the rentals, plus the stipulated termination sum, and do not cover indemnities given by the lessee to the lessor in respect of taxes imposed on the lessor or other owner liabilities imposed on the lessor, e.g. for pollution or personal injury or death caused by the equipment to third parties. Bank guarantors could not provide unlimited guarantees against these risks, since either by practice or bank regulation, bank guarantees must be limited in amount.

The awkwardness of this structure illustrates one of the differences between title finance and ordinary security. If, instead of a financial lease, the lessee acquired the equipment, borrowed money from the lessor and mortgaged the equipment to the lessor to secure the loan, then the bank guarantee would be a guarantee of the loan and, on payment, the bank guarantor would be subrogated to the lessor's rights against the lessee together with the benefit of the mortgage over the equipment. In the case of a financial lease, the lessor is the owner of the equipment and the lessee has no beneficial ownership to mortgage to the creditor. Further, it seems doubtful that the doctrine of subrogation would permit the bank guarantor, on payment, to take over the lessor's beneficial ownership of the equipment leased, but only to take over the lessor's rights against the lessee under the lease by subrogation. The lessor could of course agree to transfer title to the equipment to the bank guarantor on payment, but the impact of this on the tax treatment of the lease would have to be considered and further the lessor may be unwilling to transfer title so long as it was unsure whether or not its potential liabilities as owner of the equipment and the responsibilities of the lessee under the various indemnities had completely disappeared.

Sub-leasing

3–7   **Sub-lessee's right to possession** Where a lessor consents to a sub-lease of the equipment, it is possible that on a termination of the head-lease for a default by the lessee, the sub-lessee may be entitled to retain the equipment on the basis that the lessor's consent estops the lessor from taking possession. If the lessee were in liquidation, the lessor may be left with a claim as an unsecured creditor of the lessee unable to claim directly the hire payable by the sub-lessee which would therefore fall into the general pool available to all the creditors of the lessee. A method of protection against this eventuality is for the lessor to contract with the sub-lessee that a termination of the head-lease also terminates the sub-lease or to take an assignment of the sub-lease, coupled with an undertaking from the sub-lessee to continue to be bound by the sub-lease notwithstanding the liquidation of the head-lessee. This assignment may be registrable in some jurisdictions or may have to comply with other formalities, e.g. prescribed formal notice to the sub-lessee.

3–8   **Freeze on repossession of the head lease** Where under a rehabilitation statute, the lessor's ability to repossess the equipment is frozen and rights of forfeiture restricted (Canada, England, France, Ireland, New Zealand, the United States in certain circumstances), and the equipment has been sub-leased, the effect may be that the head lessor as owner of the equipment is prevented from terminating the lease and also from suing for unpaid rentals (because of the accompanying freeze on creditor legal proceedings or executions) while the insolvent company under rehabilitation protection can collect the rentals from the sub-lessee. In other words, the debtor profits from the equipment but does not pay for it.

In the case of an English administration order, the courts will in such a situation generally permit the head lessor to terminate unless the protected head-lessee accounts for the sub-rentals: *Re Atlantic Computers Systems plc* [1990] BCC 859. In any event, the head-lessor should take a security assignment of all sub-lease agreements to secure the head-lessee's liabilities, so as to confer a direct right of action against the sub-lessee if the head-lessee does not pay. The enforcement of this security may also of course be frozen; but in England and in the United States the secured creditor enjoys protection against complete expropriation.

Bankruptcy freezes on repossessions and on the enforcement of security are discussed in another work (on insolvency) in this series of works.

Summary terms of finance lease of aircraft

This section summarises the terms of a finance lease of an aircraft and may serve as an illustration of the terms to be found in finance leases of other "big ticket" equipment. A discussion of aircraft finance generally may be found in another work (on the comparative law of security) in this series on international financial law.   3–9

Conditions precedent to grant of lease

Documentation: corporate constitution; authorisations; official consents. Also:

— Purchase agreement between seller and lessor

— Novation or assignment of manufacturer's warranties in purchase agreement in favour of lessee

— Bill of sale transferring aircraft to lessor. This may be subject to UK stamp duty. Check VAT and other local taxes on sales

— Certificate of acceptance of aircraft by lessee

— Acceptance by process agent of lessee under jurisdiction clause

— Evidence that registration fees, taxes and customs duties in relation to aircraft have been paid

- Evidence that no encumbrances on the aircraft
- Evidence that required insurances have been taken out, and provision of brokers' undertakings, assignment notices to insurers, plus report of lessor's insurance advisers
- Copy of maintenance agreement between lessee and approved maintenance company
- Certificate of registration of lessor's title to aircraft and (if lease is registrable) of lease
- Airworthiness certificate
- Air operator's certificate and air transport licence
- Letter from aircraft registry confirming non-deletion of registration without prior notice to lessor
- Evidence that notice of lessor's title affixed to airframe and each engine
- Legal opinions

Other conditions precedent

These include:

- No default or termination event
- No prejudicial change in law
- Representations and warranties true
- Delivery of aircraft to lessor under purchase agreement

Lessee representations and warranties

3–10   Status; powers; authorities; legal validity; non-conflict with laws, contracts, constitution; no default; consents; no litigation; all taxes paid; pari passu ranking; no immunity; no withholding taxes; no stamp duties; accounts and financial information correct; no encumbrances. Warranties to remain true.

Aircraft

3–11   Aircraft includes: airframe; engines which (a) are on aircraft when delivered, (b) replacement engines which become property of the lessor, (c) removed engines which are not replaced, and (d) technical documents relating to the aircraft.

Lease and lease period

Lessor will lease the aircraft to the lessee from delivery for the specified period or earlier termination.

Quiet enjoyment

- Lessor will not disturb quiet enjoyment of the aircraft by the lessee during the lease period.   3–12

- If aircraft arrested by reason of claim against lessor-owned sister aircraft or otherwise, lessee may procure discharge at expense of lessor.

- If other lessor-owned aircraft arrested by reason of claim against lessee, lessee will indemnify owner.

Delivery

- Place of delivery (same as place of delivery by manufacturer to lessor   3–13 under purchase agreement).

- Lessee accepts aircraft from manufacturer as agent of lessor and simultaneously accepts under lease by delivery of acceptance certificate. Lessee must accept once lessor has accepted under purchase agreement.

- Lessor not responsible for delays in delivery under purchase agreement or for total loss prior to delivery.

- Lessee responsible for delivery costs and licences to export from place of delivery.

- If delivery has not taken place by specified date, lessor may cancel lease and lessee will pay unwinding costs.

Exclusion of lessor liability

- Lessee acknowledges that aircraft acquired by lessor at request of lessee   3–14 and that aircraft has been designed and manufactured to lessee's specifications without involvement of lessor. Accordingly:
  - aircraft leased "as is, where is" on delivery date;
  - no warranties or conditions or liability of lessor as to title, airworthiness, condition, merchantability, fitness for operation, or any other matter;

– acceptance by lessee is conclusive proof that aircraft is satisfactory;

– lessor not liable for personal injury, death or loss caused by aircraft;

– lessee will indemnify lessor against liabilities arising from aircraft, e.g. those which cannot be excluded.

Note: Exclusion of liability clauses must be tested against usual doctrines construing them against the lessor, non-exclusion of fundamental breach unless clear, and statutory restrictions on exclusions, e.g. Unfair Contract Terms Act 1977.

Premature termination

Lessee may terminate lease on [   ] months notice expiring not earlier than [   ] years after delivery, if lessee pays termination sum (broadly unpaid capital costs, plus unpaid rentals, plus unwinding costs, plus tax losses).

Rent

3–15 – Lessee will pay agreed rentals on agreed dates. Rentals are generally calculated as capital and other costs of purchase of aircraft plus amounts equal to interest, and adjusted for any tax benefits received by lessor, e.g. capital allowances, based on detailed assumptions.

– Obligation to pay rent is absolute irrespective of:

– non-availability of aircraft, including requisition;

– no title, not airworthy, not operational, encumbrances;

– total loss or damage;

– breach by lessor, however fundamental (except lessor's covenant for quiet enjoyment);

– any force majeure or frustrating event, however fundamental.

– But if aircraft is total loss, rent ceases when lessor receives loss proceeds (e.g. insurance, requisition compensation).

Payment of rent

– Place, currency, immediately available funds, business days

– No set-offs or deductions

- Gross-up for tax deductions. Right of lessee to terminate (as above) if gross-up operates
- Lessee to pay all value added, turnover and other taxes
- Default interest on late payments
- First right of lessor to appropriate partial payments as it sees fit

Corporate covenants

Usual loan agreement covenants by lessee, e.g. financial statements and   **3–16**
other corporate information; no change of business; pari passu ranking;
negative pledge; restriction on substantial disposals; maintenance of status;
no mergers; financial covenants, etc.

Operational covenants

Information Lessee will notify:

- casualties resulting in total loss or amounts in excess of $[   ];
- location, operation and maintenance of aircraft;
- invalidity of airworthiness certificate;
- employment of aircraft, including charters;
- disputes regarding aircraft.

Lessee will deliver logs and technical records.

Inspection Lessee to have reasonable access to inspect aircraft.

Lawful and safe operation Lessee will:

- operate aircraft in accordance with applicable laws and airworthiness certificate and only for commercial operations;
- ensure that crew are properly qualified;
- not locate or operate aircraft where safety of aircraft is imperilled, in area of hostilities, or declared war zone, or in manner which might render aircraft liable to confiscation or seizure;
- not employ aircraft in carrying prohibited or dangerous goods;
- operate aircraft as designed and in accordance with technical require-

ments and manufacturer's and official requirements and recommendations;

— not prejudice manufacturer's warranties;

— not hold out lessor as being liable in respect of aircraft or as principal on aircraft contracts;

— comply with applicable laws and pay all taxes and fees in relation to aircraft and its operation.

Title and registration

3–17   Lessee will:

— maintain and not prejudice title registration, licences and certificates, including airworthiness certificate, and title of lessor;

— not permit encumbrances on the aircraft, except:

  — liens for taxes or "ordinary course of business" aircraft liens if (a) amounts not due or properly contested, (b) no risk of arrest or forfeiture of aircraft, (c) adequate reserves available, and (d) no criminal liability on lessor;
  — encumbrances created by lessor;

— not dispose of aircraft;

— prevent arrests; discharge liens; procure releases; procure waiver of repairer's liens;

— affix prescribed notice plates of lessor's ownership and of lease on aircraft and engines;

— not operate outside prescribed geographic areas, unless lessor satisfied that no prejudice to lessor's title or insurances.

Sub-leasing

3–18   Lessee will not (and will procure that sub-lessee will not) sub-lease or charter or relinquish possession of aircraft except as follows:

— delivery to manufacturer, repairer, etc., for testing, maintenance and modification;

— operating (non-demise) charters to approved charterers (not affiliates of lessee) for use in approved jurisdictions for not more than specified periods (e.g. 12 months) including options under approved charters, on terms that:

- — sub-rentals payable periodically and monthly in advance;
- — lessee remains liable to lessor;
- — sub-lease consistent with lease, e.g. information, inspection, lawful and safe operation, maintenance, geographic operation;
- — no sub-sub-charters or leases;
- — sub-lease subject to rights of lessor, e.g. termination;
- — recognition of owner's rights not likely to be prejudiced, e.g. non-recognition of owner's title in operating jurisdictions;
- — insurances not prejudiced;
- — lessee assigns sub-lease to lessor by way of security for lessee's lease obligations;
- — sub-lessee acknowledges to lessor that sub-lease is subject to lease, e.g. termination, redelivery.

Maintenance

- — Lessee will properly maintain aircraft so as to: 3–19
    - — keep it in good operating condition;
    - — comply with airworthiness certificate;
    - — comply with official, legal and manufacturer's requirements and recommendations.

- — Lessee will deposit funds periodically in maintenance reserve account charged to lender.

- — Lessee will replace unserviceable engines and parts by equal or better items which must become property of the lessor.

- — All removed engines and parts to remain property of owner and to be marked and located in specified stores.

- — Lessee will not make structural modifications except as required or recommended by manufacturer or authority or to satisfy safety.

Temporary replacement and pooling of engines

- — Lessee may replace engines with other equivalent or better engines which   3–20 are subject to an encumbrance in favour of third parties or are owned by third parties if:
    - — no lessor-owned engine available;

—   engine is made available to lessee under a customary pooling
     arrangement and is replaced by or becomes a lessor-owned engine
     within 30 days.

— Lessee may relinquish possession of a lessor-owned engine under a customary pooling arrangement for not more than 30 days if title not transferred.

— Lessee may install lessor-owned engine on another aircraft leased to
   lessee or mortgaged by lessee if other owner or mortgagee renounces any
   interest in the engine and engine is returned in 90 days.

Insurance

3–21 — Lessee will maintain approved insurances in approved form with
         approved insurers in required amounts (on agreed value basis with
         approved deductibles) against required risks and through approved
         brokers as follows:

     —   joint names of lessor and lessee (with lessor right but not obligation
          to pay premiums);
     —   risks: loss or damage to aircraft; third party liability for personal
          injury, death or damage or loss of property; war risks; political risk
          (confiscation, non-export, refusal to deregister, etc.); mortgagee
          interest insurance;
     —   waiver of insurer's and brokers liens and set-off;
     —   waiver of insurer's subrogation to lessor;
     —   no right of contribution from other insurance;
     —   insurers/brokers to notify lessor of cancellations, variations;
     —   loss payable clauses: up to threshold figure payable to lessee until
          insurers notified to contrary when all proceeds payable to lessor;
     —   insurances to be maintained for two years after termination of lease.

     Lessee will:

— not prejudice insurances;

— operate within warranties and geographical limits of insurance;

— pay premiums and calls and produce receipts;

— renew 14 days prior to expiry;

— provide details and duplicate of insurance documents to lessor;

— procure prescribed broker's letters of undertaking to lessor and endorse-
   ment of loss payable clauses on policies;

— all insurance proceeds receivable after termination or total loss are payable to lessor, but subject to this:

- major casualties (over $[   ]) payable to lessor who will pay to lessee or repairer on damage being made good;
- minor casualties payable to lessee to apply in making good;
- third party liability to third party.

Lessee may take out additional insurance if:

– insurance does not conflict with existing insurances;

– details notified to lessor.

Power of lessor to insure on default by lessee.

Total loss

In case of:

– actual, constructive, arranged, agreed or compromised total loss;

– compulsory acquisition for title;

– requisition for use or hire for more than 90 days;

– hi-jacking, theft or disappearance for more than 30 days;

lessee will continue to pay rent until lessor receives termination sum (not later than 60 days after the total loss), less insurance, compensation and abandonment proceeds received by lessor.

Requisition for hire

If aircraft is requisitioned for hire, lessee's obligations continue, but lessee is entitled to requisition hire until end of lease period. Relief for lessee's maintenance and other obligations during requisition period to the extent lessee cannot procure performance, subject to making good thereafter. Comparable provisions for requisition of engines.   **3–22**

Indemnity

Lessee indemnifies lessor against all losses and liabilities (including personal injury) and taxes arising in relation to aircraft, before or after lease period excluding claims (not attributable to fault by lessee) caused by wilful default of lessor.

Termination

Termination events include typical credit agreement defaults, e.g. non-payment, non-compliance, breach of warranty, cross-default, insolvency, creditors processes, illegality, material adverse change. Also revocation of   **3–23** lessor's registration or unacceptable burdens placed on lessor; seizure of air-craft; circumstances in state of registration or incorporation of lessee which may imperil interests of lessor in aircraft.

On termination:

— lessor may terminate lease;

— lessor may repossess aircraft (and enter lessee premises) and lessee will redeliver;

— lessee liable to pay unpaid rentals plus discounted total future rentals (less net sale proceeds received by lessor);

— lessor will sell aircraft, using reasonable endeavours (but without lessor liability on sale agreement);

— lessor will pay to lessee, by way of rebate of rental, any excess of sale proceeds (less a commission) over lessee's liability to lessor.

Redelivery

On termination, lessee will redeliver to lessor at prescribed place and in pre-scribed condition including fuel.

Transferability

3–24   Lessor may:

— transfer title to aircraft;

— assign lessor rights.

Lessee may not assign rights or obligations under lease.

Miscellaneous

Expenses; stamp duties; notices; currency indemnity; waivers; remedies cumulative; governing law; jurisdiction; waiver of immunity.

PART II

SECURITISATIONS

Chapter 4

SECURITISATIONS: GENERAL PRINCIPLES

What is securitisation?

Summary of securitisation

The basic transaction is as follows: an owner of receivables (the originator **4–1** or seller) sells receivables to a third party (the purchaser or special purpose company or SPV). The purchaser borrows money to finance the purchase price and repays the borrowing out of the proceeds of the receivables bought by it. Hence securitisation is essentially a sophisticated form of factoring or discounting of debts. The transaction may be summarised in slightly more detail as follows:

- An originator of (usually) high quality receivables, such as home mortgage loans or consumer credit receivables, sells the receivables to a specially formed company (SPV) in return for a purchase price payable immediately on sale.

- The SPV finances the purchase price of the receivables by borrowing from banks or by a conventional bond or note issue to sophisticated investors ("funding loan"). The SPV grants security to the investors over the receivables to secure the borrowing.

- The SPV authorises the originator as "servicer" to collect the receivables on behalf of the SPV which uses them to pay principal and interest on the funding loan (investing the proceeds in the meantime). The SPV pays a servicing fee to the servicer.

- The SPV is usually a thinly-capitalised single-purpose company whose shares are held by somebody other than the originator, e.g. charitable trustees, so that the SPV is not a subsidiary which must be consolidated on the originator's balance sheet.

- In order to ensure that the receivables are sufficient to repay the investors on time, there may be various forms of "credit enhancement", e.g. a third party may give a guarantee to the SPV or the originator may agree to make a subordinated loan to the SPV.

- The loan by the investors, e.g. loan notes, are often rated by a rating agency. Usually the loan has a higher rating than would be obtainable for a direct loan to the originator.

- The SPV pays surplus income from the receivables, which is not needed to repay the funding loan, to the originator so that the originator takes the profit. The SPV may pay this profit to the originator as servicing fees or other means.

The intended economic effect is that the originator raises money from investors on the security of the receivables and continues to retain any profits from the receivables, but transfers the risk of non-payment of the receivables to the investors and removes the assets and the funding loan from its balance sheet.

Main requirements in summary

4–2   If a securitisation is to be feasible, certain minimum requirements must be satisfied. These are usually:

- **Credit** The receivables must be sufficient to cover the loan made to the purchaser to finance the purchase price. Any shortfalls or mismatches must be covered, e.g. by guarantees or other credit enhancement.

- **Saleability** It must be possible for the seller to transfer the receivables to the buyer without expense or formality or the consent of the debtors.

- **True sale** The sale must be treated as a complete and final transfer of the receivables from the seller to the purchaser so that the receivables are no longer assets of the seller and the financing loan is not a liability of the seller for the purposes of: (a) accounting rules applicable to the seller (off balance-sheet); (b) the authorities regulating the seller (capital adequacy); (c) bankruptcy of the seller (the transaction must not be recharacterised as a mortgage); and (d) tax. The rules determining what is a true sale are different in each case.

- **Other restrictions** It must be possible to set up the transaction without other burdensome restrictions or expenses, e.g. under tax laws or securities regulation.

Typical documents

4–3   The usual documents are as follows:

- **Funding loan documentation** (eurobond documentation, bank loan agreement, commercial paper documentation)

- **A transfer agreement** between the originator and the SPV covering the following: the sale of existing receivables; sale of substitute receivables; representations and warranties as to the receivables (validity, eligibility, no set-offs, status of security, etc.); an obligation on the originator to repurchase for breach of warranty; and a right to repurchase in other circumstances, e.g. the final stump amounts

- **An administration agreement** between the originator and the SPV covering the following: the setting of interest rates; arrears and enforcement procedures; the investment of SPV surplus cash; termination on an administrator default; administration fees; liability for acts or omissions; and insurance against error and employee fraud. There may be provision for a successor administrator

- **Credit enhancement documents** between a credit enhancer and the SPV, e.g. a guarantee, letter of credit, surety bond, pool policy, or subordinated loan agreement

- **Security trust deed** whereby the SPV creates security in favour of the trustee over the SPV's assets to secure the creditors providing the funding loan.

Receivables and other securitised assets

Theoretically, any kind of asset can be securitised. Common examples are: 4–4 home mortgage loans (the most common historically); commercial property mortgages; consumer receivables (car, boat and truck loans, credit card receivables, TV rentals, health care receivables, telephone charges); trade receivables; equipment leases, e.g. aircraft leases (but the sale of tax-based leases may prejudice capital allowances available to the originator-lessor); bank loans (sovereign debt, even project finance loans); and bond portfolios. Single debtor receivables have been securitised.

Some important differentiating features between these various types of receivables which impact on the documentation are: the collectibility of the receivables, e.g. home mortgage loans have better recovery rates than unsecured credit card receivables (this affects the credit-standing of the purchaser); the standardisation of the documentation covering the receivables (it is usually too expensive to study them all); and the life of the receivables. Home mortgage loans often have a nominal life of 10 to 25 years, but an average life of five to seven years because of prepayments. Consumer credit receivables tend to have a life of 30 to 90 days so they need to be constantly topped up by fresh sales to the SPV. The SPV uses the proceeds of repaid receivables to buy new receivables. Trade receivables often have a life of 30 days – but car loans may have maturities of five years perhaps.

Other factors are: (1) simplicity (e.g. home mortgage loans are easier to securitise than, say, complex project finance loans) and (2) the defences available to obligors (e.g. set-offs for defective goods) may weaken trade and consumer debts. Consumer protection laws and guidelines may affect credit card receivables and home loans.

The criteria for eligible mortgage receivables typically relate to the security, the loan to value ratio, minimum loan size, debtor income multiples, seasoning, geographical dispersion, and buildings insurance. There may be an audit of a sample.

Securitisations of other assets are possible, such as office buildings, stands of timber and oil and gas properties. Securitisation of securitisations can be achieved: receivables or bonds sold to several purchasers are resold to a single purchaser and pooled.

Securitisations of receivables from several originators are sometimes set up. Each may be too small for a single securitisation. The advantages include pooled expenses, a single operator, and standard documentation.

Objectives of seller

4–5 The objectives of these transactions fall into three main groups: (1) accounting advantages; (2) capital-raising advantages; and (3) regulatory advantages. The convergence of these three has been a great stimulus to the development of the securitisation market from the early 1980s onwards.

Financial accounting

Securitisation can result in an improved balance sheet for the seller. If accounting rules permit, the seller can raise money without the loan appearing on its balance sheet and still keep the profits from the sold receivables. The cash price is used to pay the seller's liabilities, so the seller has less assets and less liabilities and hence more borrowing room. Its financial ratios are improved, e.g. a debt to equity ratio. Return on capital is improved, because the seller has removed the asset and liability from its balance sheet, but still retains the profit.

> **Example** The seller has receivables of 1000 and borrowings of 800. The seller sells 200 of the receivables and uses the proceeds to repay borrowings so that its assets are now 800 and its borrowings 600. The cover of assets compared to liabilities has increased from 125 per cent to 133 per cent.
>
> The receivables bear interest at 10 per cent and the borrowings at 8 per cent.

Before the sale, the seller has net interest income of 36. After the sale and repayment, the seller has net interest income of 32 but earns fees of another 10 for servicing the sold receivables, so that net income is 42.

Before the sale, net income was 3.6 per cent of assets. After the sale, it is 5.25 per cent of assets – a dramatic improvement in return on assets.

Before the sale, interest income was 1.6 times interest expense. After the sale, interest income is 2.2 times interest expense, hence improving the interest cover ratio.

A securitisation may also accelerate the recognition of income or losses. If the investors receive a lower yield and the originator retains the excess on the receivables, the originator will generally be required to capitalise the expected excess yield as a gain on the sale. A sale of low-yielding assets would result in a loss. If the originator had retained the assets, the income or loss would have been recognised gradually over the life of the assets, instead of all at once.

Capital raising

Securitisation frequently has advantages in relation to capital-raising by the 4–6 seller. First, the seller raises capital immediately, rather than having to wait for the receivables to be repaid. Secondly, securitisations may offer cheaper or longer-term finance compared to finance raised directly by the seller from banks or the bond market: this is often because the receivables are of better quality than the seller's assets generally or because the assets are insulated from the credit of the seller. One possible disadvantage is that the seller might cherry-pick its best assets and thereby reduce its own credit.

Thirdly, the seller has access to wider sources of finance. For example, the seller may not itself have the credit-standing for a eurobond issue, but the SPV could issue bonds secured on the receivables which have a higher rating than the seller. Hence the seller diversifies its sources of funds and is less reliant on bank borrowings. Funding from international investors replaces that of domestic banks. Often securitisations are a reaction to a tightening of bank credit – banks may offer less credit or only offer short-term credit or insist on security or guarantees.

Fourthly, securitisation is effectively secured finance, but avoids negative pledges (assuming the purchaser is outside the group).

Fifthly, the seller can match assets and liabilities. This is safer where the receivables are exactly used to repay the funding loan. There is no mismatch of yields or timing of payment. By reason of the pass-through of payments discussed below, there is less risk of having to repay the funding before the receivables are paid.

Other related advantages are: the funding of short-term receivables with medium-term financing; the avoidance of onerous loan covenants in a direct borrowing (unusual as a sole motive); the investors look to the SPV risk, not that of originator, and hence there is no cross-default clause on the seller; the originator can earn fees from the SPV in servicing the receivables; and finally the seller transfers the risk to investors, e.g. the catastrophe risk. There have been securitisations of defaulted loans, such as sovereign debt, which have been attractive to speculative investors: those have been dubbed "vulture funds".

Regulatory

4-7   The regulatory advantages relate mainly to capital adequacy. In the case of banks and other financial institutions (e.g. building societies), the originator may have to raise extra capital under supervisory rules in order to support the receivables. This is avoided if the assets are sold. The choice facing the originator is either to raise capital or sell the assets. But the originator keeps the profit (hopefully).

Securitisations may also avoid lending limits, i.e. limits on lending to single obligors or lack of diversification.

Purchaser of assets

Special purpose vehicle

4-8   The purchaser is usually a specially-formed single-purpose company whose shares are held by charitable trustees so as to be independent of the seller and not to be a subsidiary of anybody. The usual objective is that the purchaser should not be consolidated on the balance sheet of the seller. In non-trust countries, the shares of the purchaser must be held by third parties willing to come forward.

The SPV is formed as a public company, so as to be able to issue securities non-privately. The minimum capital requirement is an extra cost. Of course the SPV may be formed in a tax haven jurisdiction although this is not available for UK home loans because the tax scheme for home loans (known as MIRAS) requires residential mortgages to be held by a UK lender.

Trusts and sub-participations

Other structures are possible.

Trust Under this structure, the receivables are transferred to a trustee which holds them first for the benefit of the investors and then for the originator. The trustee issues pro rata certificates to investors, or the SPV and the originator hold undivided beneficial shares under the trust. The originator's share is subordinated to that of the investors so that the investors have first bite – the junior share is the excess profit. The use of the trust in the United States was originally inspired by certain idiosyncratic US accounting rules and is somewhat unusual elsewhere.

Sub-participation Under this structure, the seller grants sub-participations in the receivables to investors whereby investors are paid only if and to the extent the receivables are recovered. The seller does not declare a trust or charge them to investors. Sub-participations are most unlikely to be marketable or useful since the investors take a double credit risk and the transaction may not succeed in being off balance sheet or avoiding capital adequacy requirements. The legal technology of sub-participations is reviewed in another work (on international loans and bonds) in this series.

Administration of receivables

Somebody must be in charge of setting interest rates, collecting payments   4–9
and arrears, corresponding with the debtors, and investing receipts.

Usually this task is given to the originator who wishes to preserve its customer relations. Further, consumer protection guidelines may seek to ensure that the administration of the receivables remains with the originator, as opposed to unknown (foreign) investors who, it is feared, might be less sympathetic. Also, the originator usually has the necessary systems and records.

There will frequently be a replacement administrator of last resort if the originator defaults. The documentation should reflect the need for access to or for duplicates of computer records and access to debtor documentation.

Investors in securitised assets

Investors and lenders

Investors or lenders provide the finance to the purchaser of the receivables   4–10
to enable it to pay the purchase price. These funds may come from a variety of sources: a bond or note issue (either a private placement or an issue to sophisticated investors), a bank loan, or a commercial paper issue on a revolving basis. In the case of short-term commercial paper issues, an additional lender (third party bank) provides a committed facility to fund maturing commercial paper in case a refinancing of maturing commercial paper fails to materialise.

An issue of redeemable preference shares by the SPV would be rare. They cannot be secured. But, as mentioned, the issue of trust certificates giving an ownership share in trust assets is typical of US structures. Shares in an open-ended investment company would also be unusual.

Tiering or tranching is possible. Examples are the issue of senior and junior notes, or fast-pay and slow-pay notes, or fixed notes and revolving notes.

Matching of receivables and loan

4–11   Matching so that principal and interest payments on the receivables are sufficient to pay principal and interest on the funding loan is important. Any mismatches must be covered by credit enhancement: see below.

As to **repayment** of the funding loan, the purchaser repays the loan by instalments as and when repayments of receivables are received. A bullet loan would be unusual. Eurobond investors usually require certainty of term, since they do not favour the trouble and expense of receiving and having to re-invest drips and drops. Also, any interest rate swap would be for unpredictable amounts. But in practice the maturity of the receivables is uncertain, e.g. because of prepayments. The purchaser will normally be allowed to apply repayment proceeds from the receivables in purchasing additional receivables from the originator (or in making top-up mortgage loans) but only during a limited period and subject to various conditions (e.g. the effect on the overall risk profile of the portfolio of receivables). Thereafter, repayment proceeds received will be applied to repayment of the funding loan in a corresponding amount on the interest payment date at the end of the period during which they are received. This involves a reinvestment risk up to the payment date because the interest on the repayment proceeds (which will normally be required to be invested in safe investments, often under a guaranteed investment contract) may be less than the rate on the original receivables and on the funding loan. It also means that the investors carry the risk of prepayment – the securities are prepayable and hence are not for a fixed term. Investors attach considerable importance to the average life of the investment, which is calculated on the basis of various assumptions as to, for example, the rate of prepayment of receivables, the level of substitution and the like.

In some cases prepayments have not been returned to the investors as and when received, but have instead been deposited under a guaranteed investment contract (under which a bank guarantees a specified return on all amounts deposited) until the original scheduled maturity of the relevant loan. Investors are thus protected from prepayment risk. Alternatively, the issue may comprise several tranches, one of which is repayable to the extent of prepayments and therefore absorbs the prepayment risk for investors in the other tranches.

In the case of short-term receivables (e.g. credit card receivables), the term is erratic: hence the purchaser uses the proceeds to acquire additional receivables from the originator. But the loan still has an uncertain life because the originator may become insolvent or have insufficient eligible receivables, and hence more back-stop credit enhancement is needed. The topping-up is also riskier for investors, because the identity of the receivables changes.

Credit enhancement is usually needed to cover mismatches. See below.

Generally **prepayment** of bonds is allowed only in limited cases, e.g.   **4–12** because of the imposition of a withholding tax, or if 90 per cent of the funding loan is repaid or after a specified period. Bond investors require certainty of term.

As to **interest**, the interest payable on the receivables must be more than   **4–13** the interest on the funding loan. One question is whether, under the terms of the receivables, the SPV can be substituted as the interest-fixer and whether the SPV as assignee can increase the interest rate on the receivables. The originator will however normally be authorised by the purchaser to set the interest rate on the receivables, but, except where there is an interest rate swap in place, on the basis that it may not set it below a threshold rate (to cover interest on the funding loan plus other expenses of the purchaser) unless the purchaser already has sufficient surplus cash to cover the resulting shortfall or receives a subordinated loan to cover the shortfall.

If interest on the receivables floats, but interest on the funding loan is fixed, the SPV may enter into an interest swap with a (rated) third party and pay floating in return for fixed or may enter into an interest rate floor. If the receivables are fixed, but the funding loan floats, the SPV can enter into a swap or a cap with a (rated) third party so that the third party pays the excess of floating over fixed on the receivables and investors are protected against a shortfall. Interest rate swaps (between, broadly, the rate on the receivables and the rate on the funding loan) can also be used where both rates are variable as a way of, amongst other things, providing funds to the purchaser to cover a shortfall where, e.g. mortgage rates are less than the rate of interest on the funding loan. For an explanation of these contracts, see chapter 15.

Other credit enhancement may be required to cover mismatches in interest rates and the timing of receipts, e.g. a liquidity facility.

Official guidelines, inspired by consumer protection, may require rate-fixing on house loans or other consumer credits to remain with the originator. This is one reason for the appointment of the originator as administrator.

4–14   There will be a **currency mismatch** if receivables are in one currency, but the loan in another. Currency hedging is a possibility.

Almost invariably, there is no tax **grossing-up clause** in the funding loan because of a usual rating agency requirement that the SPV should not be exposed to unidentified and uncovered extra costs. If a withholding tax is imposed on interest payable by the SPV, the SPV may prepay. Hence a tax imposition, followed by a prepayment, is an investor risk.

Security over purchaser's assets

4–15   The purchaser grants the maximum security over its assets to secure the financing loan. The assets which should be covered by the security include: the receivables; the sale agreement (especially the warranties and the repurchase obligations of the originator); the credit enhancement contracts (guarantees, subordinated loan agreement); the insurances; the administration agreement; and the purchaser's bank account and investments.

The security is fixed, but some of the security may necessarily be floating, such as the security over the bank account. The disadvantage of English floating charges that they rank after preferential creditors (certain taxes and employee benefits) is unimportant because the prior preferential creditors are limited: the SPV has no employees and is not VAT registered.

The security is given to a trustee if available.

The risk that the SPV might, in breach of a prohibition, charge or sell the receivables to a third party who notifies the debtors first is accepted by investors and rating agencies.

The grant of security over receivables is in some countries prohibitively complicated, e.g. notice to the debtors is required for the validity of the security. See para 5–2.

CHAPTER 5

SECURITISATIONS: LEGAL ASPECTS

Legal aspects of sale of receivables

Price for sale

The receivables may be sold at a discount, reflecting the risk that some of   5–1
them will be uncollectable and also reflecting the financing cost to the SPV
of funding the purchase. A discount may improve the credit standing of the
SPV. Apart from a small discount to cover the expenses of the transaction,
discounts in mortgage-backed securitisations are rare.

Assignability of receivables

If the consent of debtors is needed to the assignment of the receivables   5–2
(because under the terms of the contracts applying to the receivables, they
are personal contracts, or there are contractual prohibitions or because of
official guidelines for the protection of consumers or home-owners) the
securitisation is impracticable because of debtor inertia in replying. There
are usually just too many debtors.

Other factors relevant to assignability are whether bankers confidentia-
lity is breached, whether the SPV can fix the interest rate, and whether the
SPV can fix a market rate (as opposed to the originator's rate).

Alternatives to assignment might include a trust of the receivables, a trust
of proceeds, sub-participations (unlikely), or a novation (consent of debtors
required).

Notice will not normally be given to the debtors because of the incon-
venience and expense and because the seller generally wishes to maintain its
relationship with its customers and to continue collection.

If no notice is given to the debtors, the effect in some countries is that the
sale is invalid against attaching creditors of the seller and on the seller's
bankruptcy. This renders the securitisation impractical unless there is a

special exemption. Compulsory "notice to the debtor" prevails in France, Luxembourg, Italy, Japan (CC Art 467), South Korea and many other countries. Notice must often be formal, e.g. by a court bailiff in France. But there are exceptions to the "notice to debtor" rule in some of the hostile countries, such as France, Italy and Japan, but generally the exemptions are very restrictive. These topics are reviewed in another work (on the comparative law of security) in this series of works on financial law.

Notice is not required for validity in England, New York (*Malone v Bolstein* 159 F Supp 544 (DNY 1957 affd 244 F2d 954), or Germany.

In countries which validate assignments on the insolvency of the seller, even though no notice is given to the debtor, the absence of notice has other effects. Thus:

1. The SPV might lose priority if the seller resells or charges the receivables to a third party: this is of course prohibited and investors and rating agencies are content to rely on the SPV complying with this prohibition.

2. Debtors can continue to pay the seller. This is not an objection because the seller usually wishes to continue to collect in any event. A separate trust account may be set up and the direct debit mandates given by the debtor may be amended. There may be a commingling risk if payments are made to the seller's account. Often it will be possible for payments made by direct debit to be paid direct into the SPV's account rather than via the seller.

3. Debtors without notice can continue to acquire new set-offs and defences, e.g. if goods supplied are defective.

4. In the absence of notice, the seller and debtors can vary the terms of receivables: again one relies on the good faith of the seller.

5. It may be necessary to join the seller in an action by the purchaser against debtors (in England only the debtor can waive this, but it is a procedural technicality).

In any event, the rating agencies do not object to non-notified (equitable) assignments if valid, i.e. they are prepared to assume that originators will not act fraudulently or with gross negligence.

Other assignments might include assignments of endowment insurance, of guarantees of the receivables and of any security for the receivables, e.g. buildings mortgages. The cost of registration, such as Land Registry fees, is usually avoided by an equitable (unregistered) assignment in England. To cover the position on enforcement, the SPV takes a power of attorney to enforce and to register, and will normally have custody of or control over the title deeds.

Recharacterisation of sale as security

The sale of the receivables by the originator to the SPV must not be rechar-   5–3
acterised as security for the purposes of security and bankruptcy law. This
topic is discussed generally in chapter 2.

The question is whether the transaction is recharacterised as a loan by the
SPV to the originator secured on the receivables which are treated as still
belonging to the originator, as opposed to a true sale of the receivables to
the SPV.

If the sale is legally recharacterised as security for the purposes of mortgage law, the result is usually disastrous. The assets remain on the balance
sheet of the seller and the funding loan is a liability of the seller – the whole
object of the securitisation will have failed. Further, the security may require
registration or perfection by filing if it is not to be void on the insolvency of
the seller. The security may infringe negative pledges of the seller. The
enforcement of the security may be frozen on the insolvency of the seller (US
Chapter 11, British administration, French *redressment judiciaire*). The
bankrupt estate may have a right to use or substitute secured property
(France; US – but only if the secured creditor is given adequate protection
under BC 1978 s 361; Britain, in relation to floating charges of companies in
administration, although a universal floating charge has blocking powers).
The security may be subordinated to a super-priority moratorium loan (US,
France). The security given by the SPV to the investors would be a sub-mort-
gage limited to the "loan" by the SPV to the seller. Access by the investors to
the receivables might be subject to potentially restrictive mortgage enforcement procedures. Altogether, recharacterisation would normally be a catastrophe.

The chief factors in considering recharacterisation include:

– Whether the originator's rights to repurchase receivables in substance
   constitute an equity of redemption of mortgaged property, i.e. the mortgagor's right to get back the mortgaged property on repayment of the
   loan. The originator may desire a right to repurchase in order to end the
   transaction because, e.g. it is too onerous, or enforcement would be
   damaging, or it is no longer profitable. The originator usually has the
   right to repurchase small remaining amounts at the end of the financing
   to mop up the last drops when it is no longer economic to continue.

– Whether the extraction of profits by the originator amounts to a lender
   accounting to the borrower for the excess of the mortgaged property
   over the loan. In a true sale, the purchaser keeps the residual value
   (profit) of the purchased property, but in a mortgage the borrower
   receives back the residual value on repayment of the loan.

– Sham, i.e. the parties carry out the transaction in a different way than that contemplated by the documents, e.g. the records refer to a loan and interest, not a sale price. The parties need to make sure that this does not happen.

– Collections by the originator, i.e. whether the continued collection of the receivables by the originator negates a true sale.

5–4   **United States** Recharacterisation is mainly a US risk under UCC Art 9, which covers security interests in personal property. The main US test is whether a purchaser has recourse to the seller for losses and the extent of that recourse. Warranties as to the receivables are not usually enough. Other tests include: a right of the seller to repurchase receivables, retroactive adjustment of the sale price to reflect actual losses as opposed to expected losses, administration and collection of accounts by the originator (a buyer usually has right to manage a purchased asset), expressed intent (such as use of loan terminology instead of sale terminology), payment of any surplus to the transferor, non-notification to debtors on receivables, and the holding by the transferor of any documents evidencing the receivables.

In substance, the US courts adopt the accounting and regulatory substance-over-form tests – which examine whether the transferor has transferred the risks and rewards (profits) or whether the transferor keeps the risks and rewards. The test is elusive and unpredictable when risks and rewards are shared and the cases cannot be harmonised.

Hence, a US sale is usually two-step: the originator sells the receivables to a wholly-owned SPV without recourse and the SPV then transfers them to a trustee for the benefit of the investors. The first step is a true sale, but under UCC s 9–102, transfers of an interest in "accounts" and "chattel paper", whether or not a transfer for security or a sale transfer, must be perfected, e.g. by filing with the result that a true sale of these rights must be perfected. The second step is not a true sale because of the SPV's subordinated interest and the SPV's right to the surplus, and the trustee must therefore have its first priority security interest in the receivables perfected by filing or other means under UCC Art 9. The perfection should extend to the originator's bank account in which the proceeds are received, but perfection may not preserve commingled funds if the originator is bankrupt – see UCC s 9–306(4). In any event, the second step should qualify as a true sale for US accounting purposes under FASB 77.

In Canada, the provinces west of Quebec have personal property security statutes based on UCC Art 9.

In England, a properly documented sale of receivables, which is treated by the parties as a sale, is not a loan by the buyer to the seller secured on the receivables requiring registration, even if the buyer has recourse to the seller for unpaid receivables, even if the seller has a right of repurchase (e.g. stub assets at end), even if the profit is paid to the originator (e.g. a servicing fee), even though the seller continues to collect as agent of the purchaser, and even though the economic effect is similar to a loan secured on the receivables. Form over substance (predictability) was established in, e.g. *Olds Discount Co Ltd v John Playfair Ltd* [1938] 3 All ER 275; *Re George Inglefield Ltd* [1933] Ch 1, CA; *Lloyds & Scottish Finance Ltd v Prentice* (1977) 121 Sol Jo 847; affirmed HL, *The Times*, March 29, 1979; and *Welsh Development Agency v Export Finance Co Ltd* [1992] BCC 270, CA.

Preferences

Transfers by the originator to the SPV must not be capable of being avoided 5–5
as preference if the originator becomes bankrupt in the suspect period. These transfers include: the original sale, the sale of substitute receivables, and any credit enhancement payments by the originator. Preference law is not usually a problem if the sale is at market value and there is no transaction at an undervalue or element of gift. It is perhaps more of a preoccupation in the United States because of the width of the preference section in BC 1978 s 547.

Contractual restrictions

One should investigate whether there are any contractual restrictions bind- 5–6
ing the seller, e.g. in its loan agreements. Examples are prohibitions on substantial disposals, and wide negative pledges catching transactions having the effect of security.

Profit extraction by seller

Generally

The seller desires to continue to enjoy the profit from any surplus interest 5–7
from the receivables after the payment of interest to the investors and the other expenses of the SPV. The profit is usually the difference between the higher interest rate on the receivables and the lower interest rate payable by the SPV to investors on the funding loan plus any surplus receivables, e.g. if the original sale was over-collateralised.

Points to bear in mind are whether there is a withholding tax on profit payments, whether the payment is tax-deductible by the SPV, and whether there is any VAT on profit payments.

The profit extraction must not prejudice the off-balance sheet treatment or prejudice the true sale for the purposes of capital adequacy, or lead to recharacterisation as security as opposed to true sale for the purposes of mortgage law.

Methods

5–8   The main methods of extracting profits have included:

1.   Servicing fees for the administration of the receivables (consider VAT)

2.   Dividends via a golden share issued to the originator. One should consider whether shares convert the SPV into a subsidiary for accounting purposes, double taxation, and capital adequacy. In England, originator banks and building societies cannot have a shareholding in the SPV because of capital adequacy rules.

3.   Interest swaps whereby the SPV agrees to pay amounts equal to surplus interest to the seller. Consider the tax position on swap payments, especially withholding and deductibility.

4.   A high interest subordinated loan by the originator – a common English route. One should consider whether the interest would be treated as equity dividends, especially if interest varies with profits.

5.   The sale of receivables at par or over par with the surplus price deferred and payable only if realised. One should consider tax deductibility by the SPV and transactions at an undervalue.

6.   A receivables trust where the receivables are sold to the vehicle which holds the proceeds on trust to pay the SPV an amount equal to interest on the funding loan plus its other expenses and to pay the balance to the originator. In the United Kingdom, this may give rise to problems under the MIRAS scheme for residential mortgages.

The originator cannot have a right to repurchase surplus receivables for nothing because of the recharacterisation risk (among other things).

Solvency of purchaser and credit enhancement

Main risks

5–9   If the purchaser issues securities to investors, the solvency of the purchaser must be assured. The main potential threats to solvency include:

–   **Fees** These include initial start-up fees, fees of the administrator, trustee, rating agency, accounting, land registry and issuing and paying agency fees, the cost of credit enhancement guarantees, insurance premiums, and the like. Solutions to cover the fees include a subordinated loan from the seller (or a subordinated trust interest in the US); direct payment by the seller; share capital; and over-collateralisation.

— **Credit risk** This is the risk that the receivables are not collectible. It is not usually possible for the originator to guarantee the receivables (accounting balance sheet, capital adequacy, recharacterisation in the US). There are various possible solutions. For example the SPV is over-collateralised by the sale of more receivables than are needed to cover the senior funding loan; the extra surplus is funded by a junior issue of securities so that there is a two tier issue of securities (class B is subordinated to class A) where the seller (or a third party) holds class B and so carries the risk of loss (in return for higher yield). Or the SPV acquires receivables for less than their face value at a discount. Or third parties provide guarantees or pool insurance which cover a specified maximum of deficiencies arising from the enforcement of the receivables.

— **Interest basis risk** This is the risk of a mismatch between the interest rate on the receivables and the interest rate on the funding loan, e.g. one is fixed and the other floating, or a floating rate on the funding loan goes up, without a re-setting of the rate on the receivables. Solutions include an interest rate swap and an obligation on the originator to set interest at or above a threshold rate (unless the SPV already has sufficient cash to cover the shortfall or it receives a subordinated loan to cover it).

— **Liquidity risk** This is the risk of a timing mismatch between receivable recoveries (because of their terms or because the debtors delay payments) and the interest on and the repayment of the funding loan. Solutions: a cash fund within the vehicle, originally funded from an originator loan to the SPV on a subordinated basis and capable of replenishment from surplus income; class A/B notes structure where interest on the class B notes can be deferred if there is insufficient cash after paying interest on the class A notes; letter of credit; liquidity facility from a third party; or a guarantee or surety bond in relation to interest from third party insurers.

— **Reinvestment risk** This is the risk of a prepayment of high interest-bearing receivables when the SPV cannot reinvest the proceeds at the same rate in the market pending payment of the funding loan, so that there is a timing mismatch between the prepayments of the receivables and the next interest payment on the funding loan. The problem would be exacerbated if the funding loan is fixed term and is not prepayable on a pass-through basis. Solutions: a guaranteed investment contact with a highly-rated third party at a pre-determined rate of interest; setting the threshold rate referred to above at a level which takes into account both the likely level of prepayment and the rate of return on prepayment proceeds; cash fund as above; or a class A/B notes structure.

—   **Business liabilities** The SPV will covenant not to carry on any other business or incur any other liabilities, the intention being that the SPV should be protected from bankruptcy. But there may be involuntary liabilities – as where affiliates are liable for tax or pensions unpaid by another member of the group (this affects US structures where the SPV is a wholly-owned subsidiary selling to a trust). Other examples are: new taxation of the SPV; unexpected costs of litigation or calling a bondholders' meeting; and employee remuneration – but the SPV should have no employees since it is managed by the seller.

Forms of credit enhancement

5–10   As discussed, in order to protect the SPV from insolvency, the structure usually contemplates various forms of credit enhancement. The enhancement can be internal, such as over-collateralisation by the seller, or external, such as a guarantee from a third party. Examples are:

—   **Guarantees** or their equivalent, such as letters of credit, an obligation to purchase defaulted receivables, irrevocable and unconditional obligations to lend, such as obligations to invest, and top-slice credit insurance. These must usually come from a third party, such as a bank or surety, if the transaction is to be off the seller's balance sheet (for the purpose of the accounting and regulatory regime) and to avoid the recharacterisation risk, especially in the United States. There can be no indemnity from the originator or its affiliates. The guarantor must have a credit-rating at least as high as the rating of the SPV's securities to maintain the rating of the SPV's securities. Third party sureties charge a fee.

   A difficult negotiating issue can be whether the guarantor is secured on the receivables and whether the guarantor has the normal right of subrogation if the guarantor pays in full but the payment is insufficient. In these cases the guarantor competes with the investors by giving with one hand and taking with the other.

—   **Liquidity facilities** These are subject to usual loan conditions but they may be cheaper for the provider (and hence the SPV) than a full guarantee equivalent because of capital adequacy costs.

—   **Subordinated loans** The seller may make a subordinated loan to the SPV, junior to the investors and limited in recourse to the available assets. In the typical US trust structure, the seller has a subordinated trust interest. The loan must usually be made in advance to fund the purchase price. If to be made later, the loan must be unconditional, so that the loan is drawable by the bankruptcy trustee of the SPV without cancellation. The powers of a bankruptcy trustee to do so should be investigated. In any event, the only permissible conditions would be maximum amount and purpose. The English courts will not order specific performance of an agreement to lend but award damages only (such as the extra cost of getting the loan elsewhere).

— **Over-collateralisation** The seller sells more receivables than are needed to cover the funding loan or sells at a discount. It is preferable for the seller to have a deferred sale price for receivables, i.e. the seller is paid, say, 80 per cent on the sale and the remaining 20 per cent only if and when the receivables are collected. Hence the investors lend 80 against receivables nominally worth 100. There would not usually be transaction at an undervalue problems whereby transfers with an element of gift are voidable on the insolvency of the transferor.

— **Reserve accounts** The surplus and any difference between the interest on the SPV's bonds and the interest on the receivables is accumulated in a reserve account of the SPV.

— **Extra share capital** This is an extra cost.

Insolvency of seller

Securitisation must also withstand the insolvency of the originator, or, in the jargon, be "bankruptcy remote" from the originator. The main points are listed below.   **5–11**

True sale The sale must be a true sale for the purposes of mortgage law and not a disguised security or charge on the receivables: para 5–3.

Non-consolidation The SPV must not be consolidated with the originator on the originator's bankruptcy so that all its assets and liabilities are merged with those of originator. This involves ensuring the separateness of the SPV and attention to the rules of piercing the veil of incorporation (separate officers, no commingling, separate records, observance of corporate formalities, disclosure in financial statements, and the like.). This is more a US obstacle in two-step structures where the SPV is a wholly-owned subsidiary of the originator. In UK structures the SPV is an independent company, though managed by the originator, and consolidation on insolvency and piercing the veil of incorporation are rare. Consolidation generally, is reviewed in another work (on the principles of insolvency) in this series of works on international financial law.

Preferences Transfers or payments by the seller to the SPV must not be capable of being set aside as a preference or transaction at an undervalue on the bankruptcy of the seller. The main transactions are the sale itself, any recourse to the seller and any repurchase by the seller, any substitutions by the seller, and any payments on a subordinated loan to the SPV. Note the avoidance of "bulk sales" in some countries (stripping assets to prejudice of creditors). Preferences and bulk sales are discussed in another work in this series.

5–12 **Originator collections** There should be no material loss of or delay in the recovery of funds collected by the originator as servicing agent, if the originator becomes insolvent. There is bound to be some delay. The commingling risk in non-trust jurisdictions should be investigated. The main protection is to require frequent turnovers to the SPV, e.g. every two or three days. Alternatively, it may be possible to arrange for payments to go direct to the SPV's account. Bankruptcy stays on the replacement of the bankrupt originator because of a stay on contract termination may apply, e.g. the US Bankruptcy Code of 1978 and the Canadian Bankruptcy and Insolvency Act 1992.

Post-commencement Payments and transactions by the seller after insolvency petition against the seller are universally suspect. This is not a major commercial risk in practice.

Practical effect of originator's insolvency If the originator becomes insolvent, then a replacement administrator must be appointed. This would involve extra costs. Since the originator will be unable to subsidise an interest rate on the receivables if that rate is less than the rate on the funding loan, the interest rate on the receivables may be higher than the market rate, with the result that there may be more prepayments by borrowers, so that the reinvestment risks are increased and the average life of the funding loan may be affected.

Rating

5–13 The securities issued by the SPV must usually be rated by a rating agency to sell to investors, e.g. AA or AAA. A high rating is usually essential to sell bonds in the euromarkets. But some securitisations have been rated speculative grade, as opposed to investment grade, and some not rated at all. It is conceivable that the senior securities are rated, but any junior securities are unrated. The rating agency requirements are stringent and affect the structure.

Rating is both initial and periodical, so that it can be down-graded. A down-grading of the rating of a credit-enhancer can also down-grade the rating of the SPV's securities.

Rating agencies seek to ensure that their rating is internationally consistent, e.g. a US AAA is the same as an English AAA, notwithstanding differences in receivables and the legal regime.

Rating agencies firstly assess the overall soundness, e.g. the quality of receivables by audit. Thus in the case of mortgage loans, they will review loan to value ratios and income multiples and (to determine the likelihood of default by borrowers and the level of loss upon enforcement) the foreclosure frequency and loss severity. This analysis will determine the level of credit enhancement required to achieve the desired rating. The higher the rating, the worse the assumptions as to default and loss.

They will also review (1) the SPV's remoteness from the bankruptcy of the seller (e.g. true sale, no preferences or transactions at an undervalue, non-consolidation); (2) the credit enhancement to cover costs, possible shortfalls on the receivables, and liability risks (credit enhancers must have a comparable rating); (3) the risk of a SPV bankruptcy because of other liabilities, i.e. there must be no liabilities to third parties outside the transaction (e.g. no employees, premises, other business); and (4) the sophistication of the systems of the administrator.

Accounting

This is a swiftly moving field. The usual objective is that the receivables and   **5—14** the loan to finance the SPV are not consolidated on the balance sheet of the seller, but are independent. Hence:

— The SPV must not be a **subsidiary** of the seller. There may be special rules for the consolidation of affiliates which are not majority-owned: this usually leads to the result that the seller cannot have a significant shareholding in the SPV. See the Companies Act 1989 where a "right to exercise a dominant influence" over the SPV is sufficient in certain cases, even if the originator does not have shares in the SPV, and actual dominant influence is enough if the originator has a "participating interest" in the SPV.

— The sale of the receivables must be a **true sale**, i.e. the transferor has transferred significantly all of the incidents of ownership of the receivables to the transferee, namely the risk of loss and rewards. Transfer of risk is easy to understand – if the seller still has a liability, as where the seller guarantees that the receivables will be repaid, this ought to be recorded on its balance sheet. But the transfer of rewards is more questionable.

The theory is that if the asset producing the reward is held by a third party, the seller's right to the reward is vulnerable, e.g. because the seller does not manage and control the asset and because the asset may be taken away by events beyond the control of the seller, as on the holder's bankruptcy.

The problem is that some risks remain with the seller and the seller also wishes to extract some profit, so there are grey areas. The main questions are: (a) how much recourse or risk of loss can be imposed on the seller in the form of guarantees, repurchase liability, junior loans, reserve accounts, warranty of receivables, prospectus liability, moral commitment and the like, and (b) how much of the profits can be passed back to the seller and how, whether by a right to repurchase, servicing fees, subordinated loan, junior interest under a trust or the like. Usually the right to repurchase a *de minimis* amount (e.g. 10 per cent) at the end of the financing is not counted.

There are detailed international differences in accounting approaches towards entities which must be consolidated and the degree of transfer of risks and rewards. Accounting treatment aims at substance, not form, and so may be different from the legal treatment.

5–15   In 1994 the UK Accounting Standards Board issued Financial Reporting Standard 5 providing for, amongst other things, the consolidation of "quasi-subsidiary" SPVs and the use of a "linked presentation" in the balance sheet showing the proceeds of the funding loan deducted from the securitised receivables. There are a number of conditions to be satisfied for a linked presentation to be appropriate. Thus there must be no doubt that the originator's exposure to loss is limited to a fixed amount, the investor's claims must be limited to the securitised assets and there must be no provision for the repurchase of the receivables by the originator in the future.

US FAS 77 (Financial Accounting Standard, Reporting by Transferors for Transfers of Receivables with Recourse 1983) has a very lenient standard. The sale is off balance sheet even if the originator retains full recourse, so long as the level of recourse can be estimated (only quantification, not amount) and other conditions satisfied. But there are tougher standards for US commercial banks under the regulatory accounting principles applying to them.

Capital adequacy

The capital adequacy regime is also subject to rapid change.   5–16

Some institutions must have a prescribed minimum capital according to the size and nature of their other assets, e.g. banks, building societies (thrifts), insurance companies, and investment businesses. The principles in relation to banks are explored in another work in this series. Usually the capital adequacy requirement is avoided only if the seller has fully transferred the receivables and has no liability to the purchaser if the receivables are not collectible.

The principles adopted by the regulatory authorities are similar to the accounting principles but with a greater emphasis on the transfer of risk as opposed to the transfer of rewards. In addition, supervisors pay regard to moral obligations to support the SPV because of the special vulnerability of credit institutions to a loss of business confidence. If the test is too stringent, securitisations are dampened and the ability of credit institutions to finance themselves and to comply with capital adequacy rules is reduced.

The Bank of England requirements are designed to ensure that the origi-   5–17
nator has no legal or moral obligation to support the SPV so that the receivables have been completely and truly sold: Notice of February 1989, BD/1989/1, "Loan Transfers and Securitisation". The main requirements are:

— The originator must have no shareholding in the SPV (hence the use of an "orphan" SPV with shares held by trustees on discretionary trusts for charities; hence profits cannot be extracted by dividends). The originator must not have more than one director on the SPV's board and he must be in a minority. The originator must not fund the SPV, apart from an initial contribution and a long-term subordinated loan to fund issue expenses. Contribution and loans are deducted from the bank's capital for capital adequacy purposes. The originator must not supply any other credit enhancement, such as a guarantee or interest subsidy (although there is no objection to an interest rate swap with the SPV at "market prices"), or an obligation to repurchase receivables (but there is no objection to warranties as to the receivables and a repurchase obligation in case of breach of warranty as to the validity of the receivables and no objection to an option to repurchase if the receivables fall to an uneconomic rump of 10 per cent). The originator must not be associated commercially with the SPV, e.g. by a similar name which might imply a moral obligation to support the SPV.

— A Bank of England paper of April 1992 (BSD/1992/3) on securitisation of revolving credits, especially credit card receivables, proposes restrictive and detailed rules limiting these transactions. The main regulatory objections include: transfer of good, leaving the bad; the seller has the refinancing risk in practice; and consumer protection (transfer of consumer assets from regulated to non-regulated entity). There are special detailed rules for building societies.

The potential liability of the originator for an incorrect prospectus is not usually counted as a risk for capital adequacy purposes.

Taxation

5–18   The main taxes to be considered are:

Stamp duties Is there a stamp duty on the sale? Home loan mortgages and bank loans are usually exempt from UK stamp duty as loan capital, but this exemption does not apply to consumer receivables

Value added tax Is there any VAT on fees? Are VAT recoveries in respect of bad debts recoverable by the SPV?

Withholding taxes Can the debtors pay interest to the purchaser without tax withholding? Is withholding tax deductible by the purchaser from interest payable to the investors? Debt securities issued to investors must not be recharacterised as equity, lest interest is treated as dividends subject to withholding and not deductible

Profits tax on SPV Is there a tax on the SPV's profits? Expenses should be matched so far as possible. A tax haven location could be considered. Can the SVP deduct its expenses (initial and continuing)? Is interest payable by the SPV deductible?

Taxes on originator The main question is the tax treatment of the originator's receipt of the sale price: is it treated as an accelerated gain or loss?

Securities regulation

5–19   **Issue of securities** The usual rules are applicable to any bond issue funding the purchaser, notably whether the issue is exempt from prospectus requirements. These requirements and exemptions are reviewed in another work in this series.

Collective investment scheme A securitisation is essentially a pooling of assets for the benefit of investors and may therefore be a collective investment scheme. There is an objection in many countries to the unregulated issue of securities backed by financial assets.

In the United States, mutual funds are regulated by the Investment Companies Act of 1940. Rule 3a–7, promulgated by the SEC in 1992, introduced a new exemption to the 1940 Act (which regulates an issuer which "is or holds itself out as being engaged primarily in the business of investing, reinvesting or trading in securities" – which would include most financial assets). Rule 3a–7 excludes issuers "engaged in the business of purchasing or otherwise acquiring, and holding eligible assets" subject to various detailed conditions. Most US securitisations can benefit from this exemption. Other exemptions are available, e.g. for issuers whose securities are held by not more than 100 persons, and for issuers acquiring various trade and other specified receivables.

Japanese securities laws restrict securitisations: investments in investments are regarded as inherently dangerous. There is detailed legislation.

In Britain, technical authorisations may be required under the Financial Services Act 1986, e.g. if the administrator manages reinvestment proceeds or insurance policies – both may be managing investments requiring authorisation.

Banking and credit regulation

This area too is labyrinthine. The main issues often are: 5–20

— Whether the SPV is carrying on a regulated business, e.g. taking deposits contrary to the UK Banking Act 1987.

— Whether the SPV is carrying on a regulated consumer credit business. The securitisation involves a potential transfer of consumer receivables from a regulated to a non-regulated entity. The UK Consumer Credit Act 1974 applies a ceiling of £15,000 or less and only applies to individuals. The Act requires the licensing of credit businesses, but as the SVP does not itself usually provide credit, it may only need a debt-collecting licence. Regulated credit agreements are subject to rules as to prescribed form, content and copies; cooling-off; restricted rights of enforcement on default; duty to provide information to the consumer; no penalty default interest; consumer right of prepayment; and liability of providers of credit for defects in goods financed. The consumer credit rules may affect top-up home loan mortgages.

— Under the US Glass-Steagall Act, US commercial banks cannot act as underwriters for securities, subject to exemptions.

- US Federal Reserve Act, s 23(A): this prevents an affiliate of a bank from obtaining improper financing from the bank (insider lending). The SPV must not be an affiliate within the rules because the bank's ability to provide credit or liquidity enhancement will be reduced.

- US Reg D of the Federal Reserve Board: commercial banks and thrifts must maintain reserves against deposits and liabilities, subject to exemptions.

Miscellaneous

5–21   Various miscellaneous matters may fall to be considered, for example the UK Data Protection Act 1984. The SPV, trustee and originator may have to be registered as a data user or computer bureau.

As regards top-up mortgages in home loans securitisations, the purchaser could lend the top-up loan out of repayment proceeds; or the seller could buy back the home loan and lend the top-up amount itself or lend the top-up amount on the security of a second mortgage. A receivables trust can also be used to allow either the purchaser or the originator to make the further advance, without forcing the originator to buy back the loan or take a second mortgage.

Country notes

France

5–22   In France assignments of receivables must be notified to the debtor in prescribed form if the assignment is to be effective on the bankruptcy of the seller: CC 1690. But the Daily Act of 1981 (Law of January 2, 1981 as amended in 1984) simplified the assignment of receivables in order to facilitate the factoring of receivables and pledges of receivables to raise finance: they can be assigned by delivery of a list specifying the receivables (*bordereau*) in favour of a credit institution (which can include foreign banks). The procedure is formalistic, e.g. the instrument must bear a specified title and refer to the 1981 Act and must clearly identify the receivables. Notice to the debtors is not necessary for the efficacy of the assignment on the assignor's insolvency. If a creditor sells an asset to the assignor subject to a reservation of title clause, then that creditor has priority over the assignee of the receivable under the Daily Act on a resale by the assignor. Future claims not arising out of existing contracts can be covered, but there must be a degree of certainty that they will arise: hence the ability to assign future receivables is weak.

Securitisation (*titrisation*) is governed by Law No 88–1201 of December 23, 1988 and subsequent regulations (together the "regulations"). The rules are rigid and restrictive, mainly because of a traditional hostility to transfers of debts (protection of debtor), so that, as mentioned above, a sale is ineffective against creditors of the seller unless notified to the debtor by a court bailiff – the *huissier*.

The regulations establish a new single-purpose legal entity "*fonds commun de créances*" (FCC). Receivables can be transferred to an FCC without costly notification to debtors.

The seller of the receivables ("fund sponsor") must be a credit establishment. Only the sponsor can collect the receivables unless the debtors consent in writing *after* the original agreement to the transfer of collection duties (so it is impracticable to appoint another collection agent even if the sponsor defaults).

The FCC must be managed by a single-purpose *société commerciale* with prescribed duties and not more than one third owned by the sponsor. The FCC must deposit its assets with a French credit establishment.

There must be prescribed forms of credit enhancement (guarantee, over-collateralisation, subordinated loans) and a rating evaluation by an approved rating agency.

Any FCC certificates must have a minimum face amount of 10,000 French Francs, and be entered in book-entry form with the French Securities Clearing-house System SICOVAM. The FCC can acquire receivables and issue certificates only once – hence there can be no top-ups or substitution and no multiple offerings. Under French bank accounting rules, assets transferred to an FCC are taken off the sponsor's balance sheet if certain conditions are fulfilled. There are detailed rules for the offering of FCC certificates and for the provision of information to investors.

Since the above is so restrictive, an alternative is subrogation: the SPV pays the originator and is subrogated to the receivables; in this case no *huissier* notice is required.

Germany

There appear to be no major legal barriers, but there is a strong resistance to 5–23
the transfer of intermediation of capital away from the banks and possibly other cultural objections.

Italy

5-24   Notice to debtors is generally required for the validity of the transfer on the insolvency of the assignor. The French subrogation route is not available. But a 1991 law allows the factoring of certain trade receivables without notice.

Japan

5-25   There is an unsympathetic legal and non-legal environment – which may be influenced partly by the desire of banks not to cede borrowing business to securities firms. The main impediments – which are legal, administrative and cultural – include restrictions on securities which can be issued and the investors to whom they may be issued; limited exemptions from the requirement under CC Art 467 formally to notify the debtor on the receivables of an assignment (so one cannot securitise many receivables, such as credit card receivables); and tax disincentives. There is an exception for certain eligible transferors, e.g. leasing and finance companies, but not banks and other originators. In this case, public newspaper or official publication of record to obligors is allowed instead of individual certifications: the Law Relating to the Regulation of the Business of Specified Items 1992. The regime includes official approval of securitisations, the licensing of purchasers, and prescriptive rules, e.g. as to the investment of surplus funds and disclosure.

Spain

5-26   Spain has a special (and restrictive) law regulating mortgage securitisation funds: Law 19/1992 of July 7, 1992 which sets out tight, prescriptive and formal rules.

PART III

SET-OFF AND NETTING

CHAPTER 6

SET-OFF: GENERAL PRINCIPLES AND INSOLVENCY SET-OFF

These chapters, in this part, are based on the author's *English and International Set-Off* (1989) Sweet & Maxwell, ("EISO") to which the reader is referred for a more extensive analysis and citation.

Introduction

Set-off as a litmus test

Set-off is one of the leading, and most accurate, indicators of pro-debtor or pro-creditor attitudes to insolvency, it is a litmus test of jurisdictions. For example, in English-based countries, set-off is restricted between solvent parties (favouring payment to creditors like banks, lessors and sellers who wish to be paid without deduction so as to maintain cash-flow and to support the "pay now, litigate later" principle) and compulsory on insolvency (favouring payment to creditors who are thereby paid by the defaulter, even though they are unsecured), while in most Franco-Latin jurisdictions solvent set-off is liquid between solvent parties (favouring debtors) but prohibited on insolvency (augmenting the debtor's estate and hence favouring debtors). The contrast could not be more complete.

6–1

Definition of set-off

Set-off is the discharge of reciprocal obligations to the extent of the smaller obligation. A debtor sets off the "cross-claim" owed to him against the "primary claim" which he owes his creditor. A bank sets off a cross-claim for a loan owed to it by a depositor against the depositor's claim for a

6–2

deposit owed by the bank. A defendant sets off, against the plaintiff-creditor, a cross-claim owed by the plaintiff to the defendant.

Security function of set-off

6–3   Set-off avoids circuity of payment and achieves the aim of judicial economy by avoiding multiplicity of proceedings. But the main effect of set-off is that a debtor with a set-off is in substance "secured" in that the debtor's cross-claim can be paid or discharged by setting it off against the creditor's claim. Thus a bank can discharge a loan owed to it by setting it off against a deposit owed by the bank. The set-off discharges both claims.

Since claims are a major form of property nowadays and since creditors are often also debtors to the same counterparty, the law of set-off is of paramount importance in international financial affairs – almost as important as the law of security interests. The most common cases of set-off in other contexts include set-off by banks of loans against deposits; set-off between institutions in financial markets such as the inter-bank deposit market; netting of foreign exchange, swaps, futures, securities and repo contracts; and set-off in centralised payment systems. The amounts involved are immense and the reduction in exposures achieved by set-off, with resulting reduction in credit costs and cascade risks threatening the integrity of the financial system, are correspondingly large.

But this short list should not disguise the pervasiveness of set-off in financial and business affairs: wherever there is a series of contracts between parties, there is a potential for set-offs, and even single contracts containing reciprocal obligations give rise to a set-off possibility – banking, sales, insurance, leasing, custodianship, transportation, services.

However set-off is not security proper in that the creditor does not grant the debtor a security interest over the creditor's property in the debt owed to the creditor to secure the cross-claim owed by the creditor to the debtor, e.g. a depositor does not grant security over the depositor's ownership of the deposit claim back to the bank to secure a loan owed by the depositor to the bank. Nor is set-off a right of retention like a lien because the bank does not retain the coins or notes of the depositor: the property in the benefit of the deposit account is held by the depositor and the bank has no property to retain.

Classes of set-off

6–4   There are no universally accepted terms for the various classes of set-off and it may therefore be useful to suggest a suitable terminology. In the interests of international understanding, the terms chosen are intended to mean what they say and are not tied to the local usage of any particular jurisdiction.

The main classes – which are sufficiently distinct to justify a separate label – are as follows:

(a) **Independent set-off** This is the set-off of unconnected and independent reciprocal claims and is known variously as compensation (the mainstream Roman law and civil code term), legal set-off or statutory set-off.

(b) **Current account set-off** This is the set-off of reciprocal claims arising on demand current account, especially bank accounts, and is variously known as bankers set-off, running account set-off or combination.

(c) **Transaction set-off** This is the set-off of claims arising out of the same or closely connected transactions and is known in England as equitable set-off or abatement and in the United States as recoupment.

(d) **Contractual set-off** This is a set-off created by contract where it would not otherwise exist.

(e) **Judicial set-off** This is a set-off allowed as a defence in judicial proceedings.

(f) **Retainer or fund set-off** This is not strictly a set-off but is akin to set-off. It is the remedy whereby the trustee or other administrator of a fund, such as the estate of an insolvent or a commercial trust, can retain a dividend owed to a contributor to the fund who has not paid his contribution into the fund. Common law courts have struggled to find a term for this remedy and have sometimes called it impounding, or have given up altogether and called it *The Rule in Cherry v Boultbee*, after the leading case.

(g) **Insolvency set-off** This is the set-off arising where one of the debtor-creditors is insolvent.

Set-off, charge-backs and conditional debts (flawed assets) distinguished

Set-off, charge-backs and conditional debts (or "flawed assets") need to be distinguished.   6–5

(a) **Set-off** Set-off is the discharge of both reciprocal claims by the debtor applying the cross-claim owed to him to "pay", discharge, extinguish, acquit, the creditor's primary claim and the debtor's cross-claim pro tanto. Thus a bank applies a loan owed to it to pay a deposit owed by it – its asset to pay its liability. The bank does not retain a deposit as a lien because it has no property over the deposit: the property of the deposit is held by the depositor. Note that in set-off the debtor uses its asset to pay his liability. It is not unhelpful to get the claims the right way round.

(b) **Charge-back** A charge-back is a grant by a creditor of a proprietary security interest (by way of charge, pledge, assignment, mortgage, what you will) over the claim owed to him to secure the cross-claim he owes to the debtor. Thus a depositor may grant a charge over the depositor's property in a deposit to secure a loan cross-claim which the depositor owes the bank. On enforcement the bank applies the depositor's asset to pay the depositor's liability. The bank is for all purposes a secured creditor whereas a bank with a mere right of set-off, although he may often be in a position similar to that of a secured creditor, is not a secured creditor in law. He is not subject to registration or filing or the baggage of mortgage formalities and enforcement. Charge-backs are reviewed in another work (on the comparative law of security) in this series of books on financial law.

(c) **Conditional debt or "flawed" asset** A conditional debt is a debt which is not payable at all until an event happens. The creditor does not have an asset at all until that event occurs. The depositor's claim for his deposit is conditional on him paying his loan. This is not a set-off since, if the event has not happened, the debtor has no liability against which he can set off his cross-claim. Nor is it a charge-back because the creditor-depositor does not assign his property in the conditional debt-deposit. Flawed assets have intellectual appeal, but not if they are a result of misunderstanding set-off. There is little English case law.

These concepts are extraordinarily difficult to grasp. The reason lies in the nature of debts as property. They are the sole form of property which can only be translated into a usable form by the transfer of an asset – payment by debtor to creditor. Hence it looks as though the debtor has the asset. Hence set-off looks like the retention of an asset by way of security or by way of conditional payment. Hence the confusion. But the debtor does not have the property in the asset. The creditor has the property – the depositor owns the deposit, not the bank; the seller owns the price, not the buyer; the insured owns his insurance policy, not the insurer; the bondholder owns the bond, not the issuer. This is obvious. Therefore, if the debtor who has granted his creditor that asset, wants a pledge, the creditor must transfer his asset back to the debtor, e.g. deposit the bond or the certificate of deposit with the debtor. If the debtor wishes to make the asset conditional, the right to forfeit it must be written into that asset: the bond or deposit contract must state that it is cancelled or postponed if, say, the debtor is not paid by the creditor. If the debtor wants a set-off, he must use the asset owed to him by his creditor to knock over the asset of the creditor, like a skittle, as where the bank sets off a loan owed to it against a deposit owed by it. Of course the transactions have the same commercial effect. But the treatment of set-off, security and forfeiture are very different in financial law. It is only if the distinctions are made that one can make real progress in working out the effects. Otherwise the result is as bizarre as drafting a sale as a lease. Characterisation is crucial.

One may now pass on to matters which are less tiring to the intellect.

Insolvency set-off

Introduction

Without doubt one of the most fundamental and crucial cleavages between   6–6 jurisdictions is their attitude to insolvency set-off. A creditor with a set-off on insolvency is a super-priority creditor: the bankrupt owes him 100, he owes the bankrupt 100. On set-off the creditor is paid in full.

Policies of insolvency set-off

The old classical view espoused by the Franco-Latin jurisdictions is that   6–7 insolvency set-off is a violation of the pari passu principle because a creditor with a set-off gets paid in full, and that the set-off is like an unpublicised security interest causing assets to disappear on bankruptcy.

The arguments in favour of set-off are: (a) it is unjust that the defaulter should insist on payment, but not pay himself; (b) set-off helps creditors escape the debacle and hence mitigates the knock-on or cascade effect of bankruptcy; (c) set-off reduces exposures and hence the cost of credit; (d) set-off avoids circuity and hence reduces costs; (e) set-off prevents the debtor from being bankrupted on a debt he does not owe, if the overall position is taken into account; if he has this admittedly legitimate relief, he should not be in a better position than the creditor.

As to the view that set-off is effectively an unpublished security interest, it is not practical to require creditors who have reciprocal claims to publish this fact. There are many other cases where it is accepted that it is not realistic to publicise the fact that assets will be removed or depleted on insolvency, e.g. repossessions of leased assets, cancellation of contracts and forfeitures of mortgaged assets where it is too expensive or burdensome to require filing or registration. Financial statements themselves are based on the necessary assumption that the enterprise will continue as a going concern: a bankruptcy break-up sale results in a dramatic collapse of values and extinction of goodwill, so that creditors dealing with an enterprise must accept that bankruptcy is a spoiliator of value, a devastation far in excess of anything that set-off can inflict. The "secrecy" argument therefore appears unconvincing.

In any event, whatever view one may take about the policies, the fact of the matter is that if set-off is to be of any value as a form of "security" it must stand up on insolvency which is the time that the protection is really needed.

States allowing insolvency set-off

6–8   The majority of international opinion favours the grant of wide insolvency set-off although there is variation in the detail.

States allowing insolvency set-off by statute include the following (see EISO chapter 24 for statutory references):

Europe: Austria, Czech Republic, Denmark, England, Germany, Guernsey (but only if the parties have contracted for it), Ireland (North and Republic), Isle of Man, Italy, Jersey, Liechtenstein, the Netherlands, Poland, Scotland (case law – no statute), Slovak Republic, Switzerland, West Germany

North America: Canada (including Quebec since the Federal bankruptcy legislation overrides the Napoleonic bar on insolvency set-off), and the United States (including Louisiana which is also a Napoleonic state where the Bankruptcy Act 1978 s 553 overrides, although there are contrary decisions). Note that there is a stay on set-off under the Canadian Bankruptcy and Insolvency Act 1992 s 65.1(1) amending the insolvency set-off in BA s 75(3).

Scandinavia: Finland, Norway, Sweden

Latin America: Panama

Middle East: Cyprus, Israel

Asia and Pacific: Australia, China, Hong Kong, India, Japan, South Korea, Malaysia, New Zealand, Pakistan, Singapore, Sri Lanka, Thailand

Africa: Liberia (probably, although there is no statute), Nigeria, Zambia and probably some or all of the former British colonies (except South

Africa and surrounding South African based jurisdictions, like Zimbabwe).

Caribbean: Bahamas, Bermuda, Cayman Islands

The position in the Arabian states in the Middle East, such as Saudi Arabia, is often uncertain because of the absence of a developed bankruptcy law.

The position in the new states following the collapse of the Soviet empire appears unclear. It is believed that the new bankruptcy laws in Russia, Belarus, Khazakhstan and the Ukraine do not mention insolvency set-off, but this should be checked.

States refusing insolvency set-off

In those jurisdictions which do not permit insolvency set-off, the general 6–9 principle subject to local variations is that the reciprocal claims must satisfy the conditions of the solvent set-off rules prior to the relevant insolvency date, e.g. in the case of independent set-off both claims must be mutual, liquidated, matured and legally payable, or they must have been set off by contract prior to the insolvency date under a contract entered into prior to the preferential suspect period. Generally a contract which removes an obstacle to set-off such as illiquidity, multicurrency or immaturity, must remove the bar prior to the suspect period and the claims must be eligible for set-off before the relevant insolvency date pursuant to the contract.

If the claims do not satisfy these requirements by the relevant date, there can be no set-off and the creditor must pay the cross-claim into the insolvent's estate and prove for the claim owed to him by the insolvent. Hence if a bank owes a term deposit maturing after the insolvency date and is owed a term loan accelerated before the insolvency date, there is no set-off and the bank must pay in the term deposit and prove for the accelerated loan – something of a disaster. The bar is also unfortunate for netting agreements.

The group of non-allowing states comprise:

Europe: France (Art 107 of the Decree of December, 27 1985), Belgium, Luxembourg, Spain, Greece, Portugal. But France and Belgium have special netting statutes: see chapter 11.

Middle East: Egypt, Kuwait (probably, but there is no statutory provision), Bahrain (Art 86 of the Banking and Composition Law No 11 of 1987)

Latin America: Argentina (CC Art 862 Art 134 of the Bankruptcy Law 1955), Brazil (but this is worth checking), Chile, Colombia, Mexico (Art 128 of the Bankruptcy Law)

Africa: South Africa and surrounding states and (probably) various other states originally part of the French or Belgian dominions, e.g. Francophone north, west and central African states

Exceptional insolvency set-offs in refusing states

6–10   There are two main exceptions to the general bar on insolvency set-off in the refusing states.

(a) **Current account set-off** It seems to be universally true that current account set-off is available in the refusing states on the rationale that debits and credits are but one account eligible for compensation on termination of the banker-customer relationship on insolvency. This is true in France and Luxembourg. See also, for example, Art 784 of the Argentine Civil Code and Art 36 of the Bahrain Bankruptcy and Composition Law No 11 of 1987.

(b) **Transaction set-off** There appears to be wide acceptance of the notion in the non-allowing states that transaction set-off is permitted because it would be intolerable that, for example, an insolvent should be able to claim the price without bringing into account damages for delay or defective performance.

Under the pre-1985 bankruptcy legislation, France allowed set-off between an insurance premium and policy proceeds, between reciprocal claims arising out of supply contracts, between the price owing to the insolvent for goods or services supplied and a damages claim for defective performance or delay, and between an invoice payable by a consumer to a gas company and caution money due by the consumer. This was so even if the debt owing by the insolvent matured after the relevant insolvency order. These decisions were confirmed by statute in 1994. The principle is that the *lien de connexité* justifies the set-off. See also, e.g. Art 69 of the Chilean Bankruptcy Law and Art 128 (IV)(a) of the Mexican Code of Commerce.

If the reciprocal claims are not in fact connected by virtue of the same transaction, it appears that generally an attempt by contract to create a set-off on insolvency will fail as contrary to the policy of the bankruptcy laws. The impact on contractual set-off of preferential doctrines and long suspect periods is particularly relevant. Long suspect periods are typical of French-based bankruptcy regimes.

Insolvency jurisdiction

The insolvency set-off clause in the allowing states will apply only to entities   **6–11**
subject to the insolvency jurisdiction of the state concerned. This jurisdiction will invariably include domiciled individuals, partnerships and ordinary companies. The position as regards foreign companies depends, but
many commercial states exercise insolvency jurisdiction over foreign companies which do business locally or have local assets. Some entities may be
subject to a special bankruptcy regime, notably banks (which are not subject
to a separate regime in Britain but are in the United States), insurance companies, utilities, statutory governmental corporations, municipalities (not
subject to any British insolvency regime) and international organisations
(probably not subject to British insolvency jurisdiction).

Debts owing by the insolvent: summary

It is useful to deal separately, to some degree at least, with debts owing by   **6–12**
the insolvent and debts owing to the insolvent since different rules apply.
    The general rule is that debts owing by the insolvent are eligible for set-
off in the jurisdictions allowing insolvency set-off if all the following are
satisfied:

(a) The reciprocal claims are mutual in the sense that, prior to the insol-
    vency, (a) there are only two debtor – creditors, and (b) each claimant is
    both beneficial owner of the debt owed to him and personally liable on
    the debt owed by him: para 8–1 *et seq.* The reciprocal claims do not
    have to arise under the same transaction or connected transactions or
    transactions of the same type.

(b) Both claims were incurred prior to the insolvency date or arose out of
    contracts or other dealings entered into prior to the insolvency date,
    even if the debt matures or accrues after the insolvency date. Hence
    claims incurred by the insolvency representative on new contracts
    entered into by him in the course of administration are not eligible for
    set-off. Instead his liability is generally payable as a priority expense.
    But a claim against the estate arising from a contract entered into prior
    to the insolvency date is eligible, e.g. a claim for damages for breach of
    the contract or its repudiation by the insolvent estate. If the insolvent
    estate performs a pre-existing contract, e.g. by paying the price for a
    delivery of goods, that claim is probably eligible for set-off in England,
    but, even if it is not, it is payable as a priority claim so no harm is done.

(c) The debt owing by the insolvent must be a debt claimable in the insol-
    vency, and not invalid or excluded from proof for some reason: see para
    6–13.

(d) The claim of the creditor must be a money claim, not an in rem proprietary claim for the specific return of an asset or a proprietary priority
claim for money held on trust by the estate. In this case the "creditor" is
paid in any event by virtue of his priority claim: para 6–46 *et seq*.

(e) The claim is not excluded from set-off by rules preventing the build-up
of preferential set-offs: para 6–38 *et seq*.

In **England,** the cut-off insolvency date is the liquidation order (not petition) or earlier winding-up resolution.

Debts owing by the insolvent: provability

6–13   A debt is not eligible for set-off unless the creditor is entitled to claim it in
the insolvency – it must be "provable", "verifiable", "admissible", "allow-
able", etc.
   If a debt is provable, usually it is eligible for set-off in its provable
amount. The general pattern is that all claims are provable, whether
matured, contingent or illiquid and regardless of their origin, i.e. whether
arising from contract or under a sealed instrument, notarial act or otherwise.
   Common exclusions for non-provable debts include tort claims (provable
now in England but not in many other English-based states unless the claim
can also be brought in contract such as a claim for negligence or misrepresentation), future alimony and the like, various unenforceable debts such
as gaming debts (important for those states which treat securities or options
trading as gambling), time-barred debts, interest and rentals accruing post-
insolvency, claims by foreign authorities for taxes or penalties, claims
excluded from proof by the rule against double proof (see para 6–17) and
claims unenforceable under Art VIII 2(b) of the IMF Bretton Woods Agreement requiring that "exchange contracts" conflicting with certain exchange
control regulations of an IMF state be treated by member states as "unenforceable". Rarely, if ever, are claims by foreign creditors excluded from
proof, although foreign creditors are discriminated against in a few states:
notably in Latin America.

Unmatured debts owing by the insolvent

6–14   As a general rule applicable in the states allowing insolvency set-off, unmatured credits not requiring further performance to earn them, such as
loans, term deposits and deferred purchase credits, are provable and hence
eligible for set-off. This is because the bankruptcy, either expressly or as a

matter of necessary implication, results in a statutory acceleration of claims so that they may be presently proved for against the insolvent state.

Debts may be discounted back to reflect the acceleration and usually it is only the discounted amount which is set off. In Germany debts are discounted back at a rate varying between 4 per cent to 6 per cent p.a. In the Netherlands, claims with a fixed maturity of one year are provable at their full value; if after that year, their value is estimated. Discounting seems universal: e.g. Japan, South Korea, Panama, Italy, Switzerland, Denmark, Finland, Norway and Sweden.

In England the discounting provisions do not apply to a set-off of an unmatured debt owing by the insolvent: see IR 1986, r 11.13, as amended. In other jurisdictions which do apply discounting to set-off, it would be for consideration whether discounting applies if the creditor has a right to accelerate the unmatured credit. If so, discounting would depreciate the value of a term deposit, term loan or deferred purchase credit even though the credit does not contain an interest element (as would be the case with equipment rentals under finance leases or single sum notes bundling up both principal and interest).

Unliquidated debts owing by the insolvent

It seems to be general in the allowing states that unliquidated debts, such as   6–15
claims for damages for breach of contract, are available for set-off at their valued or assessed amount if the claim was incurred by the insolvent prior to the insolvency, or arose under a contract entered into prior to the insolvency, and provided that the claim is provable (tort claims being excluded in some states). If the unliquidated claim qualifies for transaction set-off, it is eligible for set-off, apparently universally.

Contingent debts owing by the insolvent

Many of the insolvency set-off jurisdictions permit contingent claims owing   6–16
by the insolvent to be set off at their valued amount, e.g. the liability of a guarantor to the principal creditor. This involves a valuation of the contingent debt. This is so in England (many cases) and in Germany (BA s 69), Japan (BC Arts 98–104) and the Netherlands (BA Art 130). Other examples are the liability of an insolvent guarantor to the principal creditor, reimbursement liabilities, liabilities to repurchase a debt from a creditor on a default by the debtor owing that debt, annuities, insurance liabilities (subject to any separate insurance regime), underwriting liabilities and contingent subordinated liabilities.

The Scandinavian solution appears to be that, if the debt owed by the insolvent is still contingent, the creditor must pay in the non-contingent claim he owes and if the contingency then occurs so as to crystallise the debt which the insolvent owes the creditor, the creditor is entitled to be paid the matured contingency as a preferred claim. If the winding-up has been completed, the insolvency representative must keep a reserve for the creditor's possible claim: see Denmark BA s 44, Norway BA s 8–5, Sweden BA s 121(a).

Contingent reimbursement liabilities owing by the insolvent

6–17   A special problem arises where a bank issues a guarantee or letter of credit to guarantee a debt payable by the bank's customer to the creditor and beneficiary of the guarantee or letter of credit. The bank's customer – the debtor – is liable to reimburse the bank if the bank has to pay the creditor under the guarantee. In order to "secure" the debtor's reimbursement liability, the debtor makes a deposit with the bank so that the bank can set off the accrued reimbursement liability against the deposit. The problem arises because of the rule against double-proof.

It is obvious that, if there are ten guarantors, each owing a deposit to the principal debtor, and if each could set off the contingent reimbursement liability of the principal debtor to them against their deposits before any guarantor has paid anything to the principal creditor, the principal debtor's estate would have paid the same debt 10 times before the real creditor had received one sou. Hence there can only be one proof – which must be that of the main creditor in respect of the guaranteed debt. Hence the guarantor is not allowed to prove so long as the creditor is proving. If the guarantor cannot prove, then there is nothing to set off against and he must pay the deposit to the debtor's estate. Effectively the guarantor loses his set-off.

The rule ought to be that the guarantor can set off if and when he is subrogated to the creditor's claim against the debtor – which is when the guarantor pays in full. But if the creditor has received dividends on his proof, then the creditor's proof has already been satisfied and it is too late to use it again – this would amount to a double-proof. So the latest cut-off point should be the date of the payment of dividends on the creditor's prior proof.

6–18   The English position might be that the guarantor must have paid the creditor in full before the creditor lodges his proof against the principal debtor (or perhaps before the creditor has received a dividend from the principal debtor on his proof): EISO paras 10–70 *et seq.* If he pays before the cut-off date, then he has a right of proof against the principal debtor for reimbursement (subject to any prohibition in the guarantee) and hence may set off a debt he owes to the insolvent debtor. An example is where a bank has paid a standby letter of credit issued for the account of a customer and owes the customer a deposit. If the bank pays after that cut-off date, the bank has lost its right to set off and hence the "security" of the deposit. This risk should be covered by a provision in the guarantee that the creditor must not claim against the debtor without first calling the guarantee so as not to trump the guarantor's right of proof and hence of set off. In practice, creditors usually do look to the guarantor first.

The English position with regard to partial guarantees is complex. Broadly the guarantor or issuer of the letter of credit must have paid the full claim guaranteed to have a right of reimbursement by subrogation, even if the guarantor's liability is subject to a lesser limit and the guarantor has paid up to that limit. If the guarantor guarantees 100 subject to a limit of 60, he must pay 100 to be subrogated. There are several English decisions to this effect: EISO para 10–132 et seq. Alternatively if he guarantees only 60 and pays that, then he is subrogated and has his set-off. The moral for bank guarantors is not to agree to a guarantee of all sums owing to the principal creditor subject to a lesser limit but agree to pay only a specified lesser sum. Guarantees of course often contain a clause preventing the guarantor from claiming reimbursement from the debtor in competition with the creditor: these clauses would prevent a set-off.

6–19 The US position under s 502(e) of the Bankruptcy Code of 1978 appears to be similar except that the cut-off point seems to be the time of allowance of the reimbursement claim. But the case law should be reviewed. The double-proof analysis has been applied elsewhere, e.g. in Scotland: *Henderson v MacKinnon* (1876) 3 R 608.

Similar questions arise in relation to contribution liabilities, such as the liability of co-guarantors, co-tortfeasors, co-contractors, co-directors and co-fiduciaries where each is contingently liable to pay the other if the other should pay more than his share. Until the principal creditor or the victim has been paid in full, he ought to have a senior right of proof against all the co-obligors which should shut out their contingent rights of contribution and hence any right they may have to set off a contribution liability owed to them by their co-debtor against a claim which they owe to the potential contributor. No proof, no set-off.

Foreign currency debts owing by the insolvent

6–20 It would appear to be a near universal rule that foreign currency debts owing by the insolvent are converted into local currency on the relevant insolvency date. This is so, e.g. in England (IR 1986, rr 4.91, 6.111), Germany, Italy, Austria, Denmark and the United States (see BC 1978 s 502(b)). The Netherlands Bankruptcy Act specifically allows multi-currency set-off by Art 133 (bankruptcy) and Art 260 (suspension of payments) and converts a foreign currency debt owing by the bankrupt on the day of the bankruptcy: Hoge Raad, February 4, 1977, NJ 1978 No. 66.

The question will then be whether the claim owing to the insolvent, which may be in a different currency, remains eligible for set-off and, if so, whether it is converted for set-off purposes on the same day, because if it is not, the creditor is exposed to a foreign exchange risk: see para 6–33.

Subordinated debts owing by the insolvent

6–21   A debt owing by the insolvent may be subordinated to general unsecured creditors by virtue of a rule of insolvency law or by virtue of express arrangements.

If a debt is subordinated by an insolvency rule, set-off would defeat the subordination by conferring on the subordinated creditor a priority payment. Of particular interest are: the subordination on equitable grounds of those who in effect interfere in the management of the insolvent under the US "Deep Rock" doctrine; the subordination of bank creditors in such countries as the Netherlands on the ground that they have, by continuing to lend, encouraged false credit; the subordination of creditors who have lent money at a rate of interest varying with profits (s 3 of the English Partnership Act 1890 – which does not apply only to partnerships and is paralleled elsewhere, e.g. Canada); and the subordination of sums due to company members in the nature of dividends or profits. One would expect that set-off should not defeat the subordination, but in England debts subordinated under s 3 of the Partnership Act 1890 might still be eligible for set-off: EISO para 7–217. This is because of the intense English policy in favour of set-off.

In the case of contractual subordinations or subordination trusts, care needs to be taken in the drafting to make sure that the junior creditor is not paid by set-off. This generally requires that the subordination trust must come into effect before the insolvency date so as to destroy mutuality (at least in those states, such as England, which insist on a mandatory insolvency set-off) or alternatively the junior claim must be drafted as a debt which is merely conditional on the creditor being paid, i.e. on the principal debtor being solvent. It would then have no value eligible for set-off if the debtor were insolvent.

Preferential debts owing by the insolvent

6–22   Where a creditor is entitled to be paid prior to ordinary creditors, a set-off will not necessarily improve his position because he is paid in any event. But set-off is relevant if the assets are insufficient even to pay the preferential creditors.

The prior payment of preferential creditors is universal in insolvency law, although the length of the list varies greatly. Many commercial jurisdictions treat employee remuneration and certain government taxes as preferential. Under English insolvency law, a bank or other person who pays off preferential claims for wages steps into the shoes of the employee concerned and thereby acquires his preferential status: see IA 1986 Sched 6 para 11.

In England preferential debts are eligible for set-off: EISO para 7–209 *et seq*. Where a debtor-creditor of the insolvent is owed claims by an insolvent, one of which is preferential and the other non-preferential, the English set-off is applied rateably against the preferential and non-preferential debts in proportion to their respective amounts: *Re Unit 2 Windows Ltd* [1985] 3 All ER 647. The result is that the creditor cannot appropriate the set-off wholly to the non-preferential claim so as to pay that in full and so to preserve the whole of the preferential claim (which is paid because it has priority). See also *Re EG Morel (1934) Ltd* [1962] Ch 121.

Secured debts owing by the insolvent

Where a creditor has security for a debt owing by an insolvent and the security is over property of the insolvent, he cannot both prove for the whole of the debt and keep the security because this would give him two funds to resort to, both coming out of the insolvent's estate. A secured creditor therefore has an election. He can (a) rest on his security, or (b) realise his security and prove for the balance, or (c) value his security and prove for the short form, or (d) surrender and prove for his whole debt: see the English IR 1986. **6–23**

If the mortgagee rests on his security his proof is excluded, there is no set-off. No proof, no set-off: *Re Norman Holding Co* [1990] 3 All ER 757.

If there is an unsecured balance, and the surplus is realised after the insolvency date a number of English cases have held that this is a debt eligible for set-off and is not treated as property of the estate ineligible for set-off. But the cases are inconsistent: EISO para 9–286 *et seq*.

Debts owing by the insolvent collaterally secured

Where a creditor has collateral security from a third party to secure a debt of the insolvent, the creditor can set off the claim owed by the bankrupt and does not have to resort to the security first: *Re Hart* (1884) 25 Ch D 716; *McKinnon v Armstrong* (1877) 2 App Cas 531. In other words, the rule that a creditor cannot both prove and keep the security does not apply if the security is over property of a third party because there is no duplication of remedy so far as the insolvent's estate is concerned. **6–24**

Executory contracts: claims owing by the insolvent

6–25   In the case of executory contracts with the insolvent, e.g. sale contracts, the usual result is that if the contract is cancelled (either by the trustee in bankruptcy repudiating or disclaiming the contract under statutory provisions or by virtue of a power of rescission in the contract itself or arising under insolvency law (see the rescission provisions in the English IA 1986 ss 186 and 345)), the creditor's damages are generally provable and hence eligible for set-off. They arose out of a pre-insolvency dealing and it is immaterial that the damages accrued after the insolvency. This is so in England, Germany and the Netherlands.

If on the other hand the trustee is entitled to and does perform (such as by taking delivery of commodities, securities or foreign exchange) the price or other debt payable by the insolvent estate is normally a priority claim as an expense of the administration of the estate in which event set-off is not usually needed, e.g. as in Germany and England. This result will not however assist in the case of netting schemes which rely on the set-off of gains and losses. In order to avoid "cherry-picking" it is essential that all the contracts should be capable of rescission and all gains and losses set off: see chapter 10.

6–26   Many jurisdictions give the insolvent party the right to call upon the insolvency representative to decide within a specified period whether or not he will perform – as in England, Italy, Germany, Denmark and Switzerland. Sometimes the insolvency representative must provide security for his performance, e.g. Switzerland, Denmark and the Netherlands. It is often the case that the insolvency may itself amount to repudiation, entitling the creditor to cancel, e.g. if time is of the essence.

In the United States by virtue of s 365 of the Bankruptcy Code, the trustee can, subject to court approval, assume certain executory contracts even if they contain an insolvency rescission clause. But this is subject to certain important exceptions, some of which are mentioned in chapter 11. If the trustee rejects a burdensome asset, then by s 502(9) the damages are provable as an ordinary debt.

The contract must have been entered into prior to the insolvency date. Sums payable under new contracts entered into by the insolvency representative in the course of the administration are not eligible for set-off.

Debts owing to the insolvent: summary

6–27   There are crucial differences between debts owed *by* an insolvent and those owed *to* an insolvent for set-off purposes.

In the first place there is generally no statutory method of quantifying contingent or unascertained claims owing to the insolvent. Secondly, the statutory acceleration (with or without discount) which applies to matured debts owing by an insolvent does not generally apply to debts going the other way.

The usual position is that a debt owing to the insolvent is eligible for set-off if:

(a) the reciprocal claims are mutual: para 8–1 *et seq*;

(b) both claims arose out of pre-insolvency dealings;

(c) the debt owing to the insolvent is legally valid and enforceable;

(d) the claim owing to the insolvent is a debt or money claim, not an *in rem* proprietary claim: para 6–46 *et seq*;

(e) (usually) the claim is not for the return of a preference or other bankruptcy disgorge obligation.

Legal validity of debt owing to the insolvent

It is generally true that the debt owing to the insolvent must be legally valid 6–28 and enforceable by action. If not, the insolvency representative cannot sue for it and the creditor may prove for dividends on the debt owed to him by the insolvent.

This may apply to claims which are time-barred or unenforceable on grounds of usury or gaming, claims unenforceable under Art VIII 2(b) of the Bretton Woods Agreement (applying to "exchange contracts" conflicting with the exchange controls of an IMF member) and claims unenforceable because of some formal defect such as lack of writing or absence of pre-scribed disclosure (especially in consumer credit and securities transactions).

Unmatured credits owing to the insolvent

In England an unmatured credit, such as a loan or term deposit owing to the 6–29 insolvent, is eligible for set-off if it matures during the insolvency proceedings and probably even if it is a long-dated debt. For the case law, see EISO para 7–131 *et seq*.

If there were no set-off of long term debts, such as debentures or bonds held by the insolvent, and the instrument is negotiable or transferable free of set-offs of a cross-claim owed to the issuer by the insolvent holder and if the insolvency representative sells the instrument, the transferee would take free of any set-off. This problem may not arise in relation to ordinary assignable debts because the assignee will often take subject to the set-off of the cross-claim owed by the insolvent-assignor to the debtor liable for the assigned claim: para 8–5 *et seq*.

In this connection an interesting feature of unmatured debts due to the estate is to be found in Scandinavian bankruptcy legislation. Denmark provides in BA s 45 that, if the estate assigns a claim so that the creditor forfeits his access to set-off, the estate must compensate him for the loss thus incurred. See also Norway, BA s 8–6; Sweden, BA s 121(a).

Norway is idiosyncratic in excluding from set-off a debt owing to the insolvent if it matures after the insolvency and if the debt owing by the insolvent matured before the insolvency: BA s 8–1. The rationale appears to be that the debtor would not have been entitled to a solvent set-off and so should not have it on insolvency. This is potentially disastrous for banks owing term deposits or dealers owing term margin deposits to an insolvent, but fortunately for creditors Norway's view appears to be an isolated one not adopted elsewhere (although the point should be checked).

Unliquidated debts owing to the insolvent

6–30   Where a claim owing to the insolvent is unliquidated, such as a claim for damages arising from a pre-insolvency breach of contract or tort (delict) by the creditor-debtor, England will allow a set-off: EISO para 7–135 *et seq.*

Further research would be required to establish the position in those jurisdictions (such as the Canadian provinces and Germany) which apply the ordinary rules of statutes of set-off or civil code compensation to debts owed to the insolvent: these rules require liquidity except in the case of transaction set-off or its local equivalent.

The same question may arise under the US set-off section in BC 1978 s 553. Set-off is a matter of state law and the insolvency set-off clause is merely facultative. The same problem does not arise in relation to unliquidated debts owing by the insolvent because these are generally ascertained by the process of proof.

However, transaction set-off appears to be universally available on insolvency.

Secured claims owing to the insolvent

6–31   Where the insolvent's claim is secured and the creditor is proving or claiming to prove for an unsecured debt owing by the insolvent, there is a set-off between the secured claim and the creditor's unsecured claim: *Re Deveze, ex p Barnett* (1874) LR 9 Ch 293.

Claims owing to insolvent out of executory contracts

6–32   Executory contracts which are performed by the insolvency representative after the insolvency date and which result in claims owing to the insolvent, e.g. the creditor's duty to pay the price for goods delivered, give rise to situations too complex to detail here: see EISO para 7–145 *et seq*. The main-stream English position is broadly that if the insolvent estate performs by using assets of the estate, e.g. delivering goods or foreign exchange or completing building works, so as to earn the price, the price owing to the estate is not eligible for set-off unless the set-off is a transaction set-off. This underlines the importance for netting agreements of the counterparty being entitled to cancel all contracts with the insolvent so as to set off losses and gains and hence to prevent a situation where the insolvent estate can perform profitable contracts without inviting a set-off and cancel the unprofitable contracts: see chapter 10.

Foreign currency debts owing to the insolvent

If the debts are in different currencies, the set-off requires a conversion into   6–33
the same currency, so that the claims are commensurable. Note that the debt owing by the insolvent is usually converted into the local currency automatically on bankruptcy: para 6–20.

Further investigation would be required to establish whether the lack of commensurability defeats set-off. Currency differences do not defeat insolvency set-off in England, and should not do so in countries with a strong set-off policy. If there is a problem, the contract should provide for conversion into the currency of the debt owing by the insolvent – which, as noted, will usually be compulsorily converted into local currency. The same rate should be used.

In the case of foreign currency debts owing to the insolvent, the English position is probably that the debt is converted into sterling at the spot market rate of exchange at the insolvency date for set-off purposes so as to achieve equality: see *Re Dynamics Corporation of America* [1976] 2 All ER 669.

If a later conversion date were used, the creditor may be exposed to a foreign exchange exposure and the amount of the set-off would vary. Accordingly the creditor's voting and proof rights would change according to fluctuations in the value of the debt owed to the insolvent. It would seem sensible for bankruptcy courts to strike conversion rates both ways at the same insolvency date and to use the same conversion rate.

Whether insolvency set-off is mandatory

In England and in the other jurisdictions adopting versions of the English   6–34
insolvency set-off clause, the clause is mandatory and it is not possible to contract out, unless the creditor renounces his right of proof altogether:

National Westminster Bank Ltd v Halesowen Presswork & Assemblies Ltd [1972] 80 785: *Re The Paddington Town Hall Centre Ltd* (1979) 4 AC LR 673 (Australia); *Rendell v Doors & Doors Ltd* (1975) 2 NZ LR 191 (New Zealand).

Although freedom of contract is overridden, the English mandatory insolvency set-off seems a convenient rule for most cases. The reason is that, as between solvent parties, it is often easy to find an inferential agreement that a creditor will not set off in many cases, e.g. where an account is dedicated for a special purpose. There are numerous situations where the parties wish to deny set-off in solvent dealings, but where this should fall away if one party is insolvent. An example is an agreement by a bank not to set off two accounts so that the customer is able to draw on the credit balance on one account, even if the other is overdrawn. If these agreements were to nullify insolvency set-off, the bank or other debtor's expectations would be defeated since the situations in which a counterparty would not want to set-off on the insolvency of his creditor-debtor must be rare. The result would be that parties would have to add yet another clause to their contract terminating express or implied contracts not to set off on the insolvency of the other. This would be commercially tiresome and the risk of parties forgetting to insert a term which they would obviously intend must be high.

6–35   In the case of subordinations, the mandatory set-off does not defeat the subordination if it is properly drafted. In the case of debt restructuring schemes, the bank holding the operating account of the debtor may have a set-off and it is customary for this priority recovery to be shared with other banks under loss-sharing agreements.

The rules are also significant, not only in relation to widespread contracts not to set off, but also in relation to other claims which are insulated from solvent set-off. Thus in England the maker of a promissory note may not set off a cross-claim owing to him by the first holder of the note against the claim on the note in solvent proceedings, but can do so on insolvency: EISO para 12–79 *et seq.* Hence the protection afforded by a note collapses on the insolvency of either party, as it should. This situation is to be distinguished from a case where the note has been transferred: nowhere can the maker set off a cross-claim owing to him by the original holder against a subsequent holder in due course of the note.

In a German case, the court decided that in composition proceedings relating to a bank an exclusion of set-off by the customer in the bank's general business conditions did not prevent the customer from setting off a credit balance and a loan because the general business conditions must be deemed to have fallen away: BGH decision of July 6, 1978, NJW 2244. The court sensibly implied a term as to the duration of the agreement.

In the United States, the set-off is not mandatory and may be varied, e.g. **6–36** by a creditor turning over his debt to the estate or filing a proof of claim without asserting a set-off or by acceptance of a distribution: see *Collier's Bankruptcy Manual* (3rd ed) para 553.10. The position is probably similar in Canada since the set-off is evidently also not mandatory.

In the Netherlands the insolvency set-off clause in BA Art 53 has been held not to be mandatory so that parties may contract out: HR June 28, 1985, NJ 1986, no 192; HR, Jan 16, 1987, NJ 1987, no 553.

Preferences and insolvency set-off

Because insolvency set-off enables a creditor to be paid in full ahead of **6–37** other creditors, there is the risk that transactions might be entered into between the insolvent and the creditor which are substantially preferential – as where the potential insolvent places money on deposit with a bank with a view to the money being used for a set-off. Banks may build up set-offs during the suspect insolvency period by virtue of credit transfers and other payments into the insolvent's bank account by debtors to the insolvent.

While statutory formulations vary, the general tradition is that where a potential insolvent enters into a transaction which places the solvent party in a better position than he would have been on the insolvency at a time when the other party is insolvent, then, if the transaction takes place during the relevant suspect period (ranging from 3 months upwards), the transaction may be set aside on the insolvency, unless a defence is available. The general rule in countries allowing insolvency set-off is that, although the set-off is not preferential (because it is mandated by insolvency law), a payment or transaction producing the set-off might be, e.g. a payment by the debtor into his bank account which is subsequently set-off. The topic is reviewed in another work (on the principles of insolvency) in this series on international financial law.

Prohibition on build-up of set-offs in suspect period

Many jurisdictions which provide for an enhanced insolvency set-off also **6–38** specifically prevent acquisitions of debts in the suspect period so as to build up a set-off. A debtor to the bankrupt estate may, prior to the bankruptcy, buy debts from creditors of the bankrupt with a view to setting them off. For example, the bankrupt owes a creditor 100. A debtor owes the bankrupt 100. If the debtor buys the creditor's debt, then the debtor will be able to set off and will not have to pay his 100 to the estate. If the expected dividend from the bankrupt is only 10 per cent., the creditor will be better off if he sells to the debtor for more than 10 since this is all he would get on the bankruptcy. Preference law does not catch these transactions because the bankrupt is not involved – the sale is solely between the creditor and debtor. The law seeks to prevent the set-off if it is preferential, e.g. because the bankrupt is in fact insolvent, when the equality principle should apply. But the normal preference rules are applied more cautiously because of the need to protect legitimate transactions – defences, such as the bankrupt's preferential intent, cannot apply.

In England the cut-off for the acquisition of debts to build up a set-off is now virtually non-existent. Only debts acquired after notice of petition or summoning of the relevant creditors meeting are unavailable for set-off: see IA 1986 s 323 and the IR 1986, r 4.90. In other English-based jurisdictions which still base their law on pre-1986 English Bankruptcy Acts, the cut-off for the acquisition of debts is generally the commission of the act of bankruptcy, e.g. the declaration of inability to pay debts, or its corporate equivalent, but only if the solvent party had notice of the relevant act.

Whatever the position prior to insolvency, it seems to be invariably the case that debtors to the insolvent cannot improve their position by buying up claims owed by the insolvent after the insolvency order. As a random example, see *Lawrie v Robertson* (1783) M 2581 (Scotland) which shows that this rule enjoys respectable antiquity. In England see, e.g. *Middleton v Pollock, ex p Nugee* (1875) LR 20 Eq 29.

6–39   In the United States, debts acquired by the creditor from a third party within 90 days of insolvency commencement are excluded from set-off, even if the acquiror did not know of the actual insolvency: this creates a three-month unpredictable risk period.

Elsewhere knowledge of the insolvency is commonly required so that the creditors are not surprised. Austria BA Art 20 excludes insolvency set-off where the claim of the bankrupt is acquired within the period of six months before the adjudication of bankruptcy and the creditor knows or should have known that the debtor was unable to pay. Section 55.3 of the German Bankruptcy Act excludes from set-off a claim of a debtor to the bankrupt acquired by a transaction with the bankrupt or by assignment or redemption of a creditor if at the time of the acquisition he was aware that the bankrupt had stopped payment or that an application for initiating bankruptcy proceedings had been made. Netherlands law also avoids abuse of the right of set-off by BA Art 54, a provision which applies also to suspensions of payment: BA Art 235. The Japanese BC Art 104, echoed by the Korean BA Art 95, enacts a similar principle by providing that if the obligor of the bankrupt has acquired a claim in bankruptcy knowing that there has been a suspension of payments or that a petition for bankruptcy has been filed, the claim is not eligible for set-off. But this does not apply to claims arising one year or more prior to the adjudication or bankruptcy.

Denmark and Norway have a three month cut-off for acquired claims (see Denmark BA s 42(3) and Norway BA 1984 s 8–2) and longer if the transferee acquired the claim when he knew or should have known that the debtor was insolvent.

Involuntary acquisitions in suspect period allowed for insolvency set-off

Where the acquisition of a claim against an insolvent after the cut-off point 6–40 is involuntary or arises out of a pre-existing transaction, a set-off should be allowed since the object of the rule is only to prevent voluntary improvements in position.

A claim may be acquired involuntarily where, e.g.:

(a) an indorser has to pay a negotiable instrument to the holder and thereby reacquires the instrument: see, e.g. *Collins v Jones* (1830) 10 B&C 777; *MacKinnon v Armstrong* (1877) 2 App Cas 531, HL;

(b) the obligor on a put option is required to repurchase a debt;

(c) a guarantor takes over the principal creditor's claim by subrogation;

(d) the chargor of a claim redeems the security: *Re Wise, ex p Staddon* (1843) 3 MD&D 256;

(e) an overpaid member of a bank syndicate is obliged to acquire part of the claims of banks under a pro rata sharing clause. Pro rata sharing clauses are reviewed in another book in this series (a work on international loans).

The principle is well established in English and US case law and applies even if the involuntary reacquisition of the claim takes place after the relevant insolvency date provided that the claim was held by the debtor to the estate prior to the insolvency date: EISO paras 7–244 and 14–21 *et seq*. Specific provisions appear in the German, Japanese and South Korean Bankruptcy Acts as well as in Scandinavia.

Return of property of the estate without insolvency set-off

It seems to be generally the case that where an insolvent party must return to 6–41 the estate a preference, a transaction at an undervalue, a post-petition disposal, a fraudulent transfer, a voidable transaction under the Pauliana, the post-petition fruits of execution or a liability for wrongful or fraudulent trading, then he must pay the refund or the liability without set-off of either the debt paid by the preference or another debt owed by the insolvent to the creditor. If the position were otherwise, the purpose of the recovery of property of the estate and the policies against preferential transfers, etc., would be vitiated. Property for turnover is property of the estate not liable to be consumed by set-off.

This is the position in England (subject to some refinement – see EISO para 7–262 *et seq*) and also generally in the United States: see, e.g. *US v Roth* 164 Fd 575 (CA2) – a case on a preference.

If the return of the preferential payment results in the preferred debt springing up again, this claim may become eligible for set-off as if it had never been paid: see, e.g. s 502(7) of the US Bankruptcy Code of 1978; *Re Washington Diamond Mining Co* [1893] 3 Ch 95, 111, CA (England).

Set-off in rehabilitation proceedings

6–42   Statutes providing for corporate rehabilitation on insolvency or compositions as opposed to the guillotine of liquidation may affect set-off. An illustrative list of these proceedings is to be found in another work (on the principles of insolvency) in this series on international finance.

The object of a stay on set-off is that the debtor should have access to its assets so as to carry on its business and, the argument would run, it would not be able to do this if banks could set off. On the other hand, set-off is a form of security and, if rehabilitation laws could defeat a set-off without conferring on a creditor alternative protection, set-off, on which so much reliance is placed, would cease to have any value. The annulment of the set-off leads to the effective use of the moneys owing to the estate for the purposes of the business, and the deprivation of the creditor who would otherwise have had a set-off. If this can happen, creditors would not be able to rely on set-off because they cannot control whether or not the debtor invokes a rehabilitation proceeding as opposed to a final liquidation. "Security" is useless unless it stands up on insolvency – all forms of insolvency.

Whether or not the reorganisation law deals specifically with set-offs, set-offs may be prejudiced by virtue of the extension of the maturity of debts or their scaling-down consequent upon creditor or court-approved reorganisation plans. Further, the netting of executory contracts may be prevented if the insolvency representative can forcibly assume contracts and override the counterparty's rights of rescission.

The impact of rehabilitations or compositions on set-off is reviewed in another work in this series, but the position may be briefly summarised here.

6–43   In **England** an administration order under the Insolvency Act 1986 does not stay set-offs as such, nor does it as such stay contractual accelerations of debt or contractual rescission clauses: EISO para 7–19 *et seq*. The effect of an administration therefore is not usually serious for properly drafted documents. However where a company enters into a voluntary arrangement under the Insolvency Act 1986 and the arrangement is approved by the requisite majorities of members and creditors so as to bind dissentient creditors, the effect may be to postpone the maturity of a cross-claim owed to a creditor and hence defeat a set-off: the creditor must pay in the matured debt he owes if it matures before the stretched debt owed to him. The creditor would have to apply to the court on the ground of unfair prejudice under IA 1986 s 6 and in practice plans should not be drafted so as to override set-off since this is discriminatory. The creditor should ideally draft documents so as to be able to exercise a contractual set-off before the creditors' meeting which is the cut-off point: EISO para 7–25, *et seq.*

The US Bankruptcy Code of 1978 adopts the approach of treating set-offs as "security". Set-off after the filing of the bankruptcy petition requires court approval. This is because under s 362(a)(7) of the Code the filing of a petition automatically stays the set-off, but this does not defeat the set-off. The object is that set-off should not be exercised post-petition pending an ordinary examination of the debtor's and creditor's rights. The creditor seeking a post-petition set-off must seek court relief from the automatic stay and a stay will be lifted if the court is satisfied that the right of set-off exists under applicable non-bankruptcy law and is free of the restrictions of the section, notably that preventing an improvement of position in the 90 days preceding the bankruptcy.   **6—44**

There is disagreement in the US cases as to whether a bank's post-petition freeze on the debtor's bank account violates a stay.

However, the set-off may be refused and the property (such as a deposit account) used by the bankrupt estate if the trustee can provide "adequate protection" of the creditor's interest in the property pursuant to s 363. Ordinarily this should not impair the creditor's position and is rather intended to enable the estate to use its assets but subject to protection of the creditor who is treated as a secured creditor and therefore entitled to compensating reimbursement proceeds.

The automatic stay does not in any event apply to certain claims arising out of commodities futures transactions, or options to buy or sell securities or in connection with certain repurchase agreements or to certain financial contracts: see chapter 11.

Art 1920 of the Austrian Composition of Creditors Act provides for set-off in composition proceedings parallel to those in Art 19 of the Bankruptcy Act.   **6—45**

In Italy the insolvency set-off provisions apply also to rehabilitation proceedings (*concordato preventivo, amministrazione controllata*), but there is a stay in the case of the extraordinary administration.

In the states refusing insolvency set-off, it will often be found that set-off on rehabilitation proceedings is also refused. For example, in France the bankruptcy law (Law No 98 of January 25, 1985) by Art 83 more or less totally prevents payment of debts incurred prior to the opening judgment and accordingly the continued operation of civil code compensation is forbidden unless the cross-claims are transactionally related and in certain other cases: para 11–12 *et seq.*

Under the US Chapter 11 proceedings, the trustee can invoke the provisions regarding preferences and fraudulent conveyances and thereby avoid previous set-offs which conflict with those provisions: see BC 1978 s 103, importing ss 547 and 548. The position is similar in England in relation to an administration.

Whether the insolvency provisions preventing the build-up of set-offs by acquisitions of debt in the twilight period apply also to reorganisation varies from jurisdiction to jurisdiction. These provisions do not apply to English administration orders. But Articles 162 and 163 of the Japanese and South Korean Corporate Reorganisation Laws limit rehabilitation set-off to claims which are eligible for set-off prior to the expiry of the period for report of reorganisation claims and reorganisation security rights. There is also a provision against build-ups.

Money and property claims

Generally

6–46   As a general rule, set-off is only available where there is a debtor-creditor relationship both ways, not where one of the parties has an *in rem* or proprietary claim for the restitution or delivery of his property. The international case law in common law jurisdictions is colossal. For the English case law, see EISO chapter 9. For US examples, see especially *Scott on Trusts* (3rd ed).

In this section "money claim" is used to describe a debtor-creditor relationship, whether a claim for a simple debt or for damages or otherwise, and "property claim" is used to describe all types of proprietary or *in rem* claims for the return or delivery of property, including property in the form of money.

Reasons for precluding set-off against property claims

6–47   Set-off between money and property claims is not permitted for a number of reasons. If reciprocal obligations are not commensurable or homogeneous it is not possible, without judicial action, to determine how much is to be set off, although this is not true when the property claim is, e.g. for the return of misappropriated money.

But the two most important reasons are, first, that if an obligor can convert his obligation to deliver property into a money obligation and then set off a money cross-claim, legal relationships, such as the law of sale, would collapse, and secondly where a person is wrongfully dispossessed of his property he should have a property claim against the wrongdoer for the return of his assets or their traceable product free of set-off and ahead of the wrongdoer's creditors in bankruptcy.

Illustrations of property claims

Property claims may conveniently be divided into those for tangible or 6—48 visible property and those for money.

Examples of property claims for tangible or visible property are those for property sold or bailed, including chattelised or semi-chattelised claims, such as cheques or instruments for collection and securities held by custodians or clearing houses.

The more difficult class is that comprising property claims for money because here it may also be necessary to identify the money property – a process which is straightforward if the money is represented by a bank account owed to the trustee but is less than easy if the money has become commingled or has been spent on some other assets. The identification of the money claim depends upon concepts of tracing and appropriation except that in some cases the English courts have abandoned too prim a hunt for the thimble and have simply imposed a priority claim upon the insolvent estate for the reimbursement of lost money. See *Chase Manhattan Bank v Israel-British Bank (London) Ltd* [1981] Ch 105 (mistaken payment); *Space Investments Ltd v Canadian Imperial Bank of Commerce Trust Co (Bahamas) Ltd* [1986] 3 All ER 75, PC (bank trustee).

In this class of property claims for money one may include: 6—49

(a) Claims by a principal against his agent for money received by the agent for the account of the principal if the agent must segregate and is not entitled to treat the receipt as his own, e.g. a correspondent bank, a collecting bank, a broker or a fiscal agent.

(b) Claims for proceeds of debts which have been sold or charged but which are received by the seller or chargor who is not entitled to use the proceeds as his own.

(c) Claims for the return of a mistaken payment.

(d) Claims for payments made for a special purpose, such as deposits to pay debenture interest, loans to finance a specific project which has failed, cash cover for acceptances, guarantees or letters of credit, and payments made to a debtor to ward off his pressing creditors. The trust priority claim for the money may be a resulting trust back to the payer of the money if the prescribed purpose fails. Thus, if a bank receiving cash cover becomes insolvent before paying it over or the fiscal agent becomes insolvent or the project fails, the payer may be able to claim the money – if traceable – ahead of the recipient's creditors. Alternatively the intended creditor or other recipient may have a trust in his favour as a property claim for the money, e.g. where cash cover is intended for the beneficiary of a guarantee. If neither of these apply, the payer is a mere creditor of the insolvent. See generally EISO para 9–90 *et seq* for the extensive English case law.

(e) Claims against delinquents who have misappropriated money not belonging to them, e.g. the director who pays the company's money into his private bank account, the agent who misappropriates his principal's money or the fiduciary who uses his position to gain a secret profit for himself.

If a person has a property claim for money against an insolvent, there is no objection to that person using that claim for a set-off since the reciprocal claims are commensurable. He therefore has a parallel property and money claim, e.g. for a margin deposit. But if he is also insolvent then the essential distinction between a money claim and a property claim becomes apparent because a set-off would deprive his estate of an asset which should be available to the general body of his creditors.

It is also useful to distinguish between a priority claim for money such as a preferential claim on insolvency – which is eligible for set-off (para 6–22) – and a property claim for money – which is not.

Proprietary claims for fungibles or money are almost exclusively a common law remedy if the holder is insolvent. Most civil code jurisdictions convert the proprietary claim into a debt claim if the holder-custodian is insolvent.

Tests of whether money is held in trust

6–50   The main test in England as to whether a relationship is debtor-creditor or whether the claimant has a property claim for the payment of money by its holder is whether the holder is entitled to use the money as his own. This result may be enforced by statute, especially in relation to clients accounts in securities markets and elsewhere. If there is no express direction, then US and English case law looks to such tests as to whether the recipient was required to segregate the money or pay interest on the money: EISO paras 9–57 *et seq.*

For example, a bank receiving money for the account of its customer may use the money as its own and hence become a debtor to the customer. The customer does not have a property claim for the notes or coins or for the transfer of the loan or other asset in which the bank has invested the money. There must now be few, if any, commercial states which do not accept that a bank credit balance is a money debt owing by the bank to its customer, except in the unusual case of "special purpose" or trust deposits. See EISO para 9–85 for a sampling of the case law.

Surplus proceeds of security

An important question in practice is whether a bank which has realised   6–51
security granted by a defaulting debtor can treat the surplus proceeds of sale as a money debt and set it off against another unsecured debt owed to the bank by the mortgagor on the mortgagor's insolvency. The English position is that surplus proceeds are generally regarded as money obligations but the authorities are inconsistent and confusing: EISO paras 9–286 *et seq.* A recent Canadian authority goes the other way: *Re Piscione & Sons Ltd* (1965) 1 OR 515 (Supreme Court of Ontario). This was a case where the surplus proceeds were received after insolvency. It is understood that in the Netherlands surplus proceeds are generally treated as money claims.

Fungibles

As far as the common law jurisdictions are concerned, there is normally no   6–52
set-off between delivery obligations for equivalent fungibles without agreement and this is certainly so on insolvency. However civil code countries almost uniformly allow set-off of fungible things of the same kind which are equally liquid and payable. The rules are probably less important than they might seem because they would appear to apply only to barter as opposed to mutual sales and they often do not apply on insolvency. However in both cases the contractual set-off of fungibles could be important for the netting schemes discuss in chapter 10.

Priority of set-off against tracing claims

Where a person has a tracing claim against a bank for the return of his   6–53
money, e.g. for a mistaken payment, or where he is a wronged undisclosed beneficiary, as where a director or other fiduciary misappropriates money

not belonging to him and deposits the money in his bank account, or where a seller or chargor of receivables collects them and wrongfully deposits the proceeds in his bank account instead of paying them over to the buyer or chargee, the issue arises as to whether the bank may set off, as against the property claims of the true owner (if he can identify his property) a cross-claim owing to the bank by the depositor personally.

The general position in England and the United States is that the bank may set off, prior to notice of the wrongdoing or the undisclosed beneficiary if (a) the bank was ostensibly authorised to create a debtor-creditor relationship with the depositor and (b) the bank gave value, e.g. by lending new money in reliance on the set-off: EISO paras 9–254 *et seq* and 21–48 *et seq*. If these two conditions are satisfied the bank's right of set-off will then be governed by the ordinary rules applicable to interveners as set out in para 8–5 *et seq*.

6–54   However in the United States, set-off against proceeds subject to a security interest may be affected by s 9–106 of the Uniform Commercial Code. Where a chargor creates an Art 9 security interest under the UCC, then by s 9–306(2) the security interest may continue in any identifiable proceeds of the collateral on sale, collection or other disposition, on the terms of that section. Hence if the chargor sells the collateral or collects the receivables subject to the security interest and pays these into his bank account, the bank's common law right – if it has one – to set off a cross-claim owing by the chargor to the bank as against the secured creditor's claim for the proceeds represented by the benefit of the bank account in effect assigned by way of security by the chargor to the secured creditor is modified by s 9–306 and may be overridden so as to give priority to the secured creditor if he has perfected his security interest. The terms of the section are complex and detailed and have given rise to a developing body of difficult case law which it is impracticable to analyse here, other than to flag the point.

CHAPTER 7

SET-OFF BETWEEN SOLVENT PARTIES

Independent set-off between solvent parties

Definition of independent set-off

Independent set-off is the set-off of unconnected and independent claims. It **7–1** appears that, apart from mutuality, almost universally the reciprocal claims must both be liquidated or ascertainable with certainty and both must have matured due and payable. Examples are the prices for two unrelated sales, and lease rentals on one side and deposits on the other.

Some foreign law terms are French: *compensation*; German: *Aufrechnung*; Spanish: *compensacion*; Italian: *compensazione*; Dutch: *compensatie* or *schuldvergelijking*; Danish: *modregnung*.

One of the earliest statutes of set-off was the Scottish Compensation Act 1592, followed by a Virginian Act of 1645, a Pennsylvanian Act of 1682, a New Jersey Act of 1722, the English Statutes of Set-off of 1729 and 1735 and a New York Act of 1741. By one means or another these statutes of set-off were absorbed into common law jurisdictions. In New South Wales it has been said that this set-off has been abolished (EISO para 24–5), but it would seem extraordinary if this jurisdiction did not allow the remedy.

Whether independent set-off is self-help

Jurisdictions differ markedly as to whether independent set-off is self-help **7–2** or automatic or available only in judicial proceedings. There are three main schools:

(a) **Common law school** These jurisdictions generally do not permit independent set-off outside judicial proceedings in the absence of statute or custom to the contrary. The underlying policy appears to be the special emphasis placed in mercantilist common law jurisdictions upon predictability of payment and upon the cash flow principle – policies which favour habitual creditors. In effect, payment by a creditor less the cross-

---

claim is not valid legal tender. The result is that any purported deduction of a cross-claim exposes the debtor to the default consequences of non-payment including damages, interest, contractual repudiation, forfeitures (insurance policies, chartered vessels, equipment leases or land leases), loan accelerations, enforcement of security by an "unpaid" mortgagee and bankruptcy petitions.

Jurisdictions espousing this pro-creditor bar on self-help independent set-off include many US common law jurisdictions (e.g. *US v Isthmian Steamship Co*, 359 US 314 and see *Williston on Contracts*, Vol 6 pp 543 *et seq*) and probably, the various English-based common law jurisdictions such as New Zealand, Australia, Hong Kong, Singapore, Bermuda and the Bahamas (*Searles v Sandgrave* (1855) E&B 639; *Re Hiram Maxim Lamp Co* [1903] 1 Ch 70). Scotland, as an exceptional Roman law jurisdiction may also belong to this camp: see *Cowan v Gowans* (1878) 5 R 581 (an inconclusive case).

Generally, however, these jurisdictions permit a self-help set-off by creditors customarily entitled to general possessory liens in similar circumstances, e.g. banks and brokers, although English case law is somewhat thin on this point: EISO paras 2–61 *et seq*. It may be that in this case the self-help set-off is not reciprocal, i.e. a bank may set off an unpaid term loan against an independent liability owed by the bank, but a customer may not set off a deposit owed by the bank against some independent liability owed to the bank without risking an acceleration.

7–3   The degree to which the common law jurisdictions will protect a debtor against accelerations and forfeitures if he has a set-off exercised extrajudicially seems patchy and unpredictable. As to the United States, *Williston on Contracts*, vol 6 pp 543 *et seq*, cites a large number of decisions involving forfeiture of rights under conditional sale agreements, leases and mortgages where the debtor purported to deduct the cross-claim owed to him in making payment to his creditor. There are English cases to the same effect, particularly in relation to mortgages and insurance policies. However the New South Wales case of *Stewart v Latec Investments Ltd* [1968] 1 NS WR 432 decided (without discussion of the point) that a company was entitled to set off a debt owed to it against a debenture owed by it as a self-help remedy by a simple book entry and in the old English case of *Shipton v Casson* (1826) 5 B&C 378, a debtor's self-help set-off against an instalment of a purchase price credit (apparently) precluded the creditor from accelerating the entire credit for non-payment of the instalment. In the inconclusive case of *BICC v Burndy Corporation* [1985] 1 All ER 417, CA, an English court granted relief against forfeiture of an asset for non-payment where the debtor had a set-off. In US insurance cases, the tendency now is that an insurer is not justified in declaring a forfeiture of an insurance policy for non-payment of premium if the insurer is indebted to the insured, e.g. for dividends or losses from other policies: see, e.g. *US v Morell* 204 F 2d 490 (CCA 1953).

The countervailing factor is that these jurisdictions are very ready to find an implied agreement or course of dealing permitting a self-help set-off: see, for example *Williams v British Marine Mutual Insurance Association Ltd* (1886) 57 LT 27, CA. Further a creditor refusing a set-off is likely to incur the displeasure of the court – as in the *Williams* case cited above. It may therefore be that the hard line common law attitude is on the way out.

(b) **Germanic school** Jurisdictions within this camp permit extrajudicial   7–4
independent set-off by an unconditional irrevocable declaration by the debtor exercising the set-off. Generally there is a lot to be said for this middle course. These jurisdictions include Germany (BGB s 388), Switzerland (CO Art 124), Greece (CC Art 441), the old USSR (CC Art 229), Egypt (perhaps – see CC Art 365), Japan (CC Art 505), South Korea (CC 493) and Thailand (CC Art 342). Extrajudicial declarations are also permitted in Sweden, Norway, Denmark and Finland as a result of case law. Austria, Italy, probably Liechtenstein and perhaps the Netherlands belong to this group, although this is not necessarily sanctioned by the relevant articles in the code.

As will be seen below, the declaration in the declaratory states is retroactive for most purposes so that a borrower, for example, is not exposed to an acceleration of a loan for non-payment of an instalment if he subsequently declares a set-off of a deposit, provided the deposit was due and payable before or at the same time as the instalment of the loan.

(c) **Napoleonic school** The third school comprises those jurisdictions where   7–5
set-off is automatic as soon as the requirements of independent set-off are satisfied both ways, i.e. liquidity, maturity, legal validity and mutuality. No declaration is required and the set-off extinguishes both claims, even without the volition of the parties.

This school includes France, Belgium, Luxembourg (all CC Art 1290), Louisiana, Quebec, Spain (CC Art 1202), Portugal, Argentina (CC Art 852), Panama (CC Art 1080), Brazil, Chile, Mexico, Venezuela, the Philippines, possibly Jersey (*Dyson v Godfray* (1884) 9 App Cas 726, PC), and probably Kuwait. As mentioned, Italy and Austria are no longer members of this camp.

Retroactivity of independent set-off

The question of whether set-off is retroactive to the date the reciprocal   7–6
claims were eligible for set-off is in practice more important than the ques-

tion of whether the set-off is extrajudicial, with or without a declaration. Retroactivity determines when the reciprocal claims are deemed paid for the purposes of default remedies (such as interest), forfeitures, acceleration and withdrawals, and for the purposes of limitation statutes.

The point is also relevant to the question of whether the claims remain in existence until exercise of the set-off for the purposes of moratorium statutes or the stretching by an exchange control and the question of whether a preference rule avoids a set-off effective in a pre-insolvency suspect period.

As a general rule, common law procedural set-off is not retroactive to the date the debts were eligible for set-off but is effective only at the time of judgment: see, e.g. the English case of *Re Hiram Maxim Lamp Co* [1903] 1 Ch 70. It is not clear whether common law self-help independent set-off is ever retroactive.

The Germanic school generally back-dates the set-off retrospectively to the date the debts were eligible for set-off, except for the purposes of foreign exchange conversion which (in Germany) must be taken when the set-off is declared: RG decision of December 22, 1922, 106 RGZ 99.

The Napoleonic automaticity school does not need a retroactive doctrine because the set-off is deemed to take place as soon as the reciprocal claims are eligible for set-off.

Liquidity and independent set-off

7–7   It appears that most, if not all, the leading jurisdictions require that both reciprocal claims be liquidated if they are to qualify for independent set-off so that the amount of the set-off can be ascertained with certainty: see generally, EISO paras 2–68 *et seq* and para 24–24 *et seq*.

Loans, purchase credits, equipment rentals, foreign judgments for a money amount, claims for the return of the price on total failure of consideration and the like are always liquidated as are liquidated damages clauses for fixed sums not amounting to penalties, such as demurrage; termination sums payable under financial leases; and graduated penalties under construction contracts for delay in completion.

But damages for contract breach or tort are unliquidated, as are claims for insurance losses even if there is a total loss under a valued policy: EISO para 2–108.

A guarantee of a liquidated sum is liquidated, but an indemnity against loss is not liquidated: EISO para 112 *et seq*. Probably damages for breach of a foreign exchange contract are unliquidated even though the loss is readily ascertainable by reference to transparent market prices on the screen. Damages for late payment of a debt, e.g. for foreign exchange losses, are no doubt unliquidated for this purpose.

Maturity and independent set-off generally

The general rule internationally is that independent set-off is available only 7–8
if both reciprocal claims have matured due and payable. A set-off prior to
that time would involve an acceleration of one or other of the claims contrary to its terms: see EISO paras 2–131 *et seq* and 24–26 *et seq.*

(a) **Self-help independent set-off** Where the set-off is self-help, the usual
approach in England is that a debtor has until midnight to pay (even if
payment through banking channels is impossible after close of business
– see *The Laconia* [1977] 1 All ER 545, HL) so that a set-off before that
time is improper. Thus if a bank accelerates a loan and immediately sets
off a debtor deposit without giving the borrower until midnight to pay,
the set-off is premature unless the set-off falls within the current account
set-off rules: *Marine Midland Bank-New York v Electric Graybar Co
Inc*, 41 NY 2d 703, 395 NYS 2d 403, 363 NE 2d 1139 (1977).

(b) **Judicial independent set-off** Where independent set-off is exercisable
only in judicial proceedings, then under English rules of procedure the
cross-claim must be due and payable before the creditor-plaintiff commences proceedings: see, e.g. *Edmunds v Lloyd Italico* [1968] 1 WLR
492, CA. Accordingly a cross-claim maturing later can only be pleaded
as a counterclaim which generally means that it must be related and not
independent. Some states, such as Austria, Scotland and Greece, have
more relaxed rules which allow cross-claims maturing during proceedings or even before enforcement to be raised as a defence of set-off – a
point of some importance in relation to loans maturing after a deposit
has fallen due. It is also important in relation to interveners on claims,
such as assignees, garnishing creditors and others, since the cross-claim
must qualify as a set-off if it is to be raised against these interveners:
para 8–5 *et seq.*

Creditor's claim mature, cross-claim immature

Where the creditor's claim is due, but the debtor's cross-claim is not, the 7–9
debtor runs default risks if he chooses to delay payment of the creditor's
primary claim until the debtor's cross-claim matures, e.g. the risks of loan
accelerations, contract repudiation or liability for failure to honour a
cheque. A debtor, such as a bank, owing a deposit cannot refuse to pay
merely because there is a high likelihood that the creditor-depositor will
default in payment of the cross-claim, e.g. a loan when it matures, although
anomalously s 151 of the New York Debtor–Creditor Law allows a debtor

to delay payment of the creditor's claim if certain events have occurred including the filing of a bankruptcy petition against the creditor and certain executions and attachments against the creditor.

Creditor's claim immature, cross-claim mature

7–10 Where the debtor's cross-claim is due but the creditor's primary claim is not, as where a bank loan is due and payable but a deposit owed by the bank to the depositor-borrower is not, the bank may not set off the loan since this amounts to an acceleration of the maturity of the deposit. In such a case, the set-off may be defeated by subsequent events, as where the creditor becomes insolvent in a jurisdiction disallowing insolvency set-off unless the reciprocal claims are eligible for set-off prior to the insolvency; or where the cross-claim is stretched by moratorium statute, an exchange control or creditor voting in rehabilitation proceedings so as to bind dissentient creditors (such as voluntary arrangements under the English Insolvency Act 1986); or where the cross-claim is postponed by a debenture-holder's resolution; or where an assignee, attaching creditor or other invervener claims the creditor's claim and in the jurisdiction concerned the set-off is lost against the intervener unless exercised prior to notice of the intervener; or where the cross-claim becomes statute-barred.

When does a debt mature?

7–11 The point at which a debt matures due and payable depends on its terms. A claim may be due and payable only on reasonable notice or after demand or presentation of an instrument or when a judgment is no longer subject to appeal. A bank's reimbursement claim against a customer in respect of a guarantee or letter of credit issued by the bank to a third party beneficiary is not due and payable until the bank has been called upon to pay the letter of credit or guarantee but it would seem that there is no objection to accelerating the indemnity by a call for cash cover or the like. However, as pointed out at para 6–16 *et seq*, a set-off not exercised in time may be defeated by the operation of the double proof rule if the customer is insolvent.

An unexpired grace period is not generally an objection to immediate set-off. The debt will often be treated as being due and payable when the grace period commences, but this is purely a matter of construction. Many civil codes so provide: see, e.g. France CC 1292, Kuwait CC Art 425 (2), Brazil CC Art 1014.

Communication of self-help independent set-off

In common law countries where in the exceptional case the independent set-   **7–12**
off is self-help, e.g. where the bank would be entitled to a lien in similar circumstances, it is considered that the election to set off should be communicated or otherwise clearly indicated, although by analogy with
appropriation cases, it is thought that the communication need not be formal provided the intention is plain. In Ohio it has been held that an act of
set-off is not complete until three steps have been taken:

> "(1) The decision to exercise the right, (2) some action which accomplishes the
> set-off, and (3) some record which evidences that the right of set-off has been
> exercised": see *Baker v National Citibank of Cleveland* 387, F Supp 1137 (ND
> Ohio 1974), affirmed 511 Fd 1016 (6th Cir) 1975.

But in *Pittsburgh National Bank v United States*, 657 F 2d 36 (3d Cir)
1981 it was held that under Pennsylvania law set-off occurred automatically
and that affirmative steps by the bank were not necessary to effect the set-off
where the account had been attached pursuant to a US federal tax levy. But
this latter decision may have been a case of current account set-off where, as
will be seen, notice is often not necessary: para 7–16.

In the Germanic declarative regimes, an irrevocable and unconditional
declaration of a self-help independent set-off must be communicated to the
creditor.

In the Napoleonic automatic regimes, the set-off is automatic and no
notice to the creditor is necessary.

Current account set-off between solvent parties

Definition of current account set-off

Current account set-off is the set-off of debits and credits on demand cur-   **7–13**
rent or running accounts, notably accounts between bank and customer but
also including accounts between brokers and their clients.

Characteristics of current account set-off

The set-off is idiosyncratic in that: **7–14**

(a) Everywhere it appears to be self-help from the bankers side (if not from
the customer's) since it is an off-shoot of bankers lien.

(b) Even in those jurisdictions which prohibit insolvency set-off, current account set-off in favour of the bank is universally available: para 6–10. But in the hostile jurisdictions, this may not be the case as between two separate current accounts.

(c) The set-off is generally available against assignees, attaching creditors and other interveners: para 8–14.

(d) It appears to be often the case, in England at least, that the midnight rule mentioned at para 7–8 does not apply, i.e. the current accounts can be set off immediately even though a customer has until midnight to pay the debit balance and even though debit balances are callable only on reasonable notice, e.g. *Garnett v McEwan* (1872) LR 8 Exch 10.

7–15   Because of the self-help aspect and because of the immediacy of the blending, the set-off is sometimes called combination or the two accounts are not regarded as having been set off at all but merely treated as a single running account. Still, two accounts are not one account.

Many jurisdictions have codified the current account relationship, indicating when the set-off is available, see, e.g. the Austrian ComC Arts 355–357, Japan's ComC Arts 529–534, Italian CC Art 1853 and the Californian CC s 3054.

Current account set-off is not a lien by the bank over the customer's deposit. Lien is the retention of property, but in the case of set-off the bank does not have property in the deposit: the property in the deposit is vested in the customer as the customer's asset and accordingly the use of lien terminology, though common especially in earlier cases, is pure metaphor. This point has been noted in numerous common law jurisdictions: e.g. England, *National Westminster Bank Ltd v Halesowen Presswork & Assemblies Ltd* [1972] 1 All ER 641, see especially [1970] 3 All ER 473, 487, CA; Canada, *Royal Trust Co v Molson's Bank* (1912) 27 OLR 441,448; Virginia, *National Acceptance Co of America v Virginia Capital Bank*, US DC ED Virginia, 1980, 498 F Supp, 1078; Ireland, *Re Morris* (1922) 1 IR 81, 92.

Whether current account set-off available without notice

7–16   In England a bank can set off and combine current accounts without notice to the customer: see, e.g. *Garnett v McEwan* (1872) LR 8 Ex Ch 10; *Halesowen Presswork & Assemblies Ltd v Westminster Bank Ltd* [1971] 1 QB 1, CA, 34; reversed on different grounds sub nom *National Westminster Bank Ltd v Halesowen Presswork & Assemblies Ltd* [1972] AC 785.

New York's Banking Law provides in s 9–g:

"2. No banking institution shall assert, claim or exercise any right of set-off against any other deposit account held by such banking institution unless, prior to or on the same business day of such action, notice of the set-off together with the reasons for the set off are mailed to the depositor.

3. Failure to provide the notice required by this section shall not be deemed to affect the validity of the right of set-off.''

Section 864 of the Californian Financial Code requires that notice of a set-off of certain debts owing to a bank in prescribed form be given to a natural customer.

Contracts against current account set-off

Current account set-off is not available if there is an express or implied   7–17
agreement against set-off. In England this agreement is easily implied because otherwise the customer would be exposed to sudden dishonour of his cheques, e.g. where one account is a current account and the other a loan account repayable on demand: *Bradford Old Bank Ltd v Sutcliffe* [1918] 2 KB 833.

Special purpose payments and current account set-off

The most common example of an implied agreement not to set off is where   7–18
one of the accounts is kept for a special purpose, e.g. a wages account or a credit to pay a special liability of the customer: see *Garnett v McEwan* (1872) LR Ex 10, 13; *National Westminster Bank Ltd v Halesowen Pressworks & Assemblies Ltd* [1972] 1 All ER 641, HL; *Rouxell v Royal Bank of Canada* (1918) 2 WWR 791; *Re Saugus General Hospital Inc (Massachusetts decision, 1983)*; *Re Applied Logic Corp*, 576 Fd 952, 958 (2d Cir, 1978); *US v Carlow*, 323 F Supp 1310 (DC Pa 1971) (Pennsylvania); *Engleman v Bank of America* 98, CA 2d 327, 219 P 2d 868 (California).

In England and other English-based jurisdictions such as New Zealand, Australia, Hong Kong, Singapore and Bermuda where the insolvency set-off is mandatory, the insolvency set-off clause will override any contract against current account set-off unless the special purpose designation creates a trust of the money thereby conferring on the depositor a proprietary claim not eligible for set-off: para 6–46 *et seq*.

The mandatory set-off does not apply in the United States (or probably Canada) so a special purpose designation may restrict an insolvency set-off unless, as will usually be the case, the insolvency operates as a cancellation of the special purpose designation flowing from the cancellation of the customer-bank relationship (as it usually will).

Transaction set-off between solvent parties

Definition of transaction set-off

7–19   Transaction set-off is the set-off available to a debtor where both claims arise out of the same transaction or closely connected transactions and (in England) the creditor has defaulted in performance of the very obligation for which he is seeking payment or sometimes has defaulted in the performance of some ancillary obligation. The policy is that a creditor should not be able to claim payment for something which he has not done or has done only partially: part performance, part payment. This policy overrides the cash-flow principle and the policy of predictability of payment.

Transaction set-off is a compendious term to describe the English "equitable set-off" and "abatement" developed separately by courts of equity and common law courts (fused in 1873 with equity prevailing in the case of conflict). The US equivalent is recoupment.

Illustrations of transaction set-off

7–20   Thus a buyer of securities or goods can reduce the price by a cross-claim for damages or for delay. An employer of a building contract can set off against the building price a cross-claim for deficiencies in the building work. A charterer can set off against hire a cross-claim for defects in the ship for which the hire is paid.

A client of a lawyer can deduct, from his liability to pay fees, a cross-claim for damages for negligent services. A tenant can set off a demand for damages, e.g. for non-repair, against his liability for rent and the same applies to equipment leases. A customer may deduct damages where a bank led a customer into believing that head office approval for a further loan would be forthcoming: *Box v Midland Bank Ltd* [1981] 1 Lloyds LR 434. The case law in common law jurisdictions is very considerable: see EISO chapter 4.

Unfortunately in English jurisdictions there is some unpredictability in that the set-off is not available merely because the transactions are closely connected or because both claims arise out of the same transaction. The cross-claim must directly reduce the performance for which the creditor is claiming payment. This situation affects banks taking assignments of contracts as security.

Thus a time charterer can deduct for breach of a speed warranty or for breakdown in machinery because the hire is paid for a working ship. The charterer cannot deduct for damages to the cargo by the owner's crew or for wrongful use by the owner of the charterer's cargo of oil since hire is not paid for the protection of the cargo: see, e.g. *The Leon* [1985] 2 Lloyds LR 470.

Further English and Australian courts have vacillated as to whether a transaction set-off is available in favour of the mortgagor against a mortgagee's claim for the secured loan, as where the mortgagee has allegedly sold the security at an undervalue. The case law is discussed at EISO para 4–93 *et seq.*

The reason for the vacillation is the traditional English hostility to set-off between solvent parties in order to preserve cash-flow and the security of payment to habitual creditors. One suspects that this hostility to solvent set-off is not espoused by the Franco-Latin jurisdictions which favour solvent set-off but disfavour insolvency set-off. It is therefore a matter for investigation whether these countries insist on such close transactional connexity.

Privileges of transaction set-off

The policy of preventing a creditor from claiming payment for something   **7–21** which he has not done confers on transaction set-off a number of privileges.

(a) **Unliquidated claims** The debtor can set off even if either or both of the reciprocal claims is unliquidated, such as a claim for damages: *Hanak v Green* [1958] 2 All ER 141, CA. But an Ontario court has decided to the contrary where both claims are unliquidated: *Mabir Construction Ltd v Thomas Assaly Corp Ltd* (1974) 6 OR (2d) 178. English decisions decide that, if the debtor quantifies his claim reasonably in good faith, he is not in default even if his quantification turns out to be wrong. This rule is necessary because otherwise the debtor would be exposed if he did not have sufficient facts at his disposal to quantify the damages by the time the payment from him, such as hire, fell due: see *The Nanfri* [1978] Lloyds Rep 132, CA; *The Chrysovalandou Dyo* [1981] 1 Lloyds Rep 159; *The Kostas Mellas* [1981] 1 Lloyds Rep 18.

(b) **Self-help** The set-off is self-help and therefore the creditor cannot forfeit, accelerate or withdraw or enforce security for non-payment on the due date merely because the set-off is claimed as a self-help remedy or, probably, is claimed later on in judicial proceedings, i.e. the set-off is probably retroactive for default purposes.

(c) **Insolvency** The set-off is often available on insolvency in those states which otherwise refuse insolvency set-off: para 6–10.

(d) **Interveners** The set-off is generally available against assignees, attaching creditors and other interveners regardless of liquidity or maturity, provided that the transaction was entered into prior to notice to the debtor of the presence of the intervener: para 8–13.

Transaction set-off and closely connected transactions

7–22   The degree of connection between separate transactions required to support a transaction set-off is germane. In one case a cross-claim arising out of an unconnected repurchase of a lease previously sold was held available for transaction set-off: *Bankes v Jarvis* [1903] KB 549. A bank may deduct a cross-claim for fraud arising out of an earlier drawing under a divisible letter of credit, which allows multiple drawings, against a subsequent drawing by the beneficiary under the same letter of credit: *Etablissement Esefka International Anstalt v Central Bank of Nigeria* [1979] 1 Lloyds Rep 445, CA. A charterer may deduct damages under an earlier charterparty against hire payable under a later charterparty where the owner let a vessel on three consecutive charterparties: *The Angelic Grace* [1980] 1 Lloyds Rep 288. But unconnected sale of goods transactions or separate insurance policies are not sufficiently connected.

It is therefore essential that in the case of a series of foreign exchange or interest swap contracts or investment trades, a bank should contractually agree the set-off in order to cover unpredictabilities in this area.

Contractual set-off

Definition of contractual set-off

7–23   Contractual set-off is a set-off created by contract where such set-off would not otherwise exist.

The distinctions between contractual set-off, charge-back and flawed assets are outlined at para 6–5.

A contractual set-off does not normally amount to a charge requiring registration or infringing negative pledges (other than those which specifically prohibit set-offs or any arrangements having the effect of security) since the contract does not amount to the grant of a proprietary security interest. The creditor (such as a depositor) does not grant a security interest over his property in the deposit owed to him to secure the cross-claim owed by him, such as a loan. On the contrary a contractual set-off enables the bank debtor in respect of the deposit to use its asset, namely the loan owed to it, to discharge the liability owed by it and does not involve the use of the depositor's deposit-asset to pay the loan. Some negative pledges are drawn widely enough to prohibit contractual set-offs.

Generally the purpose of a contractual set-off is to remove a bar to set-off which would otherwise exist, e.g. illiquidity or immaturity.

Types of contractual set-off

A contract to set-off may establish the following: **7–24**

(a) Self-help set-off, e.g. of independent unconnected claims. As to when independent set-off is self-help, see para 7–2.

(b) Set-off where one of the claims has not matured, e.g. set-off of an accrued loan against an unaccrued deposit thereby accelerating the payment date of the deposit; or set-off of an unmatured loan against a matured deposit, thereby accelerating the loan; or the acceleration of a reimbursement contingency in favour of a bank which has issued a guarantee or letter of credit to a third party.

(c) Set-off of independent claims where one is unliquidated and the reciprocal claims do not qualify for transaction set-off, as in the case of unrelated banking transactions or a series of foreign exchange contracts or a series of interest swap contracts. As to transaction set-off, see para 7–19 *et seq.*

(d) Set-off of a cross-claim against a creditor where the creditor's claim is otherwise insulated from solvent set-off, e.g. a claim by a creditor on a negotiable instrument; or (in England) a carrier's claim for freight; or where there might be an implied contract against set-off especially in the case of credits to bank accounts for special purposes; or a claim by a beneficiary against a bank under a letter of credit: para 7–33 *et seq.*

(e) Set-off of a debtor's cross-claim otherwise ineligible for set-off, such as a time-barred claim: para 7–38 *et seq.*

(f) Set-off of a multicurrency claim if there is uncertainty in this area: para 7–41 *et seq.*

Purposes of contractual set-off

The dominant purpose of a contractual set-off is usually to enable the   **7–25** debtor to set off a cross-claim which would otherwise not be available for set-off so as to enhance the "security" for the cross-claim and to reduce his exposure. But two other objectives are of practical importance:

(a) Where the debtor wishes to be able to set off his cross-claim as against interveners, e.g. assignees, attaching creditors, undisclosed principals and undisclosed beneficiaries: para 8–5 *et seq.*

(b) Where a party is located in a jurisdiction which disallows insolvency set-off unless granted by contract prior to the relevant suspect period. There appear to be few jurisdictions which allow a contract to confer an otherwise prohibited insolvency set-off. Guernsey is one.

Efficacy of contractual set-off

7–26   Because set-off reduces multiplicity of proceedings, the English courts are very ready to find a contractual set-off on slight grounds, e.g. *Wallis v Bastard* (1853) 4 De GM & G 251.

The contract is subject to usual contractual rules, e.g. contractual intention and consideration, and may be vitiated if it is illegal, e.g. because the contract constitutes financial assistance by a company in favour of a purchaser of the company's shares contrary to s 151 of the British Companies Act 1985 (or its equivalent elsewhere), or because the conversion of convertible debt securities results in shares being issued at a discount, or because the set-off is a contract for differences void as a wagering transaction under gaming legislation.

Insolvency rules may vitiate a contractual set-off, as where the set-off is non-mutual and takes place after the insolvency of a debtor, as in group bank account schemes and multilateral clearing systems; or because it attempts a set-off of a non-provable claim such as post-insolvency interest; or it constitutes a set-off by a bank guarantor of a reimbursement liability of a depositor against a deposit owed by the bank guarantor to the depositor contrary to the double proof rule (see para 6–17 *et seq*); or because the cross-claim which is set off is incurred after insolvency petition against the creditor; or because payment into an account giving rise to the cross-claim conflicts with preference doctrines (such as margin top-up payments); or because the contractual rate of exchange for a multicurrency set-off is not that prescribed by applicable insolvency laws.

Judicial set-off and counterclaim

Set-off in judicial proceedings

7–27   All forms of set-off are available to a defendant in judicial proceedings since one of the main objects of set-off is the achievement of judicial economy. However in summary proceedings, namely quick proceedings where the defendant has no real defence, transaction set-off of an unliquidated cross-claim is precluded. The illiquidity requires quantification at a full hearing.

Counterclaims

In many legal systems a counterclaim (cross-complaint, reconvention, *demande reconventionelle*) is treated as distinct from set-off in that it is a cross-claim which can only be raised in judicial proceedings in the interests of judicial economy. Where court rules have amalgamated set-off and counterclaim in one remedy, such as the Californian cross-complaint, this is often just a change of name and may not affect the underlying characteristics of the remedy of set-off as distinct from a counterclaim. For example:

(a) Only set-offs may be exercisable as against assignees, attaching creditors and other interveners and not counterclaims: para 8–5 *et seq*.

(b) The availability of counterclaims should be governed by the lex fori, whereas set-off should be governed by the law of the creditor's claim discharged by the set-off: chapter 9.

(c) Counterclaims are available for non-monetary claims such as injunctions, specific performance, restitution of property, or a declaration.

(d) Counterclaims may be in the discretion of the court depending upon whether the counterclaim can conveniently be determined at the same time in the interests of judicial economy without unfairly delaying the plaintiff's claim, whereas set-off is available as of right: *Hanak v Green* [1958] 2 All ER 141, CA.

7–28

Other technical differences relate to whether the court will give a balance judgment for a claim and counterclaim or separate judgment with a stay of execution, whether a counterclaim is available in summary proceedings, the time of pleading of counterclaims, costs, whether a foreign plaintiff must give security for costs, the availability of counterclaims against plaintiffs entitled to sovereign immunity, whether a foreign plaintiff submits to the jurisdiction for all counterclaims as well as set-offs, the non-availability of a counterclaim for a time-barred cross-claim or for the recovery of payments made under a mistake of law, whether a party entitled to a counterclaim is barred by res judicata doctrines (issue estoppel) if he does not raise the defence in the action, and so on.

7–29

Retainer or fund set-off

Definition of retainer

Under the English and US doctrine of retainer or fund set-off – a doctrine which has been given many different names and which is not a true set-off – where a person is liable to contribute to a fund which is not a legal entity,

7–30

such as an insolvent estate, a deceased's estate or a trust fund, and is entitled to a share of the fund as beneficiary, such as dividends or a legacy, in circumstances where set-off does not apply (usually because the trustee or administrator is not personally liable for the participation or because the contributor's share is a property claim), then in certain cases the trustee or administrator of the fund may retain the contributor's claim for his share (his dividends, his beneficial interest, his participating share) to cover the unpaid contribution.

If the contributor's share is a pro rata participation, such as dividends, the share is calculated by determining what it would have been if he had paid his contribution to the fund and then deducting his contribution from that notional share. The effect is as if the contributor had granted security to the fund over his share to secure his contribution and the security is realised by the administrator of the fund. See generally EISO chapter 8.

If the contributor is insolvent before the fund is constituted, the contribution is fixed at the amount of dividends actually receivable by the fund, not the full amount of the contributor's liability on which the dividends are calculated. This rule is based on the leading case of *Cherry v Boultbee* (1839) 2 Keen 319 and has been followed many times since.

Illustrations of retainer

7–31   The principle is extensively illustrated by US and English cases in relation to legacies where the legatee owes a debt to the deceased's estate, where beneficiaries under a trust are liable to pay money into the trust fund, where trustees are liable to the fund for breach of trust, and where a trustee overpays dividends to a creditor of an insolvent estate.

The doctrine has commercial importance in our context mainly in relation to the following situations:

(a) Where a counterparty wishes to enter into a netting agreement with a commercial trust, such as a unit trust or pension trust. As to netting, see chapter 10 *et seq*.

(b) Where a creditor of an insolvent is entitled to dividends but owes money to the estate not available for set-off, e.g. because the liability was incurred as a result of a post-insolvency dealing with the insolvency representative, such as a purchase of assets from the estate resulting in a debt becoming due from a creditor to the estate or a loan by a bank to the insolvency representative to enable him to finance the realisation of the estate: see the case law in EISO at para 8–72 *et seq*.

(c) Where a trustee of an issue of debt securities of an equipment trust, a mortgage trust or a unit, pension or trading trust is a beneficiary-creditor under the trust and is liable to contribute to the trust for default in the administration of the trust: see, e.g. *Re Rhodesia Gold Fields* [1910] 1 Ch 239.

(d) Where a creditor of an insolvent is liable to return a preference to the insolvent estate or is liable for fraudulent or wrongful trading.

Similarity with ordinary set-off

Although the contributor's claim for his share is generally a property claim   **7–32** not eligible for set-off and although there is no set-off mutuality in that the administrator of the fund is not personally liable for the payment of the share or beneficially entitled to the contribution, the doctrine adopts policies similar to set-off in that:

(a) The reciprocal claims must both be money claims, even though unliquidated. Retainer is therefore not available if, say, the share of the contributor is payable in kind: e.g. *Re Savage* [1918] 2 Ch 146; EISO paras 8–99 *et seq.*

(b) The recipient's claim must be due and payable, so that the trustee or other administrator of a fund cannot retain a share if the share is presently payable but the contribution is payable in the future: *Re Abrahams* [1908] 2 Ch 69.

(c) The claims must be mutual, i.e. the contributions and shares must be attributable to the same fund, and the contributor must be both beneficially entitled to the share and personally liable to contribute to the fund.

There are technical differences between fund set-off and ordinary set-off in relation to such matters as retainer against assigned shares, the rule against double-proof, retainer against time-barred contributions and other matters too detailed to discuss here: see generally EISO chapter 8.

Creditor claims insulated from set-off

Main insulated claims listed

Many jurisdictions recognise five classes of creditor primary claims which   **7–33** are insulated, exempt or protected to a greater or lesser degree against set-off by the debtor of a cross-claim the debtor has against the insulated creditor. These are as follows:

(a) Claims intended for the support of the creditor and which should there-fore reach him, e.g. wages, unemployment benefits, social security bene-fits and pensions. In England the insulated claim ceases to be insulated once the money has been paid into a bank account so that the bank is entitled to set off against the deposit even though the whole of the deposit is derived from a support payment: *Jones & Co v Coventry* [1902] 2 KB 1029 (pension). A similar result has been reached in Virgi-nia: *Bernardini v Central National Bank of Richmond*, 223 Va 519, 290 SE 2d 863 (1982). On the other hand in California and New York there are statutes insulating bank deposits derived from exempt creditor claims, although it is possible to contract out. The problem with the continued protection of exempt payments is that the bank may not know how much of a credit balance is eligible for set-off without burdensome administration.

(b) Claims insulated from set-off in the interests of predictability of pay-ment in international commerce. These claims include:

   (i) The claim of a beneficiary of a letter of credit against the bank issu-ing the credit: the bank may not set off a cross-claim owed by the beneficiary to the bank – a situation to be distinguished from the ability of the bank to set off a cross-claim owed by the beneficiary to the account party. See generally, EISO para 12–81;

   (ii) Negotiable instruments in the hands of the first payee: the maker of the instrument or the issuer may not set off a cross-claim owed by the first payee. Again, this case is to be distinguished from a situ-ation where the instrument has been transferred. See generally, EISO para 12–68 *et seq*;

   (iii) Freight, which in England is insulated from set-off even through this exception is highly idiosyncratic and historical. See generally, EISO para 12–82 *et seq*.

(c) Claims insulated from set-off in the public good. The main example here is tax payable to the government.

(d) Claims insulated from set-off because they arise out of the debtor's delinquent conduct towards the creditor, e.g. claims for tort (delict), fraud or breach of fiduciary duty. These claims may in any event be insulated if the victim has a proprietary claim which destroys the debtor-creditor relationship (true in common law jurisdictions), but in some jurisdictions, such as Germany, the victim's claim is insulated even if he is left merely with a claim in debt.

(e) Claims insulated from set-off by contract.

In England, certain claims which are insulated from solvent set-off cease to be insulated where the debtor or creditor is insolvent because the insolvency set-off clause is mandatory: para 6–34. Examples are creditor claims for freight, the claim of the first holder of a negotiable instrument such as a eurobond, and creditor claims where the debtor has agreed not to raise a set-off.

Further, in England it is possible by contract to remove the solvent insulation in the case of letters of credit, negotiable instruments and freight, i.e. the creditor can agree that his claim is subject to a set-off.

Contracts against set-off generally

Contracts prohibiting the debtor from setting off a cross-claim are of great commercial importance in international banking transactions. The main object is to confer predictability of payment and cash-flow, especially in chain contracts as where a financial institution pays funding deposits out of moneys received from borrowers. The policy is "pay now, litigate later". 7–34

Contracts against set-off are standard in the case of term loan agreements, particularly syndicated loan agreements where a set-off would disturb pari passu distribution by the agent bank, and in the case of debt securities intended to be marketable but which do not enjoy the advantage of strict negotiability as opposed to transferability.

The contract against set-off may be a contract against self-help set-off but not judicial set-off, or it may in addition be a contract preventing the raising of the cross-claim in judicial proceedings and also against insolvency set-off.

Efficacy of contracts against set-off

In England, contracts against set-off are generally effective except to the extent they conflict with consumer statutes or other rules of law preventing exculpation clauses or unfair contract terms and except that the courts have a residual discretion to hear cross-claims in the interests of judicial economy. This residual discretion will only in a very rare case be exercised since the policy is that the court will hold the defendant to his agreement and not permit him to obtain the effect of a set-off by the back-door method of a counterclaim in judicial proceedings or by ordering a stay of execution against him. If a debtor could avoid paying in full by forcing the creditor to sue and then obtain a stay of execution on the defence, he would have succeeded in side-stepping his agreement to pay in full without deduction: see *Mottram Consultants Ltd v Bernard Sunley & Sons Ltd* [1975] 2 Lloyds LR 197, HL; *Gilbert-Ash (Northern) Ltd v Modern Engineering (Bristol) Ltd* [1975] 3 All ER HL; contra: *PJ Hegarty & Sons Ltd v Royal Liver Friendly Society* [1985] IR 524 (obiter). 7–35

It is emphasised that a contract prohibiting set-off is ineffective on insolvency in England, Australia, New Zealand and many other common law jurisdictions where the insolvency set-off clause is mandatory: para 6–34.

Universally it appears to be possible for a debtor to contract out of all forms of solvent set-off, e.g. independent set-off, transaction set-off, and current account set-off. In the ordinary case any provisions of the code or otherwise relating to compensation and the like are not regarded as a matter of public policy except sometimes in the limited case of certain support payments. Many codes specifically contemplate renunciation of set-off by a debtor, e.g. Switzerland's CO Art 126.

Implied contracts against set-off

7–36   The renunciation of set-off can be tacit, i.e. inferred from the language or can be implied by conduct. For example in the case of current account set-off, a loan account and a current account are generally to be kept separate because otherwise the customer would have no security in drawing cheques if the loan account exceeded the credit balance: *Bradford Old Bank Ltd v Sutcliffe* [1918] 2 KB 833.

Where an account is kept for a special purpose, such as for the payment of a specified creditor or of interest on bonds or a wages account, there will often also be an inference that the account is to be kept separate: see, e.g. *Garnett v cEwan* (1872) LR 8 Ex 10, 13. In such a case the special purpose designation may convert the debtor-creditor relationship into a proprietary relationship which is in any event destructive of set-off: para 6–48 *et seq.* There are many cases deciding whether there has been an implied exclusion of set-off, e.g. where a junior creditor has agreed that his security is to rank junior, or where in certain cases a debtor has agreed to submit disputes, including his cross-claim, to arbitration and no arbitration has been held: EISO para 12–32 *et seq.* It is thought that an exclusion of set-off will not generally be implied from a statement that payment is to be made in "cash" since this may be taken to be in opposition only to "credit", not set-off.

Duration of contract against set-off

7–37   The duration of the agreement to keep accounts separate is entirely a matter of construction. In an exceptional Australian case the agreement on the facts was construed to last beyond the appointment of a floating charge receiver over the company's assets so that the receiver was entitled to continue to draw on the company's account: *Direct Acceptance Corp Ltd v Bank of*

New South Wales (1968) 88 WN (Pt 1) (NSW) 498. As mentioned, contracts against set-off may fail on insolvency: para 6–34.

Debtor cross-claims ineligible for set-off

Generally

In many jurisdictions a claim may be valid but unenforceable by action for   7–38
some reason. These may include: gaming debts; debts prescribed by limitation statutes; claims unenforceable because of non-compliance with some formal requirement, e.g. because they are not in writing, claims unenforceable under Art VIII 2(b) of the IMF Bretton Woods Agreement as arising from "exchange contracts" conflicting with the exchange controls of a member state; claims against immune creditors; and claims which are not permitted because they infringe the sovereign prerogative of the forum state, e.g. claims by foreign revenue authorities or foreign penal authorities.

Time-barred cross-claims

In relation to claims barred by limitation (prescription), a peculiar feature of   7–39
the English-based systems is that, because independent set-off is not valid tender and because the judicial exercise of a set-off does not have retroactive effect, if a debtor's cross-claim has a shorter limitation period than the creditor's primary claim, once the debtor's cross-claim has become barred by limitation, the creditor can pursue his primary claim free of the set-off except where the debtor has a transaction set-off – transaction set-offs are, subject to some refinement, perpetual defences: EISO paras 13–18 *et seq.*

According to *Williston on Contracts*, the position is the same at common law in the United States except where altered by statute: see Vol 6 pp 543 *et seq.* See especially, *Otto v Lincoln Savings Bank*, 268 Ad 400, 51 NYS 2d 561 (1944). There appears to be much variety of approach at the state level.

In Napoleonic systems espousing automatic independent set-off (para 7–5) the set-off takes effect when the debts satisfy the requirements of set-off and hence a cross-claim not barred by prescription at the time is validly set off. In the declarative Germanic regimes (para 7–4) the declaration is generally retroactive for prescription purposes so if the debtor's cross-claim and the creditor's primary claim qualify for set-off before the elapse of the time period for the debtor's cross-claim, the creditor cannot subsequently bring an action for his primary claim free of the time-barred cross-claim:

see, e.g. Germany BGB s 390, Japan CC Art 508, Greece CC 443, Switzerland CO Art 120, Sweden Statute of Limitation 1981 Art 10.

Cross-claims against foreign immune creditors

7–40   As regards sovereign immunity, it is considered that in England a debtor to a foreign sovereign creditor may as a self-help remedy (where he has one) set off his cross-claim against a sovereign creditor even though he may not be able to sue the sovereign creditor for that cross-claim on grounds of immunity and even though the result is to apply the property of a sovereign (the sovereign's primary claim as creditor) to the discharge of the cross-claim owed by the sovereign. Such a situation might arise where, for example, the bank which is owed a loan by a state also owes a deposit to the state. The immunisation in the State Immunity Act 1978 for enforcement proceedings against sovereign states and state entities (see s 13(2)) relates only to the "recovery" of property or "process for the enforcement of judgements" and it is considered that a self-help set-off amounting to payment is not within these concepts of judicial enforcement.

As regards set-off and counterclaim against a sovereign plaintiff in judicial proceedings, s 2(3)(a) of the UK State Immunity Act 1978 provides that where a sovereign creditor entitled to immunity institutes proceedings in the English courts, the creditor is deemed to submit to the jurisdiction of the English courts. The Act is silent on whether a defendant-debtor may raise a set-off against the plaintiff-sovereign but provides in s 2(6) that a submission by a state in any proceedings does not extend to any counterclaim "unless it arises out of the same legal relationship or facts as the claim". The English position therefore is as follows:

(a)   The debtor to the sovereign, e.g. the bank liable for a deposit, may raise a cross-claim if it qualifies for transaction, contractual or current account set-off and, probably, independent set-off.

(b)   The debtor may also raise a *related* counterclaim. As regards unrelated counterclaims, the debtor's counterclaim must satisfy two conditions. First it must be the type of counterclaim which the court will admit under its normal rules in the interests of judicial economy. Secondly the state or other immune party must have been de-immunised in respect of the unrelated counterclaim, e.g. because of a submission by the state by virtue of a prior written agreement in s 2(2); because the transaction is commercial within s 3(1)(a); or because the cross-claim arises out of a contract (commercial or not) which falls to be performed wholly or partly in the United Kingdom within s 3(1)(b).

As to the United States, it is thought that there is nothing in the Foreign

Sovereign Immunities Act of 1976 which prohibits a self-help or judicial set-off against a sovereign.

Multicurrency set-off

Generally

There ought to be no objection to the set-off of claims one or both of which   **7–41**
is payable in a foreign currency on grounds of incommensurability or lack of homogeneity if market rates are readily available. Nevertheless the law on the subject may not have caught up with a world of freely transferable currencies.

Payment of claims in foreign currency

The initial question is – when is a claim payable in foreign currency? In   **7–42**
many jurisdictions, where a contract debt, such as a loan, deposit or purchase price credit, is payable in foreign currency the debtor may elect either to pay in the foreign currency in question or to pay in local currency. This is the position in England. In Germany s 244(1) of the BGB states:

> "if a money debt expressed in a foreign currency is payable within the country, payment may be made in the currency of such country unless payment in the foreign currency is expressly stipulated".

There are similar provisions in Japan, Switzerland and Italy. The Netherlands too appears to adopt a similar proposition.

In England damages for breach of contract and tort damages are payable in the currency in which the loss is felt by the creditor but the rule is a flexible one: EISO para 11–11 *et seq*. The English courts may award foreign currency judgments but the judgment debtor is entitled to pay in sterling converted at the date of payment. Where the judgment must be enforced, then for practical purposes enforcement orders will usually need to be given in sterling so that the law enforcement agents know how much they have to raise out of assets in England (although this is not necessarily so). In such a case the judgment debt is converted into sterling on the date at which the court authorises enforcement of the judgment – the latest possible date. This is also the general rule in relation to the enforcement of foreign judgments or awards either at common law or under some reciprocal enforcement convention. See generally, EISO paras 11–14 *et seq*.

Multicurrency insolvency set-off

The position as regards insolvency set-off is considered at para 6–20 and 6–33 above.

Multicurrency solvent set-off

7–43 As regards solvent multicurrency set-off, there is no English case law and the position may depend upon the type of set-off, e.g. whether it is an independent self-help set-off, current account set-off, transaction set-off or whether the set-off is claimed only in judicial proceedings and in this latter case whether the set-off was a self-help set-off exercised prior to judicial proceedings and subsequently disputed, whether it is a self-help set-off exercised in judicial proceedings or whether it is a set-off not available as a self-help remedy.

As a general rule, it is considered that the courts ought to lean in favour of permitting self-help multicurrency set-off if market rates are transparent: they ought to allow a conversion at the time of the exercise of the set-off: this is because in England self-help set-off is generally allowed where the policies in favour of set-off are particularly strong and the incommensurability objection ought not to override these policies.

In France it has been decided (Paris July 19, 1943, February 5, 1944) that a foreign currency claim and a French franc claim could not be set off if independent, although some French authors doubt this and the decision has been criticised.

It has been decided in Germany that if the creditor's primary claim is in foreign currency and the cross-claim is in local currency, the debtor can convert the creditor's primary claim into local currency and hence set off but in this case the currency rate of exchange to be applied is that on the date of the declaration, i.e. the set-off is for this purpose not retroactive: RG decision of December 22, 1922, 106 RGZ 99. This is not a true multicurrency set-off because under the BGB as mentioned above the debtor is permitted to convert foreign currency into local currency in such a case.

CHAPTER 8

MUTUALITY AND INTERVENERS

Mutuality

Principles of mutuality

The doctrine of mutuality (sometimes called reciprocity or privity or the requirement of *concursus debiti et crediti*) requires that one person's claim shall not be used to pay another person's debt. 8–1

In the result, in general there must be only two claimants and each claimant must be the beneficial owner of the claim owed to him by the other (or a clear partitioned share of it) and not joint owner of the beneficial title and he must also be personally liable for the claim owed by him to the other (i.e. not liable in some representative capacity, e.g. as trustee or agent), and not jointly liable with another.

It is obvious that if, say, a bank could set off a loan owed by a parent company against a deposit which the bank owes a subsidiary, the subsidiary is expropriated in order to pay the parent. If a dealer could set off the price owed by an agent personally against a price claimable by the agent for the account of his principal, the principal is expropriated to pay the agent's personal debt.

Of course the owner of a claim can authorise the use of his property to pay the claim of another, but the authorisation must be clear. The authorisation fails on the insolvency of the authorising party because the non-mutual set-off involves a divestment of the claim owned by him which should be available to his creditors and is therefore a post-insolvency forfeiture contrary to insolvency laws. Insolvency set-offs must be mutual, notwithstanding agreement to the contrary. There is much English case law.

So far as English law is concerned, mutuality depends on the beneficial ownership of a claim, not who is the nominal, titular or legal holder of the claim and not who is nominally entitled to sue for it. There is a see-through to the real party in interest. This is so in relation to both solvent and insolvent set-off, although in the case of solvent set-off, e.g. where a bank alleges that a deposit is held in trust by a depositor for a beneficiary indebted to the 8–2 banks, the courts are inclined to order payment unless the bank can clearly prove the trust: *Bhogar v Punjab National Bank* [1988] 2 All ER 296, CA.

Hence if the nominal holder claims the beneficiary's debt, the debtor can set off a cross-claim owed by the beneficiary directly to the debtor. Any other result might enable a creditor to transfer his claim, such as a negotiable instrument, to a nominee for him who would then sue for the claim and avoid a set-off.

It is also clear that under English law the beneficial ownership must be clear and ascertained and not subject to some unresolved prior claims because this might involve an unauthorised divestment of the real owner. Secondly there is no objection to a creditor having beneficial ownership of part of a claim, provided that his ownership is a clear partitioned share and not an undivided interest: EISO para 14–48 *et seq*. Again only the beneficial ownership matters—a point which is important in relation to joint deposit accounts and to assignments of debts which do not qualify as full legal assignments.

Illustrations of mutuality doctrine

8–3   Mutuality has a very large number of applications in relation, for example, to corporate law, group trading and the veil of incorporation, joint obligations, partnerships, agency, community of family property, dealers in markets, clearing houses, trusts, deceased's estates, instrumentalities of sovereign states, the separation of governmental departments for the purposes of set-off and so on. Thus it goes without saying that reciprocal claims owing by separate corporate personalities, such as parent and subsidiary companies, are not eligible for set-off unless the veil of incorporation can be pierced and there are many international decisions upholding this basic proposition. Each case requires a detailed examination of the substantive law to ascertain precisely if sole beneficial ownership and sole personal liability apply both ways.

Global set-off between branches

8–4   Since branches of a bank are part of the same legal entity, even if in different countries or subject to a separate fiscal or regulatory regime, there ought to be no mutuality objection to set-off. Any objections that arise must be on some other ground, e.g. an implied agreement not to set off; the insolvency of the branch in a jurisdiction disallowing insolvency set-off; an exchange control inhibition; disallowance of multicurrency set-off; non-recognition of the set-off in local judicial proceedings; or the prevention of set-off of debts payable at different places if money transfer costs are not paid. Global insolvency set-off is considered in another work (on the principles of insolvency) in this series on international financial law.

In many civil jurisdictions it is usually provided that if a debtor sets off a cross-claim against a creditor's claim which is payable at a different place, the debtor is liable for the cost of transmission or for any damages suffered: see for example France CC Art 1296 (ditto Belgium and Luxembourg), Germany BGB s 319, Italy CC Art 1245, Japan CC Art 507, South Korea CC Art 494, Spain CC Art 1199. The point is not mentioned in the Swiss, Austrian or Argentine Civil Code articles on set-off.

In the case of current account set-off it has been held in England that a bank may combine current accounts in debit and credit even though the bank accounts are kept at two different branches of the same bank provided that there is no express or implied agreement or well-recognised course of dealing that they be kept separate: see for example *Garnett v McEwan* (1872) LR 8 Ex 10. The same rule ought to apply to branches in different jurisdictions but it will almost invariably be found that there is a course of dealing that the accounts must be regarded as separate. The test is whether the customer can draw on one deposit account without reference to the other.

As regards set-off in judicial proceedings, if a foreign creditor sues a debtor in England, the plaintiff will be subject to the jurisdiction in respect of related counterclaims. If the foreign plaintiff is subject to a related counterclaim he should also be subject to a defence of set-off even though independent.

In a 1938 decision of the Swiss Federal Court, it was held that a Swiss bank could set off cross-claims owed by the Spanish branch of a German bank against debts owed to the German bank in Germany. The court took the view that the degree of financial autonomy enjoyed by the Spanish branch did not destroy mutuality.

Interveners: assignees, attaching creditors, undisclosed principals, etc.

Main interveners

An initial mutuality or apparent mutuality may be destroyed by the intervention of a third party. In this chapter, these persons are generally called "interveners". The question here is whether the intervention effectively destroys a set-off available between the original creditor and the debtor. For example, if a creditor assigns the benefit of a debt owing to him, can the   8–5 debtor set off, against the assignee, a cross-claim owing by the creditor to the debtor? Thus, a bank may owe a customer a deposit, and the customer owes a loan to the bank. The customer assigns the deposit. Can the bank set off the loan owing by the customer against the deposit so as to diminish the assignee's claim for the deposit?

In view of the security function of set-off, these rules are in the context almost as important as those governing the priorities of security interests over property. If the set-off loses priority to an intervener, the debtor who thought he was "secured" is in fact unsecured.

8–6   The main interveners are as follows:

(a) **Assignees** An assignee of the benefit of a debt, whether absolutely or by way of security. Examples are: the sale of loans; the assignment of the benefit of deposits; security assignments of equipment leases, charter-parties and construction contracts; assignments of proceeds of letters of credit, bank guarantees and insurances; and recourse sales of receivables.

(b) **Floating chargees** A floating charge on crystallisation operates as a fixed security assignment of the receivables included in the floating charge.

(c) **Attaching creditors** An attaching creditor or a creditor obtaining a pre-judgment (the English Mareva injunction) restricting the removal of assets from the jurisdiction. A pre-judgment attachment may merely operate as an injunction freezing the property (including deprivations of the property by set-off) or may operate as a conditional security transfer of the benefit of a claim to the attaching creditor.

(d) **Undisclosed principals** An undisclosed principal may intervene on a contract entered into by his agent apparently as principal. In common law jurisdictions a person may enter into a contract apparently as a principal but in reality as agent provided that the contract does not exclude intervention and provided that the agent is appointed prior to the entering into of the contract. In civil code jurisdictions, generally a principal can intervene only if the agent assigns the benefit of the claim to him. Undisclosed principals are in practice important in the context of international banking transactions. Examples of undisclosed principals in this context are the lay clients of banks in foreign exchange and other money market transactions, the principals of correspondent banks in credit transfers and collections, and clients in securities transactions.

(e) **Undisclosed beneficiaries** These are similar to undisclosed principals in that the trustee does not disclose that he is a trustee acting for a beneficiary but appears as the absolute owner. Examples are: fiduciary deposits held by a bank with another bank apparently as principal but in reality for the benefit of a customer; and the assignment (whether absolutely or by way of security) of loans or other receivables or contracts where the assignor is authorised on an undisclosed basis to collect the proceeds and remit the proceeds to the assignee.

(f) **Subrogated creditors** An example is the guarantor who, on payment, takes over a security over receivables held by the principal creditor for the guaranteed debt so that the guarantor effectively becomes an assignee of the benefit of the receivables included in that security.

These interveners in effect take over a claim owed by the debtor to the original creditor – the primary claim – so that the issue is whether the debtor – who must now pay the primary claim to the intervener – can set off a cross-claim which the original creditor owes the debtor so as to reduce the primary claim. One may refer to the relevant terms as follows: 8–7

"**intervener**" means the assignee, chargee, attaching creditor, undisclosed principal, undisclosed beneficiary or subrogated claimant or other person intervening on a claim

"**original creditor**" means the assignor, chargor, judgment debtor, undisclosed agent, undisclosed trustee or other initial or apparent creditor

"**primary claim**" means the claim which is demanded by the intervener as having been transferred to him or incurred in his favour, e.g. by assignment or attachment or by his undisclosed agent or trustee

"**cross-claim**" means the claim which is owed by the original creditor to the debtor on the primary claim

"**debtor**" means the person who is liable to the original creditor on the primary claim, now taken over by the intervener

Intervener rule generally

The question of whether a debtor retains, as against an intervener, a set-off which he thought he had against his original creditor, depends upon the class of set-off and the type of intervener and is colossally complicated. Various statements of the rule in civil code articles or in the US Restatement or in the Uniform Commercial Code offer little guidance when one actually 8–8 comes down to the detail. Although it is not possible to define with particularity the rules prevailing in the various jurisdictions, it may be useful to set out some general principles. For the details, see EISO chapters 14 to 22.

Each case of intervention raises the question of whether the law should protect the debtor who is liable to have a set-off dislodged by the intervener or whether it should protect the intervener whose claim will be diminished by the set-off. The policies depend upon the class of intervener.

In the case of assignments, it may be said that the debtor should anticipate the free merchantability of claims and if he desires a set-off against the intervener he should contract for it. It is impracticable, e.g. for a discounter of debts to carry out extensive enquiries of each debtor to the assignor. The protection of these interveners may be said to encourage the availability of business capital.

In the case of attachments, arguments can be made either way. One approach is that the debtor ought not to be prejudiced by dealings between the creditor and third party. The contrary view is that third party creditors ought to have access to the assets of their debtors free of a diminishing set-off.

As to undisclosed principals, the policy should be that the principal should be subject to all cross-claims incurred before he comes out from behind the arras since he holds out his agent as principal and should not claim to be in a better position than his creature. A similar policy should apply to undisclosed beneficiaries unless the beneficiary is a wronged beneficiary in which event the rules relating to the priority of tracing claims come into play.

Broadly there are two camps.

8–9   In the **first camp** are those jurisdictions which hold that the debtor does not lose whatever set-off he would have had, as between solvent parties, provided both claims were *incurred* before he has notice of the intervention. In other words the intervener takes subject to the debtor's set-off if the debtor has entered into engagements which would have given rise to that set-off. It is immaterial that the set-off is only exercisable after the debtor has notice of the intervention, e.g. because the claims mature after notice. The result is that the debtor cannot be taken by surprise. This camp includes the Anglo-American jurisdictions, the Germanic countries and probably the Scandinavian jurisdictions – but there are many qualifications.

But in those jurisdictions, the debtor is left only with solvent set-off. He loses the enhanced insolvency set-off he would have had on the insolvency of his creditor because the claims were no longer mutual in that insolvency: the claim originally owed to the insolvent creditor is no longer owned by the creditor, but rather by the intervener. The precluded set-offs include the following, e.g.:

(a) Where the claims are independent and one of them is unliquidated. Such a set-off is available on insolvency, but not as against an intervener.

(b) Where the cross-claim matures after the intervener sues for his primary claim. On insolvency, maturity is generally irrelevant.

(c) Where the primary claim is insulated from solvent set-off but not insolvency set-off, e.g. where the primary claim is a claim for freight or a claim by the first holder of a negotiable instrument or by the original beneficiary of a letter of credit.

(d) (In England) where the cross-claim is a contingency which accrues only after notice or is an advance equipment rental falling due after notice or is an acceleration of lease hire made after notice.

The protections available to the debtor are that, in England at least and often elsewhere, if the debtor has contracted for a set-off prior to notice of the intervention, then that set-off contract is effective against all interveners, even an attaching creditor: *Hutt v Shaw* (1887) 3 TLR 354, CA. Because these jurisdictions usually allow insolvency set-off, they have no objection to a contract of set-off against other creditors, such as attaching creditors.

The **second camp** includes most of the Franco-Latin jurisdictions, minus   8–10
some and plus some (e.g. plus the Netherlands). Here the rule is that the debtor's set-off must actually be exercisable before the debtor has notice of the intervention. For example, both claims must have matured due and payable prior to notice. The rule probably springs from the original concept that set-off is not exercisable against creditors if creditors intervene before the set-off has become exercisable. This was intended mainly to prevent insolvency set-off, but it spread to a prohibition of set-off against attaching creditors and to assignees and other voluntary interveners. As a broad generalisation, therefore, a country which prohibits insolvency set-off is likely also to fall in this camp as regards interveners. The difficulty for debtors is that they can be ambushed and lose a set-off they thought they had: a debtor cannot control whether and when an attaching creditor of his creditor will attach the claim which the debtor owes to his creditor.

Because the bar on post-intervention set-off was originally a reflection of the policy that set-offs are not exercisable against enforcing creditors, whether they enforce by initiating a bankruptcy or by attachments and executions, there is a tendency in these jurisdictions to hold that a contract between debtor and original creditor contracting for a set-off is ineffective against the attaching creditor, just as it would be ineffective against the bankrupt estate of the original creditor, but this rule is not uniform and is being eroded.

8–11   Further, the general rule – that the set-off must be exercisable before notice of the intervention – is subject to two well-established exceptions, i.e. if the debtor was entitled to a current account set-off and if he was entitled to a transaction set-off – which is often much wider than the grudging Anglo-American transaction set-off. These exceptions are exactly the same as the exceptions to the rule in those jurisdictions that insolvency set-off is not available: para 6–10.

Finally, in the Franco-Latin group, the debtor is often not exposed to the intervention of undisclosed principals and undisclosed beneficiaries because both of these involve a hidden or secret ownership or trust which is anathema to countries which hold fast to the philosophy of preventing "false wealth" – where the debtor has many possessions but few assets, thereby inducing false credit, it is said.

In light of these general principles, which are subject of course to many qualifications, one may enter into a little more detail.

Set-offs exercised before notice of intervener

8–12   If the cross-claim and the primary claim have actually validly been set-off prior to notice of the intervention, the intervener takes subject to this "payment" of his primary claim. The same is true if the set-off is exercisable but has not yet been exercised. This rule applies to all interveners and no exception in any jurisdiction has been found.

Transaction set-off against interveners

8–13   The debtor can set off his cross-claim against the intervener's claim for the primary claim if the cross-claim qualifies for transaction set-off and both claims arose out of a pre-notice transaction, regardless of whether the debtor has notice of the intervention prior to the maturity of the cross-claim: EISO para 14–80.

If the position were otherwise the original creditor could defeat a debtor's cross-claim for damages by simply assigning his claim to a third party who would then take free of the set-off. The intervener should take the transaction as a whole and not take the best parts and leave behind the worst, have the benefit without the burden, the cream without the crust.

The above proposition is universally accepted: England, the American common law states, Belgium, France, Denmark. The rule appears to apply generally even to attachments. Thus a French Court of Cassation decision allowed a transaction set-off against a creditor effecting a *saisie-arrêt* : Cass Civ 1 ere April 22, 1986, Bull 1 no 98.

Current account set-off against interveners

It appears to be universally true that the debtor may set off a cross-claim **8–14**
against the intervener's claim for the primary claim if the reciprocal claims
are simple debts qualifying for current account set-off, provided that both
claims were incurred before notice: EISO para 14–81. There are two expla-
nations. One is that the claims form a single blended account and therefore
the intervener should take over the ultimate balance and should be subject
to blending by combination. An alternative and more logical explanation is
based on the proposition that both the primary claim and the cross-claim
were due and payable before notice of the intervention since current
accounts are deemed immediately due and payable for the purposes of the
set-off. Hence the set-off would in any event be available under the independent set-off rules outlined in para 7–1 *et seq.*

Contractual set-off against interveners

The mainstream view in Anglo-American, Germanic and Scandinavian jur- **8–15**
isdictions is that a debtor may set off his cross-claim against the intervener's
claim for the primary claim if the original creditor and the debtor agreed
pre-notice that the debtor could set off his cross-claim against the primary
claim and if both reciprocal claims were incurred prior to notice to the
debtor of the intervention. The intervener should take subject to the entire
transaction and should not be able to have the best without the worst or be
able to split up the transaction: EISO para 14–82. See, e.g. in England,
Mangles v Dixon (1852) 3 HL 702 (contractual set-off effective against
assignee); *Bank of Montreal v Trudhope, Anderson & Co* (1911) 21 Man R
390 (Manitoba CA) (contractual set-off effective against assignee); *Hutt v
Shaw* (1887) 3 TLR 354, CA (contractual set-off effective against attaching
creditor). If contractual set-off is available against interveners, debtors are
in a position to protect themselves against a loss of set-off on an intervention.

In Franco-Latin jurisdictions, there is some hostility to permitting a person to contract-out of the rule that unaccrued set-offs are invalid against
interveners, but this view is on the defensive. For example, in France a contractual set-off has been allowed against a garnishor: see the Rouen decision
of February 18, 1854, DP 54.2.242.

An alternative is to prohibit interventions. **8–16**
A contractual prohibition against assignments is effective in many jurisdictions (including England) to exclude an assignee's right against the
debtor. However s 9–318(4) of the US Uniform Commercial Code renders

---

ineffective terms in certain contracts prohibiting assignments of or security interests in certain accounts and general intangibles – these are defined terms and do not apply to all debts.

But in principle such prohibitions should not be effective against an attaching creditor on the ground that a creditor may not by mere contract put a debt beyond the reach of his creditors. This is considered to be the position in England and also the position under the laws, e.g. of Germany, common law Canada, Italy and Norway. Article 475 of the Netherlands Code of Civil Procedure allowing the attachment of debts is mandatory. The list of non-attachable debts prescribed by Art 2092 of the French Civil Code is probably also to be treated as exhaustive, thereby precluding non-attachability by contract.

A prohibition against an undisclosed principal should be effective in England.

Another alternative is a charge-back, but these can be unattractive for other reasons, or even unavailable. Charge-backs are reviewed in another volume (on the comparative law of security) in this series on international financial law.

The parties may provide that the debtor's liability to pay the primary claim is conditional on payment by the creditor of the cross-claim, as where a bank's liability to repay a deposit is conditional on the customer repaying a loan to the bank. If this technique of "flawed asset" is available, the intervener claiming the conditional debt gets only the flawed asset. Flawed assets *in this situation* have not been judicially approved in England and reliance appears unsafe as a protection against interveners.

Independent set-off against interveners: generally

8–17　　**English law** In England, the debtor can generally set off his cross-claim against the intervener's claim for the primary claim if the cross-claim (a) qualifies for independent set-off (liquidity both ways), (b) was incurred or acquired before the debtor had notice of the intervention, (c) became due and payable before the primary claim (or in England before the intervener sues for the primary claim), and (d) is in certain cases (such as contingencies) "due" – but not necessarily due and payable – before notice, and if the primary claim was incurred prior to notice to the debtor of the intervener. The parties cannot destroy the rights of the intervener by incurring either a new cross-claim or a new primary claim after notice to the debtor of the intervention. See generally, EISO paras 14–83 *et seq.*

The claims must qualify for independent set-off, that is, they must both be liquidated or ascertainable with certainty in most leading jurisdictions. If the primary claim or the cross-claim is unliquidated and the claims are independent, the debtor loses his set-off. An example is where a bank seeks to set off damages for breach of a foreign exchange contract entered into by a customer against an assignee of the customer's deposit.

Independent cross-claims not "due" on notice In England the courts have   **8–18** vacillated as to who to protect and hence the case law involves fine distinctions. Certain cross-claims must not only be incurred pre-notice but also be "due" pre-notice, although not necessarily due and payable. In assignment cases the English courts have held that the following independent cross-claims owing by an assignor to the debtor and incurred under a pre-notice transaction, but due, or due and payable, only after notice of assignment, cannot be set off against the assignee:

(a) **Accelerated advance rentals** Accelerated equipment or land rentals payable under a pre-notice lease agreement which the lessor contractually accelerates on a default by the lessee and which are accelerated only after notice: *Business Computers Ltd v Anglo-African Leasing Ltd* [1977] 2 All ER 741. It is considered that loan accelerations should not fall into the same category since they are not payable for future services.

(b) **Contingencies** Contingent liabilities incurred pre-notice where the contingency occurs only after notice, such as:

  (1) the contingent liability of an indorser of a bill of exchange to pay the holder if the acceptor does not pay and incurred pre-notice but due and payable after notice when the acceptor has dishonoured the bill: *Jeffreys v Agra & Masterman's Bank* (1866) LR 2 Eq 674;

  (2) the contingent liability of a principal debtor to indemnify his guarantor incurred under a pre-notice guarantee but due and payable by virtue of payment of the guarantee only after notice: *Unity Joint Stock Mutual Banking Association v King* (1858) 25 Beav 72; contra *Thompson v Miller* (1854) 4 Cr 481 (Canada).

Hence the potential cut-off may apply to all rights of reimbursement in respect of letters of credit, performance bonds and the like issued by the debtor, such as a bank, before notice of assignment but becoming due and payable by virtue of a drawing of the letter of credit or other instrument only after notice of assignment. Equally importantly, the cut-off may apply to contingent cross-claims arising from securities dealing in options and futures trading in cases where the client has deposited cash margin with the dealer and the client assigns the benefit of the margin deposit to an assignee.

On the other hand if the contingency has occurred so that the assignor's liability has accrued pre-notice, the liability is not cut off even though the liability is due and payable only after notice. This might happen if, for example, a customer is given credit for his obligation to reimburse the bank for a letter of credit paid by the bank and the letter of credit is called pre-notice so that the contingency accrues pre-notice but the customer's liability to pay falls due and payable only after notice.

This cut-off of contingencies has been applied in England to assignments, to garnishments, and to the transfer of the claim effected by subrogation (see EISO paras 16–42 *et seq*), but there appears to be no case on the point in relation to undisclosed principals. The principle will probably not apply to pre-judgment "attachments" in the form of a Mareva injunction: see *The Theotokas* [1983] 2 All ER 65.

The position appears uncertain with regard to the following:

(1)   Interest accruing post-notice on a pre-notice independent cross-claim qualifying for set-off.

(2)   An independent cross-claim constituted by the price payable by the assignor to the debtor under a pre-notice contract for the sale of property or the provision of services by the debtor to the assignor and becoming due and payable by virtue of the debtor's performance after notice of the assignment, e.g. under options and futures contracts.

(3)   An independent cross-claim constituted by the price payable by the assignor pursuant to an option granted pre-notice but exercised by the debtor only after notice.

The presence of these unnecessarily complicated rules emphasises the importance of a contractual set-off for a debtor who wishes to preserve his set-off against interveners.

Comparative law on independent set-off against interveners

8–19   It should be noted first that under common law systems an assignable debt can be sold informally without the involvement of the debtor and the assignment is effective to transfer beneficial ownership to the assignee and is valid against attaching creditors of the assignor and against his insolvency representative, regardless of whether or not notice is given to the debtor. Notice is relevant to such matters as priorities and payment to the assignee, but is not necessary for the transfer of beneficial ownership.

One exception is that in some English-based systems, if the assignee of an individual assignor has not given notice to the debtor, the debt remains in the reputed ownership of the assignor available to his creditors on his insolvency. Reputed ownership is designed to prevent the appearance of wealth and hence false credit, does not usually apply to companies and has been abolished in England.

But in other systems of law, notably France, Japan, South Korea, Chile, Colombia and others, if the debtor has not consented to the assignment or formal notice has not been served on the debtor in the prescribed manner (which may involve service by an official, such as the French bailiff or *huissier*), the assignment is ineffective as against creditors of the assignor and also on his insolvency: France CC Art 1690, Japan CC Art 467, South Korea CC Art 450. Where therefore the assignment is not properly perfected it must follow that the debtor retains whatever rights of set-off he has against the purported assignor and can ignore the assignee.

In **Anglo-American, Germanic** and **Scandinavian jurisdictions,** it seems to be generally true that independent set-off is available against interveners provided that the claims were incurred or acquired before the debtor has notice of the intervention, and provided that the claims otherwise qualified for independent set-off, e.g. liquidity and maturity. Hence the intervention does not disturb an established set-off, even if not exercisable until after notice. But, as in England, there is much detail, particularly in the US jurisdictions.   8–20

As to the common law US position untouched by statute or the UCC, see *Williston on Contracts*, Vol 3 p 176. Section 9–318 of the UCC and s 336(2) of the Restatement, Contracts 2(d) do not help when it comes to this sort of detail without examination of the case law.

Germanic codes following the German Code on this point provide that the debtor can set off against the assignee or chargee unless the debtor knew at the time of acquiring his cross-claim against the assignee that the assignee's primary claim had been assigned or pledged to a third party or the debtor's cross-claim matured after the debtor learnt of the assignment or pledge *and* later than the assigned claim. This also seems to be the Scandinavian approach. In other words the debtor keeps his set-off if he would have had a solvent set-off apart from the assignment: see, e.g. Germany's BGB s 406 (assignments) and BGB Art 392 in relation to attachments. This route also appears to be followed by Switzerland: see CO Art 169.   8–21

Some of the Spanish jurisdictions may also follow the Germanic approach – including Spain, Mexico (CC Art 2035), Chile (CC Art 1659) and Colombia (CC Art 178). But the case law should be examined.

As to attaching creditors, there seems to have been greater hesitation in the United States to permitting unaccrued independent set-offs against attaching creditors, but in both New York and Illinois statutes have been introduced which effectively allow a debtor, such as a bank, to accelerate cross-claims and to set them off against an attaching creditor in certain circumstances: see s 151 of the New York Debtor-Creditor Law and s 12–708   8–22 of the Illinois Code of Civil Procedure. Pennsylvania has no equivalent of the New York s 151 but it has been held in Pennsylvania that a garnishee bank need not have actually set off prior to garnishment: *General Electric Credit Corporation v Tarr*, 457 F Supp 935 (DC Pa 1978).

In a Japanese Supreme Court decision of December 23, 1964, it was decided that a debtor-garnishee may set off an independent cross-claim against a garnishor even though the cross-claim becomes due and payable after the attachment. It was also held that an agreement that a bank can accelerate and set off without notice all debts owing by a customer if an event occurs which indicates a worsening of the financial condition of the depositor is effective against an attaching creditor.

8–23   The general approach of many of the **Franco-Latin jurisdictions** basing themselves on the Napoleonic code is that, if the debtor has accepted or consented to the assignment, he loses independent set-offs which he could have raised as against the assignor. This is a tacit renunciation and applies even if the assigned debt has already been extinguished by the automatic operation of set-off since, having accepted the assignment, the debtor cannot be heard to say that the assigned debt has been extinguished.

But if the debtor has not accepted the assignment and the assignment has merely been formally notified to him, he can oppose set-offs accrued prior to that notification: see the Civil Codes of France, Brazil, Chile, Colombia, Egypt, Italy, Kuwait, Luxembourg, Mexico, Panama, Quebec, the Philippines and Spain.

Generally however, the reciprocal claims must be eligible for set-off prior to formal notification of the assignment if the debtor is to be permitted to raise an independent cross-claim against the assignee. This is evidently the position in France and the Netherlands: see, for example, the Louisiana case of *Bank of Louisiana v Argonaut Insurance Co*, App 1971, 248 So 2d 349. In the Netherlands it has been held that, even if the cross-claim is due and payable prior to assignment of the assigned claim, the debtor cannot set off against the assignee if the assigned claim is not due and payable at that time: *Hoge Raad* February 7, 1929, NJ 1929, p 885.

Notice of intervener

8–24   It has been seen that notice plays a crucial role in the availability of set-off against interveners. What amounts to notice?

This depends on the class of intervener. Generally in England the notice must actually be communicated to the debtor, but need not be formal. The debtor need not make positive enquiries unless there are suspicious circumstances which should put him on enquiry as to the presence of the third party's interest in the claim: EISO paras 14–94 *et seq*.

The threshold of notice varies markedly: for example in relation to market transactions a dealer might be taken to know that his counterparty may be acting for an outside principal: see *Cook & Sons Ltd v Eshelby* (1887) 12 AC 271. In relation to attachments, the garnishee does not have notice until actual service of the garnishee order nisi but in the case of Mareva injunctions mere notice of the existence of the injunction is enough: EISO chapter 18.

As to notice of assignment, an outstanding question is whether constructive notice is sufficient by the registration or filing of security interests: consider the registration of company charges in English-based jurisdictions, a UCC filing in the United States and filing under Personal Property Security Acts in some of the Canadian provinces including Ontario. It would be surprising if these filings operated as notice for the purposes of the intervener rule.

Set-off against interveners claiming insulated claims

Where the primary claim is insulated from set-off, the debtor cannot set off against the intervener. He could not have set off against the original creditor – the assignor, the judgment debtor, the undisclosed principal. Examples are where the debtor has contractually agreed not to set off – a contract which is common in term loan agreements and in the case of marketable securities – so that, if a bank assigns a loan protected against set-off by contract, the borrower cannot set off, as against the buyer of the loan, a deposit owing by the original bank to the borrower: EISO paras 16–136 *et seq.* **8–25**

Other insulated claims include (in England) freight (important in relation to bank security over ship earnings); letters of credit (important for assignments of proceeds); and first demand bank guarantees and negotiable instruments.

As to negotiable instruments, it appears to be universally true that the prime obligor of a negotiable instrument – the acceptor of a bill of exchange, the maker of a promissory note or the issuer of a bearer bond or certificate of deposit negotiable to bearer – cannot set off against a transferee of the instrument who is a holder in due course (value given in good faith without notice of any defect) any cross-claim which the prime obligor has against the first or a subsequent holder, subject to certain exceptions in the case of transfers of overdue instruments. Case law and the provisions of the Bills of Exchange Act 1882 establish this position in England: EISO paras 16–148 *et seq.* As to the United States, see Art 3 of the Uniform Commercial Code in force in all states with variations. Many civilian jurisdictions have either adopted the 1930 Geneva Convention providing a **8–26**

Uniform Law for Bills of Exchange and Promissory Notes or enacted similar provisions: see Arts 17 and 20 of the Uniform Law.

Mutuality where intervener owes debt to debtor

8–27   Apart from the question of whether a debtor can set off against an intervener a cross-claim he has against the original creditor, there is the secondary question of whether there is mutuality between the debtor liable on the intervened claim and the intervener owing a debt to the debtor.

In the case of assignments, one may take the example of a bank assigning a loan to an assignee bank which owes a deposit to the borrower. England would regard the loan and deposit as mutual: EISO paras 16–170 *et seq.*

On the other hand, if the assignment is a security assignment or charge which has not become enforceable, a set-off between the charged debt and a cross-claim owing by the chargee to the debtor would defeat the assignor's right to redeem the security and result in a realisation of the security before the secured debt is due. Until enforcement the chargee has only a limited, defeasible security interest in the charged debt and hence does not have the absolute beneficial ownership which is at the root of the mutuality doctrine. This ought to be the case even if the security assignment is in form an absolute assignment or a fiduciary assignment, unless it can be said that the assignor authorises the depletion of his assets by set-off (an authorisation which would fail on the insolvency of the assignor, assignee or debtor).

Assignments of part of the debt and set-off

8–28   Where a creditor assigns part of a debt owed by him, under many common law systems the assignment may:

(a) partition the beneficial ownership between assignor and assignee;

(b) (apparently) confer on the assignor and assignee an undivided interest in the debt as tenants in common;

(c) treat the assignor and assignee as joint beneficial owners; or

(d) assign not part of the debt itself but a share of the proceeds.

As to the English case law, see EISO paras 16–242 *et seq.*

Whichever method is used will affect set-off between the assigned portion and a debt owing by the partial assignee or the partial assignor to the debtor. The general position in England is that there is mutuality between partial assignee and debtor only if the partial assignee has an absolute and clearly partitioned share in the benefit of the assigned debt: EISO paras

16–250 *et seq*. For this purpose it is irrelevant that it is necessary to join the assignor to any action since it is the beneficial ownership which matters for both solvent and insolvency set-off, although of course the assignor should be joined in an appropriate case if the set-off is claimed in judicial proceedings.

As regards set-off by the debtor, as against the partial assignee, of a   8–29
cross-claim which the assignor owes the debtor, the partial assignee should generally be in no better position than any other assignee of a debt in accordance with the intervener rule stated above.

> In *Federal Deposit Ins Corpn v Mademoiselle of California* 379 F 2d 600 (1967), a case decided by the 9th Circuit of the US Court of Appeals, an originating bank assigned to another bank an 80 per cent participating interest in a note owed by a customer of the originator. The customer was owed a deposit by the originating bank which became insolvent. *Held*: the customer could set off the whole of the deposit against the note, even though 80 per cent of the note had been assigned. The reason seems to have been that the assignment was not notified. Jertberg J said at 664: "the unannounced transfer of an interest or sale of a participation certificate in the note should not dilute the uninformed depositor's ordinary right of set-off". Another reason was that an assignee of part of a claim takes it subject to counterclaims and defences against it.

In England the same result would be reached if the *assignee-participant* had claimed direct from the customer, but not if the customer claimed the set-off in the insolvency of the original bank since notification is irrelevant to mutuality between assignor and debtor on the assignor's insolvency.

Whether the debtor should appropriate his set-off to the assignor as opposed to the assignee's portion is an interesting point. One possibility is that he should pro rate it. *Re Inglis* (1932) 5 ABC 255 (Australia) required set-off first against the non-assigned portion but *Cavendish v Geaves* (1857) 25 Beav 163 suggests pro rata apportionment.

Successive assignments and set-off

Where a debt is assigned several times and an intermediate assignee owes a   8–30
cross-claim to the debtor, the general rule in England appears to be that the debtor cannot raise these cross-claims as against a subsequent assignee, i.e. there is no accumulation or build-up of set-offs: see, e.g. *The Raven* [1980] 2 Lloyds Rep 266. An Irish decision appears to go the other way, but is explicable on other grounds: *Re Richard Smith & Co Ltd* (1901) 1 IR 73.

Assignments of proceeds and set-off

8–31   Where an assignor assigns the proceeds of a debt but not the debt itself, it seems that the general position in England is that the assignment is to be treated for set-off purposes as a full assignment. Thus the assignment of proceeds destroys mutuality between assignor and debtor. Although the benefit of the debt is not assigned, the assignment of the proceeds denudes the claim of any value and therefore a set-off between the assignor and debtor would infringe the principle of mutuality by depriving the assignee of the proceeds of the debt.

Assignments of proceeds are common in relation to letters of credit, subordination trusts, insurance policies and non-assignable contracts, e.g. loans which prohibit assignments but not assignments of proceeds.

Floating charges, global security and set-off

8–32   Where a chargee has merely a floating charge over all present and future receivables, the English position is that rights of set-off between the chargor and the debtor to the chargor are not affected and the intervener rule does not apply until the charge crystallises on its enforcement, e.g. by the appointment of a receiver: EISO para 16–225 *et seq*. At that point the floating charge converts into a fixed charge and it is only then that the intervener rule comes into play.

Floating charges are available in English-based common law jurisdictions and have been introduced by statute into the law of Scotland and Quebec. Some civilian jurisdictions have introduced global charges over all the assets of an enterprise including receivables: see the Belgian *nantissement de fonds de commerce*, the equivalents in Luxembourg and France, and the Germanic fiduciary assignment. It is suggested that these civilian equivalents are not like floating charges in that rights of set-off may be affected as soon as a debtor has notice of the charge rather than on the crystallisation of the charge. But this point merits investigation.

CHAPTER 9

SET-OFF:
CONFLICT OF LAWS

There is little jurisprudence in England in relation to the conflict of laws on   9–1
solvent set-off and hence one can only make a number of suggestions.

Independent set-off

It is suggested that the question of whether a claim may be discharged by
independent set-off should be governed by the law of the claim which the
debtor asserts has been discharged, subject to any public policy rules, e.g.
relating to insulated debts like support payments. This will ordinarily lead
to the result that, in any judicial proceedings to test the availability of the
set-off, the court should apply the law of the plaintiff's claim – the creditor's
primary claim – to determine whether the debtor was entitled to discharge
the creditor's claim by set-off and the effect of that set-off.

Potential conflicts

The principal issues likely to be involved in conflicting rules of law in rela-   9–2
tion to independent set-off include: whether the set-off is self-help for the
purposes of withdrawals, accelerations, forfeitures, etc.; the conditions of
the availability of the set-off, such as liquidity, same currency and maturity;
whether the creditor's primary claim is insulated from set-off, such as
freight, wages or alimony; the manner in which the set-off is exercised if
self-help, e.g. automatic or by declaration; whether the set-off operates
retroactively; and the appropriation or imputation of the set-off to a plura-
lity of obligations owed by the debtor to the creditor.

Role of lex fori

The English courts may conservatively apply the lex fori to these issues. It is   9–3
considered nevertheless that the lex fori is not the appropriate system of law
since set-off is predominantly a matter of substance as a form of payment or
discharge which is a substantive matter in conflict of laws. Matters of

---

substance tend to be governed by proper law doctrines. Set-off is not primarily a procedural convenience to avoid circuity of action although the
objectives of judicial economy are present. Secondly the application of the
lex fori would make little sense where both reciprocal claims are governed
by a foreign system of law. Thirdly as a general principle of modern conflicts, the lex fori should not be applied unless there is no convenient alternative, because it elevates the rules of the home forum above all others and
might encourage forum-shopping. The homeward trend is to be discouraged
as inimical to the expectations of the parties and to the recognition of legitimate foreign interests.

However the lex fori should govern some matters which are primarily
procedural, e.g. whether a set-off which is erroneously pleaded as a counterclaim can still qualify for the advantages of set-off, the timing of the pleading of a set-off and whether or not set-off is available against an immune
creditor.

The availability of counterclaims and whether a net or balance judgment
or stay of execution are appropriate should be governed by the lex fori since
this is a matter for the convenient disposition of judicial business.

Cumulative law

9–4   Some commentators and courts in non-English jurisdictions have suggested
that the question of whether set-off is available should be determined by the
cumulation of laws, i.e. the availability of set-off depends upon it being
available under both the law governing the primary claim and the law
governing the cross-claim. But if one examines specific situations it would
seem that the application of the law of the primary claim confers a measure
of predictability in the actual result where one law allows a set-off but the
other does not: see the examples in EISO paras 23–11 *et seq.* This will
usually result in one of the parties always being the loser. The holder of the
claim which is most favourable to set-off will normally have an advantage,
whoever brings suit. A somewhat inconclusive English case supports the
application of the law of the creditor's primary claim to determine the availability of set-off: *Allen v Kemble* (1848) 6 Moo PPC 314, PC. The law of the
primary claim is the solution adopted in Germany.

Interveners

9–5   As a general proposition, not perhaps applicable to all cases, the question of
whether a debtor may set off, as against an intervener, a cross-claim which
the debtor has against the original or apparent creditor ought to be governed by the law of the debt claimed by the intervener – the assignee, the
undisclosed principal, the undisclosed beneficiary.

Assignments In relation to assignments, for example, where a debtor has a   9–6
cross-claim against the assignor qualifying for set-off, the question of
whether the assignee is subject to this set-off should be determined by the
law of the assigned debt. The assignee should be able to look to that law in
order to ascertain what set-offs he may be subject to. He cannot examine the
laws of all potential cross-claims. The debtor should be able to look to the
law of the obligation he owes to ascertain his vulnerability or otherwise to
loss of set-off. This rule would be consistent with the rule proposed above in
relation to independent set-off in the absence of assignment. This at least
seems to be the solution adopted by the 1980 Rome Convention on the Law
Applicable to Contractual Obligations: Art 12 provides that the law governing the assigned right shall determine "the relationship between the assignee
and the debtor".

Undisclosed principals Similar principles should apply to undisclosed prin-   9–7
cipals, i.e. the law governing the obligation owed to the agent by the third
party which the undisclosed principal seeks to take over on intervention
should determine whether a cross-claim which the third party has against
the agent personally is available for set-off against the principal. If an undisclosed principal allows his agent to deal with third parties without disclos-
ing his capacity, he should take the risk of the system of law under which the
agent contracts with third parties.

Attachments In the case of attachments, while the English courts generally   9–8
apply the lex situs to determine if the debt is capable of being garnished, i.e.
is within the jurisdiction, and to determine questions of the validity and
effect of attachments or garnishments by foreign courts, it is considered that
the question of whether the garnishee can set off, as against the garnishor, a
cross-claim which the garnishee has against the judgment debtor should be
governed either by the lex fori or by the law of the attached claim. It would
be more attractive, in the interests of the garnishee, to apply the law of the
attached claim (so that everybody knows where they are) but often judicial
enforcement is seen as the province of the lex fori. It is not considered that
the lex situs of the attached debt should control.

Insolvency set-off

General

As noted in chapter 6, one group of states permits insolvency set-off while   9–9
another group does not except in the case of connexity or current accounts.
In addition:

---

1. States which allow insolvency set-off usually restrict the preferential build-up of set-offs in the twilight: para 6–38.

2. US law stays set-offs as from an insolvency petition.

3. A set-off may be affected by a moratorium on or a discharge of the claim owed by the debtor on his bankruptcy or by virtue of a composition.

9–10   The position is complicated because of the large number of possible situations. Broadly there are 12 basic situations. The two base cases are, e.g.: (1) the bank is owed a loan by the home forum (principal place of business and place of incorporation) of the debtor and owes a deposit for the benefit of the foreign branch of the debtor; and (2) (in reverse) the bank owes a deposit for the account of the home forum of the debtor but is owed a loan for the account of the foreign forum where a branch of the debtor is located.

These basic cases must be examined in three situations, namely, (1) where both jurisdictions allow the set-off, (2) where the home forum does allow set-off, but the foreign forum does not, and (3) where the home forum does not allow set-off, but the foreign forum does.

Then the position has to be examined (1) from the point of view of the home forum and (2) from the point of view of the foreign forum.

Of course one could take the analysis further and posit cases where proceedings have been commenced in one forum but not the other, hence multiplying the permutations to a total of 24. This is one reason that set-off law is so crushingly complex. One cannot go through all these, but one can review some of them to suggest the guiding principles.

Home forum rules

9–11   It seems to be generally true that the home forum will apply its own rules to the availability of set-off on insolvency, including its rules as to preferential build-ups (but see below as to fraudulent preferences) and stays on set-off. This is so in England.

Home forum permits set-off, but foreign forum forbids set-off One may take first the case where the home forum permits insolvency set-off, but the foreign forum does not. If the creditor could have proved for his claim in the English proceedings, then, by the language of the insolvency set-off clause in IR 1986, r 4.90, he is entitled to the set-off even if the foreign forum prohibits set-off. This should be so even if the claim owed to the creditor was incurred through a foreign branch of the debtor. Thus if a bank is owed a loan through the French branch of an English-incorporated debtor and owes a deposit to the debtor in England, then it is considered that the bank could set off the loan against the deposit, even though France prohibits insolvency set-off: the bank is entitled to prove for the loan in the English proceedings. The governing law of the claims is irrelevant.

If conversely the loan is owed through the English office, but the deposit is for the account of the French branch, the result is the same, even though France might maintain that the deposit is a local asset which should be available in an ancillary proceeding in France. This should be so even if the bank is French because the French bank can prove in England. If both states allow a set-off, then the English courts will permit the set-off: consider *Macfarlane v Norris* (1862) 2 B & S 783 summarised at para 9–14.

> In the English case of *Re Hett, Maylor & Co Ltd* (1894) 10 TLR 412, a company in liquidation in England owed a debt to its bank (apparently in England although this is not clear from the report) and the bank owed the company a credit balance at its Manila branch. *Held*: set-off.

However if the foreign forum prohibits the set-off, then the creditor may be subject to the foreign forum's sanctions to recover the amount set off, e.g. a requirement that the creditor who exercised a set-off bring the proceeds into account in claiming dividends until all other creditors have received equal amounts, (equalisation), injunction or recovery suit against the creditor.

Home forum forbids insolvency set-off, but foreign forum allows set-off 9–12

The converse case is where the home forum forbids insolvency set-off, but the foreign forum allows it. If the bank creditor owes a deposit for the account of the home forum of the debtor and is owed a loan through a foreign branch of the debtor, then one can expect the home forum to disallow the set-off. If the bank nevertheless sets off, the home forum can claim the unpaid deposit from the bank if it has jurisdiction over the bank.

If the bank creditor is owed the loan for the account of the home office and owes the deposit to the foreign office, then in the eyes of the home forum the bank is entitled to a dividend on the loan because set-off is disallowed. The home forum is interested in the deposit held for the account of the foreign forum because it may be entitled to a turnover of foreign assets, including the deposit, and a set-off would deprive the home forum of the eventual proceeds of the deposit.

The upshot of the rules is that creditors should ensure that the set-off is available in all applicable jurisdictions, because, even though the relevant forum may allow the set-off, the creditor may be subject to recovery measures if he sets off when he should not have done so in the eyes of the prohibiting forum.

If a foreigner nevertheless sets off contrary to a home prohibition, the home forum is left with indirect methods of enforcement, e.g. equalisation, injunction or recovery suit against the creditor if subject to the jurisdiction, and contempt of court or other penalties.

Attitude of foreign local forum to home forum rules

9–13   This question concerns the attitude of the foreign local forum to the rules on set-off of the home forum where the debtor company is subject to bankruptcy proceedings at its seat or domicile.

The home forum's views will be of no impact in the foreign local forum if the local forum does not recognise the home forum's bankruptcy proceedings at all.

9–14   **No concurrent proceedings in foreign local forum** If the home forum allows insolvency set-off and bankruptcy proceedings have not been commenced in the foreign local forum, there will not usually be a conflict because the set-off is not stayed in the foreign local forum where normally solvent set-off rules will apply. All countries appear to allow solvent set-off. It is true that the solvent set-off rules may not be as wide – e.g. no set-off of unconnected claims where one of them is unliquidated – but the creditor claiming the set-off can get it, one way or another, e.g. by claiming the set-off in the home proceedings.

> In *Macfarlane v Norris* (1862) 2 B&S 783, a creditor was indorsee and holder of a bill of exchange accepted by the debtor. The debtor became bankrupt in Scotland. The creditor owed the bankrupt the proceeds of sale of goods sold by the creditor on behalf of the bankrupt. Under the law of Scotland, there was an insolvency set-off. The Scots trustee sued the creditor in the English courts. *Held*: set-off. There would have been a set-off under both English and Scots law, but it seems that the court applied Scots law as the law of the place where the bankruptcy proceedings were taking place.

Where the home forum does not allow insolvency set-off and no bankruptcy proceedings have been commenced in the foreign local forum which allows a solvent set-off, the proper solution is for the foreign local forum, if it recognises the home bankruptcy, to apply the law of the claim for which the home forum's administrator sues because this is a matter of discharge. If that is governed by the home forum's law, then the local forum should forbid the set-off. If it is governed by some other system of law which allows set-off, then the local forum should allow the set-off. But the principles are obscure and the English courts might apply the lex fori. There is some international support for the cumulative law amongst academic writers but not in the case law.

A German court has applied a foreign bankruptcy prohibition on set-off to deny the German creditor's set-off.

> In a German BGH decision of July 11, 1985, a Belgian debtor became bankrupt in Belgium. A German creditor had a set-off in respect of a debt governed by German law. Set-off was prohibited on a Belgian insolvency but was permitted under German law, including German bankruptcy law. *Held*: the Belgian bankruptcy was universal and the set-off should be disallowed.

Concurrent proceedings in foreign local forum If there are concurrent pro- 9–15
ceedings in the local forum and the home forum allows insolvency set-off, then it is to be expected that the local forum will not permit the administrator to sue for a debt locally in defiance of his own set-off: see *Macfarlane v Norris* (1862)2 B&S 783 summarised above.

It would be extraordinary if in a situation where both jurisdictions permit insolvency set-off, the foreign local forum should refuse set-off. They presumably would only do so if a claim is owed for the benefit of a local branch, if that claim would be removed by the set-off (so that local creditors do not get the benefit of it) and the policy of protecting local creditors overrides the set-off policy. This would discriminate against foreign creditors and would show a strong xenophobic policy in favour of local creditors and a weak set-off policy. This is not the English view.

As for the various other permutations, the principles discussed above in relation to the home forum's approval should apply with appropriate modifications to reflect the ancillary nature of the local proceedings.

The British comity provision in IA 1986, s 426, which requires the English courts to give assistance to courts in designated countries, is unlikely to override the English conflicts rules because the section specifically requires that the court has regard to the rules of private international law. As it happens, most of the designated countries also allow insolvency set-off so the question is less pressing. The US comity provision in BC 1978 s 304 is not expressly limited by a requirement that the courts have regard to the rules of private international law.

Postponement of maturity by foreign insolvency proceedings

If the effect of the foreign insolvency proceedings is to postpone the matur- 9–16
ing of a cross-claim by virtue of a legal moratorium or otherwise, the postponement will be recognised by the English courts if the cross-claim is governed by the foreign law concerned in accordance with the general principles of English conflicts doctrine that the proper law governs discharge. If the result is that the cross-claim matures after the foreign insolvency

representative brings his action, the cross-claim ceases to be available for set-off. However if the cross-claim is governed by English law the foreign moratorium law should be ignored since it does not arise under the governing law of the cross-claim: see *Gibbs & Sons v Société Industrielle et Commerciale des Metaux* (1890) 25 QBD 399, CA.

Similar principles apply if the cross-claim is deemed not merely postponed by a foreign moratorium but discharged by a foreign bankruptcy. If the foreign bankruptcy law discharges the cross-claim, it would be deemed by the English courts to be validly discharged if the cross-claim is governed by the law of the country of the bankruptcy but otherwise not. If the cross-claim is discharged the creditor has no cross-claim available for set-off: see *Gardiner v Houghton* (1862) 2 B&S 743; *Bartley v Hodges* (1861) 1 B&S 375.

CHAPTER 10

NETTING:
GENERAL PRINCIPLES

Introduction

These chapters review the role of netting for the safety and efficiency of markets and seek to identify the legal principles governing the legal efficacy of netting.   **10–1**

It is proposed to state the main principles in one place, although this may involve some repetition of what has gone before, so that the reader's torment in finding all the scattered pieces may be reduced.

At its simplest, netting is the ability to set off reciprocal claims on the insolvency of a counterparty. If party A owes party B $100 million and party B owes party A $100 million and if party B becomes insolvent, then if party A can set off, his exposure is zero. If he cannot, his exposure is $100 million.

Over recent decades there has been an explosion in the size of markets. Apart from the traditional markets for the sale of commodities (such as produce, metals and oil) and the securities markets, these markets include the money and foreign exchange markets, payments systems, and newer markets involving futures, options, interest swaps and the like.

The daily volume in these markets is colossal, especially in the world's financial centres. Thus, foreign exchange contracts alone in London exceed $300 billion per day and the total daily world volume is probably in excess of $800 billion. The result is a potentially huge exposure of market participants, and those who finance those participants, to the failure of a major participant with consequent risk of cascading insolvencies – the domino or systemic risk. There might be pressures on the public purse to rescue the situation so that the risk might be passed back to the citizen and taxpayer.

Objects of netting

The objects of netting are: **10–2**

– To reduce those exposures and hence to protect the integrity of financial institutions and the financial system. The reduction in risk can be

---

dramatic, e.g. more than 90 per cent. The reduction in exposure is reflected in reduced capital adequacy costs and an improved balance sheet.

— To reduce transaction costs, such as the cost of maintaining credit lines and margin to cover gross exposures, and to reduce the cost of processing a multiplicity of gross contracts.

Since the exposures are so large, a high degree of legal predictability is required – the same degree of certainty one would expect of a mortgage.

Netting is primarily (but not exclusively) a matter of insolvency law, not the governing law of the contract concerned. It is on insolvency that netting must stand up – the ability to net prior to insolvency, but not on insolvency, is as futile as a mortgage which is invalid against creditors of the debtor. The contract must, of course, be valid outside insolvency law, but generally this does not present significant legal problems in the ordinary case beyond the usual precautions applicable to all contracts.

Netting is often merely another term for set-off. But the term "netting" is used by the markets because in many cases the process involves more than just a set-off of debts.

The recognition of netting for the purposes of bank capital adequacy ought to follow the law, i.e. if the law permits netting, then the supervisory authorities ought to allow it for capital adequacy purposes. Indeed, the main emphasis of the authorities is on clear legal opinions. This approach is considered to be justifiable. But each legal community in each jurisdiction must reach a consensus which is convincing.

There is a tentative international summary in chapter 13.

Categories of netting

10–3   There are two main categories of netting – settlement netting and default netting . These are summarised before a more detailed analysis is made.

10–4   (a) **Settlement netting** The first type of netting is settlement netting. The object is to reduce settlement risks, i.e. the risk that one party pays a currency and the other party becomes bankrupt before paying his currency, as where one bank pays yen in Tokyo and the other bank fails before paying dollars at New York opening: sometimes known as the *Herstatt* risk, after the failure of a German private bank in 1974. Although possible, it is administratively impracticable in the ordinary course of business to arrange simultaneous payments through national payment systems. The settlement or delivery risk is reduced if obligations for the same asset falling due on the same day are netted so that the only obligation of the counterparties is to pay a net balance. Settlement is a gross risk and the reduction in the exposure can be colossal.

Example: Bank A sells Bank X £50 for $100. A few days later Bank A sells Bank X $100 for £51, to be paid on the same day as the first contract. If, on the day Bank A pays his £50 and $100 under the two contracts, Bank X becomes insolvent before paying his $100 and £51, Bank A has lost those gross amounts. But if the reciprocal amounts were netted when the second contract was entered into, Bank A's exposure would be £1.

This type of netting is variously called "settlement netting" or "delivery netting" or "payments netting". It is referred to in this section as "settlement netting".

(b) **Default netting** The second type of netting is default netting. Its object is to reduce exposures on open contracts if one party becomes insolvent before the value date. 10–5

Example: Bank A and Bank X have two open foreign exchange contracts with each other. One shows a profit of 5, the other a loss of 5. If Bank X becomes insolvent before maturity of the contracts, and if Bank A could cancel and set off the losses and gains, Bank A's exposure to Bank X would be zero. If on the other hand the cancellation and set-off were not possible, Bank A would have a gross exposure of 5.

This is sometimes known as the "replacement contract risk" or "market risk" and flows from fluctuations in exchange rates. This type of netting is variously referred to as "close-out netting" or "default netting" or "open contract netting" or "replacement contract netting" – the precise vernacular or colloquialism does not matter. The essence of the netting is that the innocent party revokes all his unperformed contracts with the insolvent and sets off gains and losses on those contracts. It is referred to in this paper as "default netting".

Settlement netting

As mentioned, settlement netting is intended to reduce settlement risks, i.e. the risk that one party pays or delivers and the other becomes bankrupt before he pays or delivers. The risk arises because it is often impracticable to arrange simultaneous payment and delivery in the ordinary course of business. 10–6

Settlement netting is a contract to net, in advance of the settlement date, reciprocal obligations for the same class of asset for the same settlement date. The netting can equally be applied to payments, foreign exchange deliveries, commodities (e.g. coffee or iron or gold) and fungible securities.

Settlement netting raises relatively few legal issues when compared to default netting and is straight-forward from the documentary point of view.

10–7   One of the main legal issues concerns preferences, i.e. insolvency doctrines providing for the disgorge of a transfer which the debtor makes in favour of a creditor in the suspect period prior to the opening of the formal insolvency proceedings and which prejudice other creditors of the debtor. The main object of these rules is to prevent transfers by a debtor who is actually insolvent which prefer the transferee ahead of other creditors. The agreed early discharge or "payment" of reciprocal obligations must not be a preference voidable on insolvency.

The essence of a preference is improvement in the position of the creditor, i.e. the result of the transaction is that the creditor's position is better on the insolvency of the counterparty than it would have been if the transaction had not occurred. The transaction must usually have taken place in the suspect period (varying in the different countries from three months to 18 months) and at a time when the counterparty is actually insolvent. Preferences are reviewed in another work (on the comparative law of insolvency) in this series on international financial law.

It will generally be found that, if the contracts concerned would be eligible for the second type of netting discussed below (default netting), settlement netting does not improve the position of the creditor. This is because the position of the insolvent on a close-out is the same, whether or not settlement netting had taken place. In other words, the net balance after a close-out would be exactly the same amount, event if the gross obligations had not been netted by the contract. Hence the settlement netting does not prejudice the insolvent's other creditors.

However, some jurisdictions treat as automatically preferential and inopposable to the bankruptcy estate all prepayments made in the suspect period, whether by cash, assets or set-off and all payments by abnormal means, e.g. France (BA 1985 Art 107), Belgium (C Com Art 445), Luxembourg (ditto), Greece (CC Art 537), Denmark (BA Art 67), Sweden (BA s 10) and much of Latin America. The literal language of the statute does not require a showing that the other creditors of the bankrupt are prejudiced because it is assumed that a prepayment of an unmatured debt in the suspect period is automatically preferential. But it would be a perversion of the policy of preferences if a transaction could be set aside even though the bankrupt estate was not diminished by the transaction.

10–8   Apart from this, often the principle applies only to the prepayment of claims which would have matured after the judicial declaration of insolvency. If they matured before the insolvency, the prepayment is not relevant. One should apply instead the preference rules applicable to the payment of claims which mature before the opening of the proceedings. Usually, these could validly have been netted prior to the insolvency, so there is no harm in the prepayment. As regards transactions which have value dates after the start of the insolvency proceedings, if the previous netting is invalid and the gross obligations must be restored, then the creditor can ensure that he does not deliver the gross amounts to the debtor's insolvency administrator without receiving a corresponding gross delivery.

It is therefore hard to see how these adverse preference rules could create a danger, provided that default netting is allowed.

There are no preference obstacles in England to settlement netting (because England allows default netting and also for other reasons).

Default netting

Default netting is intended to reduce exposures on open contracts if one party should become insolvent before the settlement date. See the example at para 10–3.   **10–9**

From the technical point of view, the legal conditions for the efficacy of this type of netting depend upon the class of contract. Although there are a number of variants, most market contracts fall into one of the following two categories:

(a) The first is a contract involving the payment of a vested debt or unliquidated claim. Here, it must simply be possible to set off the reciprocal claims on the insolvency of the counterparty. Examples of this class are (i) claims for simple liquidated debts, such as loans and deposits already made, and (ii) claims for unliquidated or contingent debts, such as claims under contracts for differences (typical of futures and options markets and derivatives) and claims under interest caps and floors. This is something of a simplification, but it will suffice.

(b) The second category includes executory contracts to deliver property or money – the civilian synallagmatic contract. Here, it must be possible to do two things:

- It must be possible to rescind, cancel or terminate all open or unmatured contracts with the defaulting counterparty.
- It must be possible to set off resulting losses and gains over the whole series of mutual contracts. Strictly, set-off is not required if the creditor can cancel and keep the profit on contracts profitable to him: para 10–13.

Examples of the second type of contract include (i) contracts for the sale   **10–10**
of commodities, bullion, securities or other property, and (ii) contracts for the exchange or delivery of money, such as normal foreign exchange contracts, interest swaps, and obligations to place a deposit.

English case law has established that foreign exchange contracts fall into this category in the sense that each party's claim against the other is for damages if the other does not perform – usually the extra cost of buying the defaulted currency in the market. They are not reciprocal debts. In other words, the remedies under a foreign exchange contract are the same as the remedies under a contract of barter of goods, e.g. exchanges of peas and beans. See *Re British American Continental Bank Ltd, Goldzieher & Penso's Claim* [1922] 2 Ch 575; *Lisser & Rosenkranz's Claim* [1923] 1 Ch 976; *Bank of India v Patel* [1982] 1 Lloyds LR 506.

It is thought that normal interest swaps would fall into the same category. This characterisation entirely accords with the practices of the markets concerned.

The difference is exemplified by the remedy of a depositor against a bank for non-payment of a deposit of 100 (debt claim for 100) and the remedy of a borrower against a lender for failure by the lender to make a loan of 100 (extra cost to the borrower of getting the loan elsewhere, e.g. 5, but not 100). Although both are claims for money in the amount of 100, the remedies and the amounts payable on a default are very different since the contracts are different in nature.

10–11   The basic distinctions between executory contracts and debt contracts may be further developed as follows:

(a) **Damages** If a party defaults under an executory foreign exchange contract involving, say, $100 for DM 170, the innocent party can claim damages. These damages are generally a small fraction of the gross amount, e.g. 5, namely, any extra replacement cost of getting the currency in the market. He may alternatively be entitled to specific performance in some jurisdictions (a right which would not normally be available in England) but in volatile markets specific performance will often not be a practical or attractive alternative. In many jurisdictions a party can waive specific performance by contract. By contrast, if a debtor fails to pay a debt of 100, he is liable for the full 100 as a minimum. Proof of loss, mitigation, penalties and other damages rules for breach of contract do not apply to debt claims.

(b) **Rescission** If one party to an executory contract to exchange money becomes insolvent before maturity, then in many (though not all) jurisdictions the solvent counterparty can cancel his executory obligations to deliver and take delivery. He can cancel in the same way that he can cancel an open contract to deliver generic goods which have not yet been identified, delivered or paid for. But if a party entitled to a debt becomes insolvent, it is believed that few, if any, of the developed jurisdictions will allow the solvent party to cancel his obligation to pay that debt into the insolvent estate. Unlike the benefit of an executory contract, the debt is a vested asset of the insolvent's estate and creditors cannot snatch away assets after the insolvency has commenced.

(c) **Insolvency set-off** Executory obligations to exchange money should not be set off in their gross amount under the insolvency set-off rule in those countries which allow insolvency set-off. If a foreign exchange contract is for $100 against DM 170, one does not set off the nominal gross amounts after conversion into sterling. The solvent party cancels. Only the damages of 5 should be eligible for set-off. If on the other hand the parties owe each other debts, such as deposits of US$100 and DM 170, these are set off on insolvency in their gross amount, perhaps after conversion into the local currency (as in England). It is true that the conversion of the gross amounts of the executory foreign exchange sums into local currency at current market rates followed by their set-off might sometimes result in a net sum similar to the amount of the damages, but this will often not be the case.

(d) **Currency conversion and discounting** Insolvency rules whereby debts payable by the insolvent are converted into local currency at the date of the opening of the proceedings and whereby future contractual claims are discounted back at a prescribed rate should not apply to the gross currency delivery obligations under executory foreign exchange contracts. The conversion rule should however apply to losses payable by the insolvent on closed-out contracts.

(e) **Cancellation and acceleration** If a borrower becomes insolvent, then the debt claim for a loan is accelerated, either by the bankruptcy statute itself or by a term of the contract. The whole principal amount of the loan becomes prematurely due. But if a party to an executory foreign exchange contract becomes insolvent, the gross currency amounts are not accelerated. The contractual maturity date is not advanced to the date of the opening of the proceedings. Instead, the contracts are cancelled (if permitted) and it is the damages for breach of contract which are immediately due.

It is not relevant that an executory contract relates to foreign currencies   **10–12** since executory contracts to pay money may be performable in the domestic currency without disturbing the results of the characterisation. Conversely, debts may be payable in foreign currency and are not thereby converted into executory payment obligations.

The characterisation does not involve treating foreign currency as a commodity or goods. There must now be very few, if any, legally developed jurisdictions which treat a foreign currency obligation as an obligation to deliver goods as opposed to money. The main relevance of the so-called "commodity theory of money" is that the remedies for breach of a foreign exchange contract and the position of the parties are similar to those applying to contracts for the barter of goods. But a foreign exchange contract is not, as a result, a contract for the exchange of commodities. Contracts of barter and foreign exchange contracts share the same remedies, but the subject of the contracts is different, one money, the other goods.

It is believed that the above principles of characterisation apply in the main commercial jurisdictions. Although they may be conceptually difficult in the case of foreign exchange contracts or interest swaps, the characterisation is crucial to the position on bankruptcy because the availability of insolvency set-off is not enough for netting of executory contracts: it is also necessary to be able to cancel the contracts on insolvency. An erroneous characterisation will only lead to muddle. There is, after all, nothing odd or strange or new about a contract of barter.

10–13   There is one important further consequence of the characterisation. This is that default netting may be possible even in countries which do not have insolvency set-off in the case of executory contracts. Although it is stated above that, in the case of executory contracts, it is necessary to be able both to rescind outstanding contracts and to set off losses and gains, the ability to set-off is not necessary if it is possible for the solvent party to cancel contracts which are profitable to the estate on the insolvency of the counterparty and to keep the profit. By way of illustration, let us take the previous example where the solvent party has two contracts with the insolvent counterparty. One contract is profitable to the insolvent to the extent of 5. The other contract is loss-making from the point of view of the insolvent to the extent of 5. If the solvent party is able to cancel and rescind the contract which is profitable to the insolvent, then the solvent counterparty can himself realise that profit by selling the assets in the market for an extra 5. He keeps the 5. The counterparty will of course repudiate the loss-making contract, leaving damages of 5 payable to the solvent party. But that 5 is already covered by the profit of 5 on the other contract and so the exposure is zero. Set-off is not necessary because the solvent party has not agreed to pay the profit of 5 to the insolvent, i.e. payments are not, in the vernacular, two-way and instead the solvent party can "walk away": see para 12–1.

One may therefore sum up by stating that if the contract is an executory contract as described above and if under the local insolvency regime the solvent party can, pursuant to an express clause, cancel and rescind contracts which are profitable to the insolvent estate without accounting for the profit, then default netting can still proceed even in the absence of the insolvency set-off in the jurisdiction concerned. This does however aid netting in the case of non-executory contracts, e.g. obligations to pay a debt in the sense described in para 10–9. Here, there is no rescission, but there must be set-off.

Cherry-picking

If the solvent counterparty is not able to rescind all the open contracts and   **10–14** to set off, then the insolvency administrator of the other party may be able to "cherry-pick", i.e. claim selective performance of the profitable contracts and repudiate the unprofitable contracts. The result would be that it would not be possible to net out the loss and gain of 5 and 5.

In one group of countries, cherry-picking is seen as fair: they say that the insolvency administrator ought to be able to claim profits so that he can enlarge the estate available to unsecured creditors, or at least to employees as preferential creditors. But in another group of countries, it is seen as unjust that the insolvent defaulter should be able to insist on payment of profits, but nevertheless refuse to pay losses – dividends payable by insolvent estates are rarely more than 10 per cent and often much less or zero. Contrary to the view in debtor-orientated countries, their policy is to help creditors to escape the debacle. They support this policy by the view that it is unreasonable that a defaulter should be paid, but not pay.

Default netting in England

English insolvency law allows default netting as against ordinary banks and   **10–15** corporates.

As mentioned, in the case of one class of transaction, both rescission and set-off must (normally) be available and in the other class only set-off is necessary.

As to *rescission*, there is no objection to the cancellation of an executory contract for the sale of unidentified assets under an express rescission clause operating on default, including insolvency. If a seller agrees to sell grain not yet identified for delivery in three months and the buyer becomes bankrupt after one month, the seller can cancel the contract if the contract allows him to do so. The same principle applies to foreign exchange contracts.

English insolvency law does not nullify these rescission clauses. Case law supports this conclusion and indeed close-outs under the rules of stock exchange and commodity markets have given rise to a long series of cases going back to the nineteenth century, none of which challenged the efficacy of the close-out. A claim under an executory contract of this type by the insolvent is not treated as an asset of the estate which cannot be removed on insolvency. In *Shipton, Anderson & Co (1927) Ltd v Micks Lambert & Co*

[1936] 2 All ER 1032, the court upheld a buyer's right to rescind a commodity contract on a seller's stoppage of payment under an express clause contained in the rules of the commodity market concerned.

10–16   If there is no express rescission clause, netting is still possible, but the solvent party's position is different. The debtor's insolvency will often amount to an implied repudiation entitling the counterparty to cancel in any event. If in the circumstances there is no implied repudiation (e.g. because the insolvency administrator immediately gives adequate assurances of performance), it would normally still not be possible for the insolvency administrator to compel the creditor to perform by an action for specific performance since specific performance is not generally available for contracts for unascertained assets readily available elsewhere in the market. The innocent party would at the most be obliged to pay damages (if the insolvency administrator is ready and willing to perform), but these damages would be eligible for set-off against losses payable by the defaulter on other repudiated contracts.

The result would merely at worst reflect the common market practice of two-way payments, i.e. each side accounts to the other for profits. Two-way payments are discussed in para 10–13.

10–17   As to *set-off*, it has been seen that the English policy in favour of insolvency set-off in IR 1986, r 4.90 is so strong that the set-off is mandatory. Insolvency set-off has been statutory since 1705. In the case of the first class of obligation (vested non-executory claims), the claims are set-off. In the case of executory contracts, all losses and gains arising from pre-petition cancelled contracts between the parties would be brought into account and a net balance would be payable either way. This set-off operates to net losses and gains on executory contracts entered into prior to the insolvency order and also to set off ordinary debts, even though the contracts are closed-out or the debts mature after the insolvency date. The claims do not have to be connected or arise out of the same or related transactions or under the same master agreement.

10–18   Rescission of executory contracts and set-off are not affected by an administration order or voluntary arrangement under the Insolvency Act 1986. Both are, broadly, corporate rehabilitation procedures as an alternative to final liquidation. Administrations stay creditor proceedings and steps to enforce security or to repossess, but not self-help contract rescissions of this type or set-off. However, in the case of a company voluntary arrangement (a type of composition), there should be an appropriate event of default allowing a close-out before the creditors meeting to approve the proposal for a voluntary arrangement. The event should crystallise on notice of the creditor's meeting being given. This is to avoid the counterparty being bound by a creditor resolution effectively overriding the set-off, e.g. by imposing a moratorium on default claims payable by the insolvent so that matured claims payable to the insolvent have to be paid to him without set-off. Even if this were to happen, it is thought that the creditor deprived of his set-off might in principle succeed on an "unfair prejudice" application to the court on the grounds that the composition is discriminatory. But there is no case law on this provision.

Default netting: international comparison

International comparisons reveal a great diversity of approach to the rescission of executory contracts and set-off on insolvency.   **10–19**

Broadly speaking, one group of states (which includes England) allows creditors to protect themselves against a potential defaulter, e.g. by rescinding contracts and by set-off. These jurisdictions regard it as inequitable that the insolvent should be able to insist on performance when he himself refuses to perform. But another group seeks to preserve assets of the debtor's estate with a view to the rehabilitation or protection of the debtor, e.g. by preventing the rescission of profitable contracts and by limiting insolvency set-off. In the end, there is a fundamental split between pro-creditor and pro-debtor approaches, a split which is at the root of legal disharmony and which is so deep in the history of legal cultures that harmonisation is superficial unless one crosses this ravine.

As to *rescission* of executory contracts, most developed bankruptcy laws   **10–20**
give the insolvency administrator the right to accept or reject contracts of the insolvent, so that the main question is whether the administrator, in calling for performance of profitable contracts, can ignore a cancellation clause in the contract itself. There seem to be only a few states which expressly nullify rescission clauses. These jurisdictions include Canada (under recent legislation), France, New Zealand (under the optional statutory management procedure which can only be initiated by the government and which is extraordinary) and the United States. As to special netting statutes, see below.

Conversely, it is believed that countries such as Germany, Austria, Japan, Belgium, Italy, Switzerland and many others (as well as numerous states basing their insolvency law on the English model) do not nullify rescission clauses in executory contracts of this type.

Of course, many states do not allow rescission on bankruptcy of some protected contracts, notably leases of real property and (sometimes) equipment leases, but these cases are based on objections to penal forfeitures. In the case of executory contracts for the sale of generic unidentified assets, if the bankrupt is credited with gains, there is no forfeiture of an asset.

There is a more detailed review of the position on contracts on insolvency in another work (on the comparative law of insolvency) in this series on international financial law.

10–21   As to *set-off*, it has been seen that a bloc of jurisdictions forbids insolvency set-off altogether, subject to limited exceptions. These include France, Luxembourg, Spain, Greece and their related jurisdictions including most jurisdictions in Latin America (except Panama) and in the former French dominions. Insolvency set-off is seen as contravening the pari passu principle and as unpublicised "security" and hence the creditor must pay in what he owes and prove for what he is owed. But in these countries, it is commonly the case that insolvency set-off is available if the cross-claims are connected or if they arise in the same current account.

On the other hand, insolvency set-off of mutual claims is specifically permitted by statute in the majority of the leading jurisdictions, including England, Germany, Japan, Austria, Switzerland, Italy, Norway, Denmark, Finland, Scotland (non-statutory), Sweden, the Netherlands, the United States, and, again, the numerous jurisdictions basing their insolvency law on English bankruptcy legislation, such as Australia, Hong Kong and Singapore. Poland and the Czech and Slovak Republics allow insolvency set-off, as does China in its recent bankruptcy legislation. Recent insolvency legislation in Australia has not affected set-off (or contract rescission). The tradition here is that the debtor should not demand payment if he declines to pay and that the non-publication of "security" is either not a serious issue in practice or is not important enough to override this unconscionability.

10–22   The contrast is shown by the fact that in England insolvency set-off is not merely permitted, but is mandatory and the parties cannot contract out, whereas in France insolvency set-off is prohibited and one cannot contract in. This division goes back for centuries – long before Napoleon in both countries and is therefore fairly indelible. Of course one may legitimately dispute which solution is morally the most justifiable or economically the best, but that discussion can safely be left to the philosophers of bankruptcy law: the present task is merely to record.

Insolvency set-off is reviewed generally in chapter 6.

Rehabilitation statutes

10–23   The netting must be effective in the case of a rehabilitation statute as well as on final bankruptcy. Rescue laws pose a greater threat to netting than final bankruptcy because the objective is to ensure survival. Set-off removes cash available to the debtor and the cancellation of essential contracts might inhibit the continuation of the business. But bankruptcy necessitates a choice.

Apart from traditional compositions and moratoriums, from the mid–1970s there was a vogue for rescue proceedings which freeze or stay creditor rights, although the international experience of the more debtor-protective laws has shown a poor rate of success. Some of these do not affect set-off or contract cancellation clauses, e.g. the English administration order introduced in the Insolvency Act 1986, the Australian voluntary administration and deed of company arrangement under the Corporate Law Reform Act 1992, and the Japanese Corporate Rehabilitation Law of 1952 which was based on the US Bankruptcy Act of 1898, as amended, (which was more creditor-protective than the US Bankruptcy Code of 1978). Whether the 1990 Irish examinership freezes set-offs should be considered.

Other statutes do impose stays on both set-off and contract cancellations, **10–24** e.g. the Canadian commercial reorganisation of 1992, the French *redressement judiciaire* of 1985, the New Zealand statutory management of 1989, and the US Chapter 11.

The Italian *liquidazione coatta amministrativa* does not stay set-off (BA Art 201, applying the set-off in BA Art 56), but set-offs are stayed under the *amministrazione controllata* and the *amministrazione straordinaria* and possibly also contract termination: see Supreme Court, May 9, 1969, n 1588.

In the case of the traditional moratoriums (which are not much used), it needs to be considered whether a majority creditor vote can stretch the maturity of claims payable by the bankrupt so that the counterparty is obliged to pay to the bankrupt matured claims which are not stretched. The result is a loss of set-off. The destruction of the set-off would often be discriminatory because the creditor who is deprived of his set-off suffers a greater disadvantage than ordinary unsecured creditors without a set-off. Often the set-off is expressly preserved, e.g. under the German *Vergleich* (VO s 54) and the Italian *concordato preventivo* (BA Art 169, applying BA s 56). If it is not expressly preserved, it may be saved by the usual general requirement that creditors of a class must be treated equally by the terms of the composition plan.

There is a general review of rehabilitation statutes in another work (on the comparative law of insolvency) in this series on international financial law.

Contractual enhancements: automatic cancellation, connexity, novation

Markets responded to the potential bars on rescission and set-off in the hos- **10–25** tile jurisdictions by two contractual devices:

1.   The first is a provision that all contracts between the parties are auto-

matically deemed to be cancelled and losses and gains set off *immediately prior* to the institution of insolvency proceedings. The hope is that a cancellation and a set-off automatically deemed to take place immediately prior to the insolvency would not be subject to the nullification of rescission clauses and the bar on insolvency set-off which come into effect on the opening of the insolvency proceedings – they have already occurred. This is the origin of the automatic termination clause.

2. The second device is to seek to take advantage of the common exemption from the bar on rescission and set-off (in countries hostile to netting) which exists in favour of connected transactions. For example, an insolvent cannot claim the price for goods sold without allowing a deduction for defects in the goods – the classic connexity situation which is recognised everywhere. The insolvent would be demanding payment for something he did not supply, or supplied defectively. A master contract entered into between the parties provides that all of the individual trades between the parties are governed by the umbrella master agreement and all those trades are connected transactions as part of the same business relationship. The theory is that, although the insolvency administrator may be able to cherry-pick by selective performance of individual contracts and repudiation of the rest, he could not do so in the case of a single transaction, i.e. he could not claim to take the benefit of one part of the transaction without also assuming its burden if it is all one bargain. He should not be able to take the cream without the crust, the cherry without the pip, the rose without the thorn. Plainly connexity between different contracts for different value dates and for different products is more remote than in the case of a single transaction. The contractual connexity is sometimes reinforced by a provision that all new contracts between the parties are "novated" so as to form a single contract with existing contracts. These contractual provisions are the origin of connexity by master contracts and of "netting by novation".

The key question is whether a private contract – whether automatic termination on contractual connexity or novation – can defeat a bankruptcy statute which expressly nullifies set-off or rescission or both. If the contracting-out defies a statutory prohibition, it must be capable of strong and convincing legal justification if the requirement of predictability is to be satisfied. Although ingenuity has its place, it would seem desirable that markets should not have to resort to legal witchcraft.

Automatic cancellation, connexity and novation are not necessary for the validity of default netting under English law.

CHAPTER 11

SPECIAL NETTING STATUTES

Special netting statutes

Such is the priority accorded to the legal validity of market netting, that at least 12 jurisdictions have enacted special provisions of varying scope which enhance netting on insolvency. The jurisdictions include: **11–1**

Austria	s 22 of the Bankruptcy Act (mandatory rescission of certain market contracts)
Belgium	Article 157 of Law of April 19, 1993 (netting between credit institutions)
Britain	Part VII of the Companies Act 1989 (applying mainly to certain recognised organisations and largely declaratory of existing netting law)
Canada	s 65.1(7) to (9) of the Bankruptcy Act, inserted in 1992, applying to certain financial contracts
Cayman Islands	Amendment of December 1993 to Companies Law
France	Articles 1 and 2 of Law No 93–1444 of December 31, 1993, amending Law of March 28, 1885, on futures transactions
Germany	Section 18 of the Bankruptcy Act of 1879 (mandatory rescission of certain market contracts). Article 15(1) of the Second Financial Markets Promotion Act 1994 applying to financial forward transactions
Italy	Article 76 of the Bankruptcy Act of 1942 (mandatory rescission of certain market contracts)
Japan	Article 61 of the Bankruptcy Law (applying to exchange quoted merchandise)
Netherlands	Section 38 of the Bankruptcy Act (mandatory rescission of certain market contracts)

Sweden	Section 1 of Chapter 5 of the Financial Investments Trading Act, in force 1995
United States	Sections 555 and 556 of the Bankruptcy Code of 1978 (applying to certain market contracts); s 212 of the Financial Institutions Reform, Recovery and Enforcement Act of 1989 (applying to certain contracts of federally insured banks and savings institutions); 1990 amendments to Bankruptcy Code (applying to swaps); FDIC Improvement Act of 1991.

11–2　　　The provisions in Germany (prior to the 1994 changes), Austria, the Netherlands, Japan and Italy are all similar. These provisions seem to have been based on the notion that in volatile markets an insolvent party should not have to wait to see if the insolvency administrator wishes to perform, particularly if it was unlikely that the defaulter would be able to perform. Originally, the netting clauses applied only to contracts in commodities markets and not expressly to financial contracts: this is because the sections are of respectable antiquity (1879 in Germany) when financial markets had not surmounted commodities markets in terms of size. To that extent they are quite limited. But in certain cases the provisions have been extended by case law to contracts for the sale of securities and in Italy the provisions have been applied to foreign exchange contracts by case law. The other jurisdictions might take the same view. In any event, it is believed to be the case that, in these five countries, it is not necessary that the contract comes within the special netting clause since the insolvency laws do not nullify express rescission clauses and set-off is statutorily permitted on a general basis – in the case of final bankruptcy proceedings. Hence the sections are effectively a codification of netting of particular contracts, but without excluding the availability of netting of other contracts.

11–3　　　The netting statutes in Belgium, Canada, France and the United States only apply to the specific contracts between the specific institutions specified in the legislation. Legislation was necessary in those jurisdictions, because the insolvency statute specifically prohibited rescission clauses or set-off or both. The United States Bankruptcy Code of 1978, for example, is generally regarded as debtor-protective and froze most rescission clauses under the automatic stay provision. It was this stay which originally led to the development of the contractual devices reviewed at para 10–25.

England, by contrast, has had statutes mandating insolvency set-off continuously for nearly 300 years and it has not been necessary to deal with rescission clauses since that is the law in any event. The 1989 legislation in favour of certain recognised institutions and exchanges was largely declaratory so far as netting is concerned.

The following sections give more detail of special statutes enhancing netting. Note that, in the case of Britain, Germany, Italy, Japan and the Netherlands, the special netting statute does not exclude netting generally, while in Belgium, Canada, France and the United States it is usually necessary for the transaction to be within the netting statute.

Netting legislation in Belgium

In Belgium, there appears to be no objection to contractual insolvency cancellations, but insolvency set-off is prohibited except in the case of connexity. Accordingly, Art 157 of the Law of April 19, 1993 provides:

11—4

> "(1) Bilateral and multilateral set-off agreements, together with express default clauses providing for set-off, between two or more credit establishments or between credit establishments and settlement or clearing agencies may, in the event of insolvency or any other situation of distribution to creditors (*situation de concours*) be enforceable against creditors, provided that both the credit and the debt to be set off existed in the same right (*patrimoine*) prior to the onset of the insolvency or other such situation, regardless of the contractual payment date, their purpose or the currency in which they are denominated.
>
> Agreements of the type referred to, in the first paragraph which were concluded after the date determined by the court to be that of the cessation of payments (*cessation de paiements*) of the debtor or during a 10-day period prior to that date, are not valid against other creditors if they relate to a debt previously contracted but not yet due.
>
> For the purposes of this paragraph, the *Banque Nationale de Belgique* and the *Institut de Réescompte et de Garantie* are deemed to be "credit establishments".
>
> (2) Without prejudice to paragraph (1) above and Articles 445 to 449 of Book III of the *Code Du Commerce*, payments, transactions and acts carried out by a credit establishment and payments made to such establishments on the date of the adjudication of its insolvency, will be valid provided that they are made before the moment of the judicial declaration of insolvency or if they are carried out without knowledge of the credit establishment's insolvency.
>
> For the purposes of paragraph (1), settlement or clearing agencies which deal with transactions between credit establishments shall be treated in the same way as credit establishments.
>
> (3) The King may, in respect of such payments and transactions as he determines, extend this Article to other categories of financial institution."
> [unofficial translation]

The statute is quite narrow because, apart from clearing houses, the contract must be between two credit establishments so that banks cannot net as against ordinary corporates under the statute. However even though insolvency set-off is generally questionable under Belgian insolvency law (a position which is being eroded by the case law), it does not seem to be objectionable in Belgium to cancel executory contracts with an insolvent even if these contracts would be profitable to the insolvent. If this is correct, it would be possible in Belgium to net executory contracts for the reasons given at para 13–15. By contrast, France is different because there is a specific freeze on contract rescissions by reason of insolvency.

Netting legislation in Britain

11–5   Part VII of the Companies Act 1989 (ss 154 to 191) was enacted to reduce the possibility of domino insolvencies occurring by enhancing the effect of the techniques employed by the market of netting out exposures to defaulting counterparties, and by protecting margins and protecting security given to support the obligations of market participants.

In many respects Part VII is declaratory of existing English law with some improvements at the edges. Its main effect was to reverse certain changes to 1986 insolvency freezes on security in the event of a rehabilitative administration. Much of the detail remains to be mapped out in regulations yet to be made.

11–6   **Application of Part VII to clearing houses** This statutory enhancement applies to market contracts connected with investment exchanges and clearing houses provided that these institutions have rules complying with the requirements of Part VII and otherwise fall within the requirements of Part VII. There is a limited extension of the protection to off-market contracts.

Effect of Part VII The general effect of Part VII is to establish the principle that, if the institution closes out the contracts of the defaulter, all the losses and gains on the contracts are netted out so as to be reduced to a net sum which is either provable in the insolvency of a defaulter or payable to the defaulter. The institutions must have default rules which enable this to be done.

Part VII also contains detailed provisions which severely restrict the following ordinary insolvency rules:

(a) the liquidator's power to disclaim contracts and the ability of the court to rescind contracts: s 164;

(b) rules avoiding post-petition disposals: s 164;

(c) rules avoiding preferences, transactions at an undervalue and transactions defrauding creditors: s 165; and

(d) the statutory freeze on proceedings after an insolvency: s 161(4).

Market charges Another of the aims of Part VII is to strengthen the validity **11–7** and priority of charges given to support the obligations of market participants towards exchanges and clearing houses, whether for delivery risks or for market exposure risks.

The main changes effected by Part VII are:

(a) the removal of the freeze on the enforcement of security arising if an administration order is made: s 175(1). The reason is that in volatile markets it is essential that there should be quick realisation of an insolvent's position;

(b) the removal of the power of a receiver appointed in respect of a floating charge to dispose of charged property: s 175(3);

(c) protection of the recipients of security if charged property is received post-petition: s 175(4); and

(d) improvement of the priority of market charges; ss 177–180.

Margin Part VII enhances the priority and validity of margin deposits. The **11–8** protection is broadly achieved by limiting the ordinary insolvency powers of disclaimer, protecting margin received post-petition and modifying the rules in situations where the provision of margin might otherwise be a preference or a transaction at an undervalue. In addition there are provisions protecting the priority of margin over prior rights: these are in some respects declaratory of existing law.

Territorial scope Part VII includes a limited provision for co-operation between specified insolvency jurisdictions.

In addition there is provision for the statutory non-recognition or blocking of certain orders of foreign insolvency tribunals or acts of foreign insolvency representatives to the extent they involve something which would be prohibited in the United Kingdom by virtue of Part VII s 183(2). Provisions of this type may give rise to confrontation between jurisdictions but the official policy seems to have been that the urgency of the need to safeguard organised markets should override comity and courtesy. This blocking does not affect the recognition and enforcement of judgments under the EC Judgments Convention: s 183(3).

Netting legislation in Canada

11–9   In Canada, the Bankruptcy and Insolvency Act 1992 amends the Bankruptcy Act by nullifying clauses whereby a party may terminate a contract on the insolvency of the counterparty. A new s 65.1(1) provides:

> "Where a notice of intention or a proposal has been filed in respect of an insolvent person, no person may terminate or amend any agreement with the insolvent person, or claim an accelerated payment under any agreement with the insolvent person, by reason only that:
> (a) the insolvent person is insolvent; or
> (b) a notice of intention or a proposal has been filed in respect of the insolvent person."

11–10   But by subsection (7) the freeze in s 65.1(1) does not apply:

> "(a) in respect of an eligible financial contract; or
> (b) to prevent a member of the Canadian Payments Association established by the Canadian Payments Association Act from ceasing to act as a clearing agent or group clearer for an insolvent person in accordance with that Act and the by-laws and rules of that Association."

By subsection 8 "eligible financial contract" means

> "(a) a currency or interest rate swap agreement,
> (b) a basis swap agreement,
> (c) a spot, future, forward or other foreign exchange agreement,
> (d) a cap, collar or floor transaction,
> (e) a commodity swap,
> (f) a forward rate agreement,
> (g) a repurchase or reverse repurchase agreement,
> (h) a spot, future, forward or other commodity contract,
> (i) an agreement to buy, sell, borrow or lend securities, to clear or settle securities transactions or to act as a depository for securities,
> (j) any derivative, combination or option in respect of, or agreement similar to, an agreement or contract referred to in paragraphs (a) to (i),
> (k) any master agreement in respect of any agreement or contract referred to in paragraphs (a) to (j),
> (l) a guarantee of the liabilities under an agreement or contract referred to in paragraphs (a) to (k), or
> (m) any agreement of a kind prescribed:

'net termination value' means the net amount obtained after setting off the mutual obligations between the parties to an eligible financial contract in accordance with its provisions."

Subsection (9) provides: **11–11**

"For greater certainty, where an eligible financial contract entered into before the filing by an insolvent person of:
(a) a notice of intention, or
(b) a proposal, where no notice of intention was filed,
is terminated on or after that filing, the setting off of obligations between the insolvent person and the other parties to the eligible financial contract, in accordance with its provisions, shall be permitted, and if net termination values determined in accordance with the eligible financial contract are owed by the insolvent person to another party to the eligible financial contract, that other party shall be deemed, for the purposes of paragraphs 69(1)(a) and 69.1(1)(a), to be a creditor of the insolvent person with a claim provable in bankruptcy in respect of those net termination values."

Netting legislation in France

No termination on grounds of bankruptcy The French bankruptcy legis-   **11–12** lation contained in the Decree–Law of January 25, 1985 provides in Art 37 that no contract may be terminated by a contracting party on the sole ground that bankruptcy proceedings have been initiated against the other party. Contractual provisions to the contrary are unenforceable. The inter-pretation given by case law of this provision has been ample; thus, contrac-tual provisions enabling one party to terminate the contract because the other party ceases its payments to its creditors have been held to be unenfor-ceable, even in the absence of bankruptcy proceedings at the time of termination.

In addition, insolvency set-off is effectively prevented by Art 33 of the 1985 Act: the judgment opening bankruptcy proceedings automatically results in the prohibition of payment of all debts which have arisen before such judgment.

However, a more flexible approach has been taken by case law (both before and after the 1985 Act) if the relevant debts arose from the same con-tract and this was codified in 1994. By extension, netting has been upheld between debts which, although arising under contracts which were legally distinct, were closely interrelated (*connexes*).

Finally under Art 107 of the 1985 Act, all payments made during the so-called "suspect period" (a period of up to 18 months before the judgment opening the bankruptcy proceedings (such period being determined by the judge) may be avoided as fraudulent if they have been effected otherwise than by using a "usual method of payment in business transactions". Netting which arises by operation of law in relation to reciprocal debts which are certain, determined in their quantum and which have matured fall outside the scope of this provision. Contractual netting of debts relating to terminated transactions is, on the other hand, considered to be potentially problematic as it may be an unusual method of payment which is voidable under Art 107.

Articles 1 and 2 of Law No 93–1444 of December 31, 1993, amend the Act dated March 28, 1885, on futures transactions.

11–13   The relevant provisions of the Act, as amended by the new statute, are as follows:

> "Article 1:
>
> All futures transactions (*marchés à terme*) on government or other securities, on securities, goods or commodities as well as all transactions on interest rates, indexes and currencies are legal. No one can rely on Article 1965 of the Civil Code [unenforceability of gambling contracts] to avoid the obligations arising thereunder, even if they are settled by the mere payment of a difference.
>
> Transactions on goods and commodities which are not physically settled may only be entered into between two or more parties, at least one of which is a credit institution or a non-resident institution having a comparable status or Caisse des Dépôts et Consignations.
>
> Article 2
>
> Reciprocal debts relating to the transactions referred to in Article 1, when such transactions are entered into in the context of the general regulation or special regulations referred to in Article 6 of this Act or in Article 6 of Act no. 88–70 dated 22nd January, 1988 on stock exchanges or when such transactions are governed by a master agreement which complies with the general principles of a national or international market master agreement (*convention-cadre de place*) which organises the relationships between two or more parties, at least one of which is a credit institution, an institution or enterprise referred to in Articles 8 and 69 of Act no. 84–46 dated 24th January, 1984 as amended on the activities and control of credit institutions, an enterprise governed by Article L310.1 of the Insurance Code, a stock-broking firm governed by Act no. 88–70 dated 22nd January 1988, or a non-resident institution having a comparable status, may be netted in accordance with the valuation methods provided for in such regulations or such master agreement.
>
> Such regulations or such master agreement may provide for the automatic termination of the transactions referred to in the previous paragraph when one of the parties is subject to one of the proceedings contemplated by Act no 85–98 dated 25th January, 1985 on recovery and judicial liquidation.

The provisions of this article apply notwithstanding any statutory provisions to the contrary." [unofficial translation]

The netting accordingly is available only if three conditions are all satisfied:

1. the transaction is within Art 1 (which appears to cover most securities, commodities, foreign currency and derivatives transactions);

2. one of the parties is within the specified list of protected persons; and

3. the transaction arises under the specified regulations or the prescribed type of master agreement.

Protected parties

Under Art 2 of the Act, the transactions referred to in Art 1 have the benefit **11–14** of the Act only to the extent that such transactions are concluded between two or more parties, at least one of which is either:

(a) a credit institution, i.e. a bank, financial company (*société financière*) or securities house (*maison de titres*);

(b) an institution or enterprise referred to in Art 8 of Act no 84–46 dated January 24, 1984, as amended on the activities and control of credit institutions, i.e. the *Trésor Public, Banque de France*, the financial department of the postal administration (*La Poste*), IEDOM and IEOM, the two money institutions for *départements and territoires d'Outre-Mer*;

(c) an institution or enterprise referred to in Art 69 of the same Act, i.e. *agents des marchés interbancaires*;

(d) an enterprise governed by Art L 310–1 of the Insurance Code, i.e. any company involved in the insurance sector and which is as such subject to State control; and

(e) a stock-broking firm governed by Act no 88–70 dated January 22, 1988.

Article 2 expressly extends the definition to foreign institutions having a comparable status to any one of the above. The notion of "comparable status" is not defined by the Act.

Only one party to the specified transaction must have the required status, whether or not such party is French. It follows that a foreign bank may enter into cash-settled transactions on commodities with a French industrial company and have the benefit of the provisions of the Act validating the termination and close-out netting provisions of the relevant master agreement.

Protected transactions

11–15   The Act covers transactions referred to in Art 1 only to the extent that such transactions arise under:

(a) the General Regulations of the Stock Exchange Council, i.e. all transactions arising in the organised market of a French stock exchange;

(b) special regulations referred to in Art 6 of the Act, i.e. transactions arising in the organised futures market (MATIF);

(c) special regulations referred to in Art 6 of Act no. 88–70 dated January 22, 1988, on stock exchanges, i.e. all transactions on a French stock exchange or on the organised options market;

(d) a master agreement which complies with the general principles of a national or international market master agreement (*convention-cadre de place*). Although the language is not altogether clear, this is meant to cover master agreements entered into using recognised national or international standard forms such as those published by the French Bankers' Association (AFB) or the International Swap Dealers Association or the British Bankers Association.

11–16   A number of additional comments may be made.

The new paragraph 2 of Art 2 of the Act expressly validates provisions providing for the automatic termination of a protected transaction in circumstances where the French counterparty is subject to bankruptcy proceedings. Although only automatic termination is referred to, it is considered that voluntary termination in these circumstances would also be upheld. The ability to terminate applies "notwithstanding any statutory provision to the contrary". Article 37 of the 1985 Act (which freezes contract terminations on insolvency) is thus excluded.

It appears that the netting of different transactions is permitted – cross-product netting – if the transaction is a protected transaction.

The statement that the "provisions of this article apply notwithstanding any statutory provision to the contrary" avoids the obstacles arising from the bankruptcy legislation.

The reference to the "valuation methods provided for in such regulations or such master agreement" is a recognition that the parties will be allowed to compute the termination values of their transactions in accordance with the provisions of the applicable master agreement, i.e. liquidated damages clauses are validated.

Netting legislation in Germany

In Germany, BA 1879 s 17 provides that the insolvency administrator can   **11–17** call for performance of unperformed contracts, but on demand by the other party must state "without delay" whether he will perform. If he does not do so, he cannot insist on performance. Case law has upheld rescission clauses in unperformed contracts which (it is thought) can therefore operate to defeat the call for performance by the insolvency administrator.

BA 1979 s 18 reads:

> "(1)   If goods, which have a market or exchange price, are stipulated to be delivered at a certain time or within a certain period and this point of time occurs or period lapses after the commencement [*Eroffnung*] of the bankruptcy proceedings [*issuance of the court's bankruptcy order*], no performance can be demanded, but only a claim for non-performance can be asserted.
>
> (2)   The amount of this claim is determined by the difference between the purchase price and such market or exchange price which is quoted at the place of performance or at the pertinent representative trading centre for transactions with the stipulated time of performance on the second business day after the opening of the proceedings.
>
> (3)   If such market or exchange price cannot be determined, the provision of the first subsection is not applicable."

Section 18 is mandatory. A contractual clause which provides that damages are to be assessed in another way or on a different date is not enforceable.

If s 18 is applicable to the contracts in question, cherry-picking between different contracts is not possible because the administrator cannot demand selective performance of any of those contracts and therefore cannot choose to maintain the profitable contracts and repudiate the loss-making contracts.

The section appears to apply to open or executory or unperformed con-   **11–18** tracts for any type of asset which have a fixed term where time is of the essence. The policy of the section appears to be that, if the assets are traded in a market where prices may be volatile, the innocent party should not have to wait to see if the bankrupt's administrator will perform. It is understood that the section was regarded by some commentators as applying to contracts for the sale of securities and foreign exchange.

Insolvency set-off is permitted by BA 1879 ss 53 and 54 and the *Vergleichsordnung* s 45.

11–19   A new German Bankruptcy Act was passed in 1994 and was scheduled to come into force on January 1, 1999. However a new netting section, based on a section in the Act, was brought into force on August 1, 1994. The section expands the principles of BA 1879 s 18 which remains in force until January 1, 1999, alongside the expanded provision.

Article 15 of the Second Financial Markets Promotion Act (*Zweites Finanzmarkförderungsgesetz*) of July 26, 1994, provides:

"(1)   If it was stipulated that obligations under financial transactions which have a market or an exchange price are due to be performed at a certain time or within a certain period of time, and if such time or the expiration of such period occurs after the institution of bankruptcy proceedings, then in lieu of performance only a claim for non-performance may be asserted. The term "financial transactions" shall include in particular transactions relating to:

    1. the delivery of precious metals;
    2. the delivery of securities or similar rights, unless it is intended to acquire an interest in another enterprise for purposes of creating a permanent connection to such enterprise;
    3. payments in any foreign currency or any currency unit;
    4. payments the amount of which is determined, directly or indirectly, by the price of any foreign currency or any currency unit or the rate of interest on money claims or the price of other goods or services;
    5. options and other rights for delivery or payments to Nos. 1 to 4 above.

If individual contracts relating to financial transactions are combined in a master agreement which it has been agreed may be terminated for breach of contract only in its entirety, then all such individual contracts shall constitute a single contract providing for reciprocal obligations.

(2)   The claim for non-performance shall be determined by the difference between the agreed price and that market or exchange price which on the second business day after the institution of the proceedings prevails at the place of performance for contracts entered into with the stipulated performance time. The other party may assert such claim only as creditor in bankruptcy proceedings.

(3)   The provisions set out in subsections (1) and (2) with respect to the institution of bankruptcy proceedings shall apply *mutatis mutandis* to the institution of judicial composition proceedings or reorganisation proceedings." [unofficial translation]

Netting agreements were probably in any event honoured by German insolvency law and so the section is largely clarificatory. It appears likely that transactions which are settled on any certain date after the date the transaction is entered into are covered, e.g. the typical foreign exchange spot transaction, which is customarily settled two days after conclusion of the deal. As to the transactions covered, the definition of financial transactions is generic and not limited so that frequent amendment to cope with new financial products is not required. The listing in paragraphs 1 to 4 of Art 15(1) covers particular examples only and is not exhaustive. Thus ordinary commodities, in addition to the precious metals mentioned in paragraph 1, should be included. Repos and stock-lending should be within the ambit of paragraph 2, which includes dematerialised securities and certificates of indebtedness not constituting securities. The exemption to paragraph 2 relates to acquisitions of a permanent participation in an enterprise because these are not financial in nature. Paragraph 3 covers foreign currency trades, including those involving ECU and other currency units. Paragraph 4 includes various swaps, such as interest rate swaps, cross-currency swaps, commodity swaps and index swaps. Evidently options, other than those enumerated in paragraph 5, should be covered.

It is probably the case that the method of calculation in Art 15(2) is mandatory, but it remains to be seen whether a different contractual method could override. It is considered that the reference to "market or exchange price" includes all cases where there is an available market price, even though quotations in the market may differ. The claim for the difference should be calculated in DM.

Note that under the last paragraph of Art 15(1), financial transactions under a master agreement are treated as a single contract, provided that on a breach all the transactions are terminated, not only some of them.

Netting legislation in Italy

In Italy the position is similar to the German BA 1879 s 18: see BA 1942 Art   **11–20** 72 and Art 76 dealing with compulsory rescission of market contracts.

Article 76 of the Bankruptcy Act provides as follows:

> "Stock exchange contracts which terminate on a date following the date of declaration of insolvency of one of the parties are rescinded at the date of the declaration of insolvency. The difference between the contract price and the value of goods or stocks at the date of the declaration is, if resulting in a credit [to the insolvent party] to be paid to the insolvent's estate and, if resulting in a debit [to the insolvent party] is provable as a debt in the insolvency by the counterparty."

A finding by the Court of Appeal in Milan in the case of *Williams & Glynns Bank AG v Banca Privata Italiana* dated October 17, 1986, confirms that contracts for the exchange of currencies would be classified as "stock exchange contracts" and therefore would be governed by Art 76. The section is mandatory. Note that the bankrupt is credited with gains. This section also applies to a *liquidazione coatta amministrativa*: BA Art 201.

Apart from this, insolvency set-off on final bankruptcy is permitted by BA

Art 76, but may be stayed on *amminstrazione controllata* or *amministra-zione straordinaria.*

Netting legislation in Japan

11–21   In Japan, the familiar pattern is followed: Art 61 of the Bankruptcy Law applies to term contracts for exchange quoted merchandise and provides for their compulsory rescission on bankruptcy. It is generally thought that rescission clauses in executory sales contracts are effective outside this section. Insolvency set-off is allowed: BA Art 98 *et seq.*

It is considered that a reorganisation under the Corporate Reorganisation Law does not affect rescission. A narrower set-off is permitted on reorganisation under Art 162 of the Corporate Reorganisation Law.

Netting legislation in the Netherlands

11–22   In the Netherlands the position is governed by the Bankruptcy Act s 37 which is similar to the former German provisions. Section 38 provides for the compulsory close-out of certain market contracts and states (in case of bankruptcy):

> "If, in the case referred to in [s 37] the delivery of commodities which are traded on a forward exchange market has to be made on a fixed date or within a stated period and if such date occurs or such period expires after the adjudication of bankruptcy, the agreement will be terminated by operation of the adjudication of bankruptcy, in which case the other [solvent] party may, as a general creditor, submit a claim for damages. If the estate suffers damage as a result of the termination, the other [solvent] party is obligated to reimburse that damage."
> [unofficial translation]

BA Art 237 applies the same principle to a suspension of payments. The Article is mandatory.

Apart from this, it seems that in the Netherlands there is no general insolvency bar on the contractual cancellation of executory contracts for the sale of generic assets on insolvency. Insolvency set-off is permitted by BA s 53. Hence s 37 appears to be a codification of the general position for contracts of that type.

Netting legislation in Sweden

11–22A   In Sweden a provision in the Financial Instruments Trading Act (1991:980), which came into force on April 1, 1995, was brought in to clarify that agreements on close-out netting are binding in Sweden, although this was probably the position in any event.

Chapter 5 s 1 of the Act provides:

"If two parties have agreed an agreement, when dealing in financial instruments, similar rights or obligations or currencies, that obligations arising between them shall be settled net and if such agreement means that all outstanding obligations shall be settled in the event of one of the parties becoming bankrupt, then that agreement is binding on the estate of the party in bankruptcy and on the creditors in the bankruptcy.

If an agreement according to the first paragraph stipulates that all outstanding obligations shall be settled net in the event of a resolution about a proceeding of judicial composition concerning one of the parties, then that agreement is binding on the creditors whose claims would be included in the judicial composition." [unofficial translation]

The first paragraph clarifies that a close-out agreement is binding on the estate of the party in bankruptcy and on the creditors. The second paragraph clarifies that a close-out agreement is binding on the creditors in the event of judicial composition proceedings (*offentligt ackord*).

The Act applies applies to bilateral agreements on netting if the agreement provides that all outstanding obligations (matured or non-matured) shall be settled in the event of one of the parties becoming bankrupt. The Act can also apply to clearing houses, such as OM Stockholm, if the clearing house is a party to each contract. Neither of the parties to the agreement is required to have special status or to be a financial institution.

The Act applies to agreements on netting of trades in financial instruments, similar rights or obligations or currencies and covers both delivery and payment. The purpose of the reference to "similar rights or obligations" is to clarify that the Act include obligations arising from dealings in OTC-instruments.

The trustee in a bankruptcy will consequently be prevented from cherry-picking. The Act permits close-out netting between obligations arising from different kinds of instruments (cross-netting). The Act also overrides previous doubts as to whether Swedish law allowed a set-off between claims in different currencies: under the section, this is no bar to netting under a close out agreement.

Netting legislation in Switzerland

It is understood that Swiss legislation on the subject has recently been proposed although it is thought that netting contracts are in principle effective on a Swiss insolvency. **11–23**

Netting legislation in the United States

11–24 **US insolvency law** The US Bankruptcy Code of 1978 (the "Code") governs the bankruptcy of most US companies other than US federally-chartered and State-chartered commercial banks and savings and loan associations insured by the Federal Deposit Insurance Corporation (FDIC) ("FDIC-insured Institutions"), uninsured US State-chartered commercial banks and savings and loan associations ("Uninsured Institutions") and US insurance companies. Thus the Code, in addition to covering US industrial and commercial trading companies, covers many financial institutions which are neither FDIC-insured Institutions, Uninsured Institutions nor insurance companies, including:

– US bank holding companies

– non-bank affiliates of US bank holding companies

– US investment banks

– US brokers and dealers

– US "futures commission merchants" (companies authorised to deal in exchange-traded futures contracts)

Any US company which would be subject to the Code in the event of its insolvency is referred to here as a "Code Debtor".

FDIC-insured Institutions are subject to separate insolvency rules which, depending on the circumstances, may be either the FDIC receivership or the FDIC conservatorship provisions.

The insolvency of an Uninsured Institution is largely governed by the laws of the State where it is organised. The insolvency of a US insurance company is not governed by a unified code but by a miscellany of various US federal and state laws.

This outline does not deal with the effect of US bankruptcy law on branches, agencies or other offices in the US of non-US counterparties. US bankrupcty law may affect these operations.

11–25 **Bankruptcy freezes** Section 365(e) of the Code provides that, notwithstanding any provision of an executory contract or of otherwise applicable law to the contrary, an executory contract of a Code Debtor may not be terminated or modified at any time after the commencement of formal proceedings under the Code solely because of a provision in the contract that is conditioned on the insolvency or financial condition of the Code Debtor, the commencement of a Case under the Code or the appointment of or taking possession by a trustee (which term includes the Code Debtor itself when the original management continues to manage the Code Debtor as "debtor in possesion") in a case under the Code or of a custodian before the commencement of a case under the Code.

In other words, provisions in a contract whereby the contract can be terminated by the solvent counterparty on the insolvency of the Code Debtor are void and the trustee can "cherry-pick", that is, affirm contracts favourable to the insolvent and reject contracts unfavourable to the insolvent.

This provision is a direct statutory nullification of early termination clauses and a direct statutory sanction of cherry-picking.

There is also an automatic stay under s 362 of the Code which effectively prevents the solvent counterparty setting off (and therefore netting) claims owed by and to the Code Debtor. Section 362 reinforces s 365(e) by prohibiting the solvent counterparty from declaring the Code Debtor in default.

Prior to the legislative changes described below, market participants attempted to avoid the foregoing restrictions and prohibitions by including in their documentation (the 1987 ISDA Agreement being a classic example):

— a very wide bankruptcy event of default designed to permit termination at the earliest possible sign of danger, hopefully well before the commencement of a case under the Code;

— a provision *automatically* terminating the contract on the occurrence of any of the events covered by the bankrupcty event of default; and

— where the bankrupcty event of default is triggered by commencement of a case under the Code, *backdating* the automatic termination so that it is deemed to take effect immediately prior to the commencement of the Case.

Not surprisingly, there was considerable doubt among US bankruptcy lawyers as to whether this attempt to get round the mandatory provisions of the Code was effective. But netting was allowed for some contracts in the securities markets by virtue of ss 555 and 556 of the Code.

June 1990 Amendments to the Code In June 1990 the Code was amended　**11–26** to:

— permit an exemption for "swap agreements" from the automatic stay under s 362 of the Code so as to permit early termination of transactions and set-off of resulting claims (which is the essence of netting); and

— protect "swap agreements" from the effect of the trustee's power to cherry-pick.

"Swap agreement" is defined fairly broadly in the amending legislation and includes interest rate and currency swaps, forward rate agreements, commodity swaps, interest rate options, forward foreign exchange, caps, collars and floors, currency options and "any similar agreement" (including any option on any of the foregoing).

Similar amendments to the Code (some enacted prior to June 1990) cover commodity contracts, forward contracts, securities contracts and repurchase agreements.

FDIC-insured Institutions As noted above, the insolvency of an FDIC-insured Institution is governed, according to the circumstances, by either the FDIC receivership or the FDIC conservatorship provisions. Prohibitions and limitations similar to those in ss 362 and 365(e) of the Code normally apply under the FDIC receivership and conservatorship provisions.

11–27 **FIRREA** In August 1989, Congress enacted the Financial Institutions Reform, Recovery and Enforcement Act of 1989 (FIRREA).
The effect of FIRREA is:

— in the case of an FDIC receivership, to validate the early termination and netting provisions of any "qualified financial contract"; and

— in the case of an FDIC conservatorship, to validate the early termination and netting provisions of any "qualified financial contract" *except* where the right to terminate is exercised solely on the basis of the appointment of an FDIC conservator.

"Qualified financial contracts" is defined to include:

— any securities contract

— commodity contract

— forward contract

— repurchase agreement

— swap agreement

— any similar agreement that the FDIC determines by regulation to be a qualified financial contract.

11–28 **The FDIC Improvement Act of 1991** In December 1991, Congress enacted the Federal Deposit Insurance Corporation Improvement Act of 1991 (FDICIA).
FDICIA affects not only FDIC-insured Institutions but also certain Code Debtors (such as US brokers and dealers) falling within the definition of "financial institution" referred to below.
The effect of FDICIA is:

— To validate any "netting contract" (that is, an agreement providing for close-out and netting) covering *any* contractual payment obligations (not necessarily only foreign exchange or derivatives transactions).

— *Provided* that the agreement:
  — is made between two "financial institutions";
  — is governed by US federal or State law; and
  — provides for *full two-way payments* on early termination – for two-way payments, see para 12–1 *et seq*. There is some controversy as to whether the Act requires this, but the better view seems to be that it does.

"Financial institutions" is defined to include:

— any US depository institution (whether or not it is FDIC-insured);

— US registered brokers and dealers and futures commission merchants;

— US branches of foreign banks (whether or not FDIC-insured);

— other institutions as determined by the Board of Governors of the US Federal Reserve System (the Federal Reserve Board) under delegated rule-making powers.

FDICIA includes provisions strengthening multilateral netting in clearing   **11–29**
systems satisfying requirements set out in the Act.

FDICIA also covers netting through clearing systems for "contract markets" (namely, the principal US futures and options exchanges) designated pursuant to the Commodity Exchange Act. The netting contract for a clearing system must be governed by US federal or State law.

In early 1994 the Federal Reserve Board used its rule-making powers under FDICIA to expand the definition of "financial institution" to include any entity, whether or not US-organised, which deals in or makes a market in one or more "financial contracts" (defined to include interest rate, currency, equity and commodity derivatives and spot and forward foreign exchange contracts) if the entity had outstanding on any day in the previous 15–month period "financial contracts" having a total of at least

— $1 billion in aggregate notional principal amount, or

— $100 million in aggregate gross mark-to-market value,

with counterparties other than affiliates of the dealer. Some aspects of the rule are not entirely clear, particularly with regard to the precise application of the above test. FDICIA clearly, however, provides much better netting protection where it applies than the netting provisions in the Bankruptcy Code or FIRREA.

Areas of special concern Set out below are some areas of special concern   **11–30**
relating to the US amendments.

1. With regard to US brokers and dealers, apparently some issues may

arise under the Securities Investor Protection Act of 1970 which may affect the netting benefits of the Code amendments.

2. As to FDICIA, netting agreements, in order to fall within FDICIA, must be in writing, must be governed by US federal or state law and apparently must provide for "full two-way payments".

3. Under the FDIC receivership provisions, the FDIC can choose not to liquidate a failed bank but instead enter into a "purchase and assumption" transaction whereby another FDIC-insured Institution purchases specified assets and assumes specified liabilities of the failed institution. The FDIC must in this case transfer all qualified financial contracts with a counterparty to the new institution. This is probably not a serious risk in practice because presumably the FDIC will only transfer assets and liabilities to a solvent institution and there can be no cherry-picking between those contracts which are transferred and those which are not. Because of the possibility that the FDIC might exercise this power, the close-out rights are effectively stayed upon the occurrence of the receivership until the FDIC has decided whether or not to exercise this transfer power. The FDIC has stated that it will as a matter of practice make a decision within one day of the receivership commencing.

4. Because, as noted above, FIRREA expressly excludes from the validation of bankruptcy-related early termination provisions an early termination based on the appointment of a conservator, there is a concern that there may be a cherry-picking risk if the relevant contracts are not closed out prior to the appointment of the conservator.

5. Note generally that netting problems (because of unamended bankruptcy freezes) continue to apply to insolvencies of US insurance companies and Uninsured Institutions, except where such entity qualifies as a "dealer" under FDICIA.

CHAPTER 12

NETTING:
OTHER ASPECTS

This chapter reviews other miscellaneous aspects of netting.

Two-way payments and walk-away clauses

If a bankrupt defaults on an executory contract, then he is liable to the   **12–1**
creditor for damages – normally the extra cost to the creditor of obtaining
the asset elsewhere in the market, compared to the contract price. If on the
other hand the contract is profitable to the defaulter, but the creditor cancels, then the creditor can himself sell the asset in the market at a profit.

If the creditor agrees to pay any profit to the defaulting insolvent, then the
default payments are two-way – the insolvent pays losses and receives
profits. If the creditor can keep profits, then he effectively walks away. In
such a case, all that is necessary for the effective netting of executory contracts is that the creditor can rescind; he does not also need to set off since
he does not need to pay profits to the defaulter.

Many organised markets operate on the basis of full two-way payments
and indeed the rules of the traditional London metals, commodities and
stock markets have so provided since the early years of this century, if not
before.

As a matter of law, full two-way payments are not necessary for the val-   **12–2**
idity of the netting of executory contracts under English law, even though
the effect of walk-away clauses is to deprive the insolvent estate of an asset
in the form of the profit on the contract. This is not a penalty under English
law, nor is it regarded as a void attempt to snatch away an asset of the insolvent which should be available to his creditors. Indeed, the cases on close-
outs in the commodities markets reveal a judicial antipathy to two-way
clauses whereby the insolvent is entitled to gains on his default – the clause
must be clear if the defaulter is to have a benefit.

This English policy in favour of the walk-away (keeping the profits) is so
strong that in one case the court suggested that the interpretation of a clause
which requires gains to be paid to a defaulting party under a two-way clause

is contrary to "natural justice": *Cassir, Moore & Co Ltd v Eastcheap Dried Food Co* [1962] 1 Lloyds Rep 400, 402. See also *Adair & Co v Birnbaun* [1938] 4 All ER 775, where Mackinnon LJ expressed strong doubts about the validity of a clause allowing a seller to profit from his default. There are many other cases, mainly relating to the commodity exchanges.

But the cancellation of a vested asset of the insolvent (such as a deposit or (probably) a claim under a contract for differences), as opposed to the profit under an executory contract, would offend insolvency law. This is not a flaw, because these claims are eligible for set-off and cancellation is not required.

12–3 The position in other jurisdictions varies. Under certain of the statutory regimes mentioned above, full two-way payments are compulsory in the case of the contracts to which the legislation applies. In jurisdictions which do not adopt the English views of two-way payment, it may be prudent to provide for full two-way payments in order to meet potential insolvency objections to asset-deprivation. If the bankrupt estate is credited with gains, there can be no penal forfeiture.

But the availability of walk away could be crucial in those countries which forbid insolvency set-off. If the contract is an executory contract and if the rescission is permitted, pursuant to an express clause, of all contracts with the insolvent, even if they are profitable to the insolvent, then the exposure of the solvent party is effectively netted out since the solvent party can cover losses payable by the insolvent party by the profits which the solvent party realises on a sale of the defaulted asset in the case of the profitable contract. While a large number of states are hesistant to grant insolvency set-off, many of these do not object to the cancellation of contracts with the defaulter in which event the absence of insolvency set-off is not fatal – but only in the case of executory contracts. This point is discussed in more detail at para 10–13.

12–4 Unhappily, the BIS central banks and a draft EC Directive relating to capital adequacy require full two-way payments if the netting is to be recognised for bank capital adequacy purposes. The supervisory regime does not follow the law, presumably because of a desire to protect insolvent institutions. This may be an example of a political compromise between pro-creditor and pro-debtor states.

Interveners

12–5 The safety of the netting of losses and gains on open contracts would be threatened if an intervener, who takes over the benefit of the counterparty's contract, could claim the contract free of netting against other contracts.

The main interveners are attaching creditors (whether prejudgement or post-judgment), assignees and chargees of the counterparty, and undisclosed principals of the counterparty. An example is where a judgment creditor of the counterparty attaches claims owing to the counterparty, or some of them. The question is whether the innocent party may cancel contracts, the benefit of which the intervener has taken over, and set off losses on other contracts owing by the original counterparty so as to reduce the claim taken over by the intervener.

For a general review of set-off against interveners, see para 8–5 et seq.

There seems invariably to be no objection to cancelling contracts taken over by an intervener, but there should be an appropriate event of default. Hence the only question is whether the innocent party can set off against the intervener.

These interveners do not present a problem in England in a properly **12–6** drafted netting agreement because the general position is that the intervener will take subject to the close-out and set-off if, before the innocent party has notice of the intervener, (a) the contract to set off has been entered into and (b) both of the contracts giving rise to the reciprocal claims have been entered into. In other words, a subsequent intervener cannot upset a contractual set-off which would have been exercisable if he had not intervened. The unnotified intervener loses priority to a close-out which has already been contractually set up, even though the close-out is exercised after the intervention. See, e.g. *Hutt v Shaw* (1887) 3 TLR 354, CA.

The position appears to be similar in Germany (BGB Art 392), New York (s 151 of the New York Debtor-Creditor Law) and Illinois (s 12–708 of the Code of Civil Procedure). In Japan case law appears to have adopted this solution: see the Japanese Supreme Court decision of December 23, 1964.

In a number of jurisdictions, however, the set-off must be exercisable **12–7** prior to notice of the intervener, i.e. the cancellation of contracts so as to mature the claims must take place before that time. This is often impracticable, e.g. the innocent party cannot be sure of being able to rescind prior to receiving notice of an attaching creditor. This adverse rule prevails in France and related jurisdictions (based on the French CC Art 1298) and possibly in Denmark. In Italy, consider CC Art 2906, para 1 and Art 2917; Supreme Court n 2466 of 1970. In the Netherlands, set-off against the attaching creditor seems to be disallowed (see s 127(2) Book 6, New CC) but ought to be permitted in the case of a pre-existing contract to set-off: see HR January 20, 1984, NJ 1984, 512. The basis of the rule that attaching creditors take free of set-offs seems to be that set-off is not opposable to creditors, including attaching creditors.

As regards assignees and chargees, it is believed that most developed jur-

isdictions will give effect to a contractual clause which prohibits assignments, whether by way of sale or by way of security. This is the position in
England: *Linden Gardens Trust Ltd v Lenesta Sludge Ltd* [1993] 3 All ER
417, HL. One exception is the United States but only in relation to certain
claims: Uniform Commercial Code s 9–318(4).

12–8   In practice, the main question concerns the attaching creditor because
normally a contractual prohibition on assignments is ineffective against a
court order of execution. But there is increasing acceptance of the proposition that a contract to set-off is effective even against an attaching creditor.

For various reasons, the attaching creditor has often not been viewed as a
major risk. The attachment of market contracts by judgment creditors is
extremely rare. But one cannot rely only on the practical remoteness of the
occurrence. The legal protections stem from two sources. First, the law in
certain of the adverse countries mentioned above protects transactionally
related claims – "connexity" – on the grounds that the attaching creditor
should not be able to take the benefit of part of a transaction without being
subject to the burden. Secondly, there is a much greater recognition that a
contract to set off should be binding as against the attaching creditor who
appears on the scene at a later date, even though as against the bankruptcy
trustee, such a contract is ineffective. Further, if the master agreement does
not provide for full two-way payments and the innocent party is allowed to
rescind contracts and keep the profit, then an attaching creditor would be
left with nothing to attach. For an explanation of this, see the discussion at
para 10–13.

12–9   If a problem remains, the first question is whether a court would have jurisdiction to attach an amount (or a collateral deposit) owing by the counterparty to the other party subject to the attachment. Some jurisdictions apply
the situs rule to competence over attachment of foreign claims and will
permit attachment only if the debt is located within the forum state. If the
claims owing by the counterparty are governed by a foreign system of law
and are payable by a foreign debtor, then the local court may have no jurisdiction to attach. But unhappily the rules are often unpredictable, e.g. where
the claim is physically payable within the jurisdiction of the other party, or
where the claim is denominated in the other party's home currency.

One possibility is to subject the claim to a foreign system of law in a
favourable country and to provide for exclusive jurisdiction in that country,
e.g. England. For example, the choice of law should be recognised under Art
3(1) of the 1980 Rome Convention on the Law Applicable to Contractual
Obligations and the exclusive jurisdiction clause under Art 17 of the Brus-
sels and Lugano Judgments Conventions in the case of contracting states
(most of western Europe). Outside the conventions, the international tend-

ency is to give effect to express choices of law and derogations from jurisdiction, at least if there is some connection with the chosen law and forum.

If the court in the unfavourable country claims jurisdiction to attach the claim, the court ought to apply the governing law of the attached claim to the question of set-off against that claim: see, by analogy, Art 12 of the Rome Convention of 1980.

If the court applies its own law (lex fori) to this question, then the position may be saved by the fact that the attaching creditor would normally be obliged to recover the attached claim from the counterparty in which event he ought to be bound by the exclusive jurisdiction clause obliging him to recover in the favourable jurisdiction. In principle, the attaching creditor ought not to be able to take free of a clause, which is otherwise effective, and which is one of the terms of the attached claim. He would then be forced into the favourable jurisdiction with the favourable set-off rule.

Mutuality

The law obviously cannot permit a counterparty faced with a liability to use **12–10**
somebody else's debt to set off against that liability: the counterparty would be expropriating a third party's property to pay the counterparty's debt.

Hence, the doctrine of mutuality. For insolvency set-off to operate, it is everywhere the rule that the reciprocal claims must be mutual. This means that there must be only two debtor-creditors: each must be personally liable on the claim he owes to the other and each must be solely and beneficially entitled to the claim he is owed by the other, i.e. each is liable on one, owner of the other. A typical example of non-mutual debts are claims owed by and to parent and subsidiary. Mutuality does not mean that the debts have to be connected or in the same currency or of the same type. See generally, para 8–1 *et seq.*

Agency

A common application of the mutuality rule arises where a party is acting as **12–11**
agent.

It appears universally true that netting is not possible in broker markets where counterparties act as agents on behalf of their clients, notably in securities markets if the obligations owed by a counterparty to the agent are held by that agent as fiduciary or for the benefit of his outside client and do not belong beneficially to himself. Any set-off against that claim would not be possible on insolvency because it results in the principal's claim being used to pay the agent's personal liability, contrary to the principle of mutuality.

It is immaterial that, as is commonly the case, market agents have personal liability to each other since mutuality requires, not only reciprocal personal liability, but also that each party owns the claims owed to it by the other beneficially for itself and not on behalf of outside clients.

Dealing with this risk might require institutional changes in traditional agency markets with consequent redistribution of risks. It would require the removal of agency in favour of principal relationships and hence (amongst other things) an increased exposure of outside lay clients to their brokers.

Netting contracts should prohibit the parties from contracting as agents and require each party to hold its claims for its own account. These clauses are generally considered effective in the case of agency under English law: *UK Steamship Association v Nevill* (1887) 19 QBD 110 (undisclosed principal).

Multilateral netting

12–12　Under a system of multilateral netting, market participants agree that, not only will bilateral claims between mutual counterparties be netted out, but also that all claims owed between one party and all other counterparties are to be netted so that each party owes or is owed only a single balance to or by the rest of the market. The commonest application of multilateral netting is to payment systems, but these schemes exist in other contexts, e.g. airline netting and electricity pool netting.

From the legal point of view, if the netting does not take place prior to an insolvency petition against a relevant participant, the netting is vulnerable because the multilateral netting inevitably involves a set-off of non-mutual claims. A non-mutual set-off always leads to the divestment of the asset of an insolvent contrary to insolvency law and the use of one person's money to pay another's debt. The English case of *British Eagle International Airlines Ltd v Air France* [1975] 2 All ER 390, HL is only one example of the nullification of an attempted multilateral set-off.

Techniques can be developed to mitigate this risk or avoid it altogether, e.g. by the use of cross-guarantees or a clearing-house acting as a principal on all market bargains.

12–13　If a clearing-house is used, all trades between market members are deemed to be trades with the clearing-house as principal. Thus if A agrees to sell to B, then this is treated as a sale by A to the clearing-house which in turn sells to B. The effect is that all trades which a defaulting member would otherwise have had with the other members – and which could not be netted on insolvency because of the lack of mutuality – become instead trades between the defaulter and the clearing-house which are mutual and hence eligible for netting. This mutualisation can result in a very substantial enhancement of netting.

There are various routine contractual techniques whereby trades between members can be converted into trades with the clearing-house, e.g. acceptance by conduct, agency or novation.

Since the clearing-house is principal on all transactions, it is usually essential for the members to provide it with credit support.

The insertion of a clearing-house as principal is now standard procedure in many organised futures markets and has been inaugurated for inter-bank foreign exchange.

Inter-group and inter-branch netting

Inter-group netting is the netting of contracts entered into by the creditor   12–14
with one company in the counterparty's group against contracts entered into with another company in the same group, e.g. parent and subsidiary.

This type of netting is universally ineffective on the insolvency of one of the companies, because the claims are not mutual. See para 12–10. But the necessary mutuality can be created by each company guaranteeing the other. These guarantees must of course be valid, e.g. by satisfying any "corporate benefit" requirement. The guarantee should also withstand the universal rule that gifts or transactions at an undervalue by an insolvent party in the suspect period are voidable on insolvency proceedings.

Inter-branch netting is the netting of contracts entered into by the creditor with different branches of the counterparty where the branches are not separate legal entities. There is no mutuality objection to this type of netting since the contracts are all with the same legal entity. But see below as to the position where the branches are in different jurisdictions.

Global inter-branch netting

Global inter-branch netting is the netting of contracts with different   12–15
branches of the same counterparty in different countries, e.g. the netting of contracts with the head office of the counterparty in Ruritania as against contracts with a branch of the counterparty in Kinglandia.

If the branch is a separate subsidiary, then the netting is not possible because of lack of mutuality. A guarantee may resolve this problem.

In other cases, prudence requires that the laws of both countries should allow netting. One reason is that the insolvency laws of many countries require creditors to return to the insolvent estate any excess recoveries they obtained abroad which they would not have obtained in the local insolvency, so that the creditor who nets against the foreign branch validly in accordance with foreign insolvency laws, but in defiance of head office law, may be exposed to a recovery action in the jurisdiction of the head office. Another is that the rules governing international conflicts of law in insolvency matters are shifting and, in many jurisdictions, unresolved.

12–16   Even if both jurisdictions allow netting in the case of local transactions, it is necessary to establish that one of the jurisdictions does not override its normal validation of netting by insisting that local assets should be preserved for local creditors, notably the tax authorities and local employees. This might be relevant if, say, the contracts with the local branch produced a gain in favour of the branch, but the contracts with the foreign head office produced a loss payable to the creditor. If the creditor sought to set off the loss against the gain, the creditors of the local branch would be deprived of the gain.

Nationalistic policies favouring local creditors to the detriment of foreign creditors appear here and there (e.g. in Latin American countries), notwithstanding that they lead to discrimination against foreign creditors. The foreign creditor is discriminated against because he is deprived of a protection he would have had if he were a local creditor.

It will generally be found that a country which overrides its normal netting in this case has a strong protectionist policy and a weak set-off policy.

12–17   English insolvency law seeks to treat all creditors equally, whether English or foreign, and the case law involving global set-off supports a non-discriminatory approach. Netting is a strong English policy and insolvency discrimination against foreigners is consistently disapproved of in judicial pronouncements. See, e.g. the international set-off case of *Re Hett, Maylor & Co Ltd* (1894) 10 TLR 412.

See para 9–9 *et seq* for more details.

Cross-product netting

12–18   Cross-product netting is the netting of different types of contract, e.g. interest swaps and foreign exchange contracts.

Under English insolvency law, there is no objection to cross-product netting: the contracts do not have to be of the same type. This seems to be generally true in those countries which are sympathetic to netting.

Cross-product netting may be more problematic in jurisdictions which are hostile to netting, but which allow it in the case of connexity. This is because connexity may be more difficult to establish if the contracts are of a different order.

In the case of countries like the United States, Canada and France where netting is limited to specific transactions, the contracts must come within the applicable legislation.

Cross-currency netting

In some jurisdictions – which otherwise permit insolvency set-off – it needs **12–19** to be considered whether set-off is permitted if the obligations are payable in different currencies. Many commercial countries compulsorily convert claims owing by the insolvent into local currency, so that the claim owing to the insolvent may be in a different (foreign) currency.

English insolvency law permits cross-currency set-off: both claims must be converted into sterling at the date of the winding-up order. It is thought that this is also the case in the Netherlands: see BA Art 133 (bankruptcy) and Art 260 (suspension of payments). There appears to be a measure of international consensus on this point in legal doctrine in a number of jurisdictions which favour insolvency set-off. A contract which converts claims into the local currency on insolvency so as to establish equivalence could be considered.

For more details, see paras 6–20 and 6–33.

Special counterparties

Netting is primarily, but not exclusively, governed by insolvency law. In **12–20** many countries, the insolvency regime may differ according to the character of the debtor. In particular, there may be special rules for banks, insurance companies, statutory public companies, savings institutions, co-operatives and municipalities. These rules may override normal creditor protections in the interests of rehabilitating the debtor.

There is no special regime in England for bank insolvencies which is relevant in this context. The position with regard to other special institutions, like insurance companies, is detailed.

The availability of netting against non-corporate trusts, such as unit trusts, is also a specialist subject, largely because set-off is replaced by the more refined concept of retainer: para 7–30 *et seq.*

Netting against sovereign states is a matter for ordinary contract law since states are not subject to forced bankruptcy laws. In the senior jurisdictions, a state may usually waive sovereign immunity and, in any event, immunity should not normally be a bar to netting. This is because netting does not involve judicial action or judicial enforcement against a sovereign but is self-help. This, at least, is the position under English law: para 7–40.

Margin

12–21   Transactions in organised markets are usually subject to a margin requirement whereby traders must provide the counterparty (or the clearing-house)
with security to cover exposures. The security may take the form of initial
margin plus variation margin: variation margin must be provided if there
are fluctuations in market rates which increase the exposure.

Margin may be by way of cash deposit, securities or letters of credit. The
international legal regime governing security is studied in another work in
this series. Repos have been developed in an attempt to circumvent some of
the inconveniences of security law: para 1–5.

Build-up of set-offs in suspect period

12–22   In most jurisdictions which permit insolvency set-off, there is an additional
rule preventing build-ups of set-offs in the twilight period. For example, a
debtor owing 100 to the prospective bankrupt buys a claim of 100 owed by
the bankrupt to the creditor. The debtor then has a set-off. The creditor is
content to sell at a discount since otherwise he could expect only a tiny dividend on his claim.

Usually, the set-off statute prohibits a set-off resulting from this transaction after the parties become aware of the bankrupt's financial difficulties,
sometimes with a maximum suspect period, e.g. six months. The English
suspect period in IR 1986, r 4.90(3) is very short – notice of petition or of a
notice summoning a creditor's meeting. See, e.g. the US Bankruptcy Code of
1978 s 553, as amended (90 days improvement test); Austria BA s 20 (six
months); Germany BA s 55; Italy BA Art 56 (12 months); the Netherlands
BA s 54; Japan BC Art 104; Norway BA 1984 s 8–2 (three months).

Occasionally, the principle applies not only to acquired debts, but also to
new debts contracted with the bankrupt. This is not considered a significant
commercial risk because it appears to be usually – if not always – the case
that the third party must be aware of the counterparty's actual insolvency or
of steps to commence proceedings.

For more details, see para 6–38 *et seq.*

Post-insolvency transactions

12–23   Contracts entered into after insolvency petition may be vulnerable. Insolvency laws generally restrict or completely nullify certain contracts entered
into by the insolvent after commencement. The business by the insolvent is
frozen and only the insolvency administrator can undertake transactions. In

practice, the problems arise with greater force in relation to payments or deliveries by the bankrupt after the commencement of proceedings.

There may be a time gap between the institution of insolvency proceedings and the creditor becoming aware of those proceedings. This is because the publication of petitions for insolvency and the like – by registration at an official registry, by notice in a court or gazetting in an official journal – must inevitably follow the event.

In view of these factors, some jurisdictions protect the "involuntary gap **12–24** creditor" who transacts with the insolvent in good faith without notice of the institution of the proceedings, e.g. the US Bankruptcy Code of 1978. English case law suggests that creditors acting in good faith without notice will be protected but the present guidelines are insufficient to assert this.

Some insolvency jurisdictions backdate the opening of insolvency proceedings to zero hour on the day of the court order opening the insolvency. Any payments made on that day by the insolvent before the bankruptcy order, but after zero, may be recoverable by the estate, but without a reciprocal right of the counterparty to recover in full payments made to the estate. English compulsory liquidations commence at the time when the petition is presented and the zero rule does not apply.

In any event, the potential guillotine effect of the opening of proceedings is part of settlement risk. Ultimately the guillotine must come down. This emphasises the importance of settlement netting so that the only amounts at risk are the net amounts.

Preferences

Generally All developed insolvency laws have provisions whereby a prefer- **12–25** ence by the insolvent of one creditor within a suspect period can be set aside. Preferences are one aspect of the fundamental policy of pari passu distribution and give effect to the policy that the equal payment of creditors should come before charity. These preferences are variously called fraudulent transfers, transactions inopposable to the insolvent estate, reversible transactions or transactions capable of nullification or avoidance on insolvency. The traditional example is the Paulian action. The comparative law is discussed in another work in this series on international finance.

Transactions affected The transactions which fall for consideration are as **12–26** follows:

(a) **Settlement netting** See para 10–7 above.

(b) **Compensating contracts** The question here is whether the entry into of a compensating contract by a counterparty is preferential if this has the effect of reducing the exposure of the bankrupt to the counterparty. In the case of foreign exchange contracts, it is considered that the mere entry into of a contract will not reduce exposures on existing contracts on a close-out, provided that the contract is at market value. This is because a market value contract shows neither a gain nor a loss when it is entered into – its effect on a subsequent close-out is neutral. The contract will only have an effect if there are subsequent fluctuations in rates of exchange which produce a loss or gain. Hence the question of whether a party is preferred may depend upon whether a counterparty's expectations as to future fluctuations in currency values, which turn out to be justified, can convert a trade which is initially non-preferential into a preferential trade. Any such rule would seem unreasonable.

The preference rules are more relevant where the debtor owes the creditor an unpaid debt and the creditor then buys an asset from the bankrupt and sets off the price against the unpaid debt. In effect the unpaid debt is paid by the asset. Some countries based on Napoleonic bankruptcy law regard this as a voidable payment because it is made by abnormal means.

But in many English-influenced states, even if this were preferential, the transaction is usually saved by the "intent" rule – the debtor must intend to prefer. Usually in markets the debtor merely intends to do a deal. For an example, see the Australian case of *Donaldson v Couche* (1867) 4 WW & AB (L) 41 (Victoria).

12–27 (c) **Payments to the counterparty** The question here is whether a payment or delivery by the bankrupt on existing contracts on a value date in the suspect period could be a preference. Usually these will be exempted by an exemption for payments in the ordinary course of business or matured payments pursuant to an existing contractual obligation. This is an ordinary business risk which applies to all payments to banks and is not a risk which jeopardises netting. The same applies to payments of net amounts pursuant to pre-insolvency voluntary or involuntary close-outs. Only the net amount is at risk.

Liquidated damages clauses

12–28 Some netting contracts set out a method of calculating losses and gains on a close-out. In England, liquidated damages clauses which are a genuine pre-estimate of losses likely to be suffered on a breach are not a penalty: the rule is liberal and these clauses are not struck down unless clearly excessive. There appears to be general agreement on this issue amongst developed legal systems.

Currency conversion An ancillary point is whether it is acceptable to use a reference currency for losses and gains such as US dollars.

As a matter of contract law, it would seem that generally the calculation of losses either way can be made in the currency in which the loss is felt or which the parties reasonably determine in advance.

As to insolvency law, there might be a mismatch if the jurisdiction requires that losses payable by the insolvent be converted into local currency at a different rate or on a different date than that applying under the contract, e.g. an official market rate when the insolvency is judicially declared. Conversion of foreign currency debts into local currency appears universal in developed jurisdictions, e.g. in Austria, Denmark, England, Germany, Italy and the United States. This is not considered to be a major issue. See generally, para 6–20.

Discounting Many insolvency laws require that certain debts payable by the insolvent and maturing after the insolvency must, for the purposes of the creditor's claim against the bankrupt estate, be discounted back at a prescribed rate of interest from the date the claim would otherwise have matured, e.g. Denmark, Germany, Italy, Japan, the Netherlands, Scandinavia and Switzerland. The aim is to reflect the acceleration of the debt caused by the insolvency. This prescribed rate may be different from the discount rate used in a liquidated damages clause in the contract. However the discounting rule should not apply because the claims are not debts which are accelerated on insolvency, but damages which are payable immediately under cancelled executory contracts: see para 10–11.

Gaming laws

Gaming laws in some countries might call into question contracts for differences. But gaming legislation is on the defensive. Some countries have specific legislation exempting certain contracts from the gaming legislation, e.g. Britain (1986), Belgium (1934, 1939), France (1985, 1994), Germany (1989) and the Netherlands (1986).

Exchange controls and blocking orders

A party's obligations may be frozen by a local exchange control or blocking order. Under standard forms of contract a termination event will be deemed to have occurred, even after the specified grace period. Parties are relieved from their obligations during the period of any force majeure.

Without this provision, the general position under English law would be that a foreign exchange control or foreign blocking order would not be deemed to affect a contract governed by English law, but this is subject to Art VIII 2b of the Bretton Woods Agreement which requires recognition by the court and IMF member states of exchange controls conforming with IMF Regulations and applying to "exchange contracts". Although decisions in England and elsewhere – but not all countries – have restricted the meaning of "exchange contracts" it is likely that foreign exchange contracts will fall within this definition everywhere. In that event, if the contracts did not deal with the issue, a foreign exchange control imposed by an IMF state might have to be recognised by municipal courts. The comparative law on Art VIII 2b is reviewed elsewhere in this series of works.

The position as regards foreign freezing orders is complex but the English courts lean against recognising them unless the contract must be performed within the territory of the legislating state and it is illegal for the contract to be performed there. This topic too, is reviewed elsewhere in this series on international financial law.

These are usual banking risks which apply as much to ordinary banking transactions as netting contracts.

CHAPTER 13

NETTING:
INTERNATIONAL SUMMARY

Summary of policies

It is difficult for financial institutions to carry on a global business where   **13–1**
legal rules are a mosaic or a patchwork of national colours. Traders cannot
be expected to be lawyers as well.

Any international regime, in the ideal, would be consistent, harmonious,
natural and simple. It would not require constant reference to lawyers. It
would not require legal device or artifice in netting contracts. But of course
the ideal is difficult to achieve internationally.

The insolvency laws of a jurisdiction will naturally reflect wider policies,
of which the availability of netting is only one. But for states which are
persuaded of the merits of netting, or which wish to ensure that their institutions are not disadvantaged, there seem to be at least two possible legal
approaches.

Under the first approach, netting law would be the same for all contracts   **13–2**
and for everybody, big bank or small trader, corporation or individual. The
advantages of this approach are that it is non-discriminatory, can meet market changes without the need for amendment, and is simple to understand.
This is the English approach and (it is believed) the approach adopted in
such countries as Germany, the Netherlands, Japan, Switzerland and
Sweden. On occasion, the law might have to be changed by legislation in
specific and narrow areas to iron out inconsistencies, e.g. to neutralise the
impact on netting of a rehabilitative or composition law, to correct an ambiguity, or to bring special counterparties within the netting law.

Under the second approach, netting is treated as a privilege conferred
only on certain institutions and certain types of contract, but not available
to the citizen at large. This is the approach adopted in Belgium, Canada,
France and the United States. The advantage is that the state can continue to
adhere to its general insolvency attitudes. Possible disadvantages are that
the law is often complicated, particularly if the legislator is endeavouring to
limit the scope of the privilege, that the rules might be over-rigid and ill-
equipped to absorb rapid market developments, that the world still has the

mosaic problem, that statutory particularity sometimes leads to ambiguity and that the scope of the relaxation is too narrow.

International summary

13–3 While it is unsafe for an English lawyer to trespass on the legal domains of others, it is believed that the present international situation may be summed up tentatively as follows:

(a) It is believed that the following jurisdictions (amongst others) allow default netting as against banks and corporates generally without discrimination on final bankruptcy:

> Australia
> Austria
> Cayman Islands
> Denmark
> England
> Germany
> Hong Kong
> Italy*
> Japan
> Netherlands
> Scotland
> Singapore
> Sweden
> Switzerland

> *Italian rescue proceedings may affect netting.

13–4 (b) The following countries might not permit default netting on bankruptcy (except in the case of connexity) but have specific statutory exceptions for special cases:

> Belgium
> Canada
> France
> United States

The exception in (e) below might apply to Belgium for situations not covered by the Belgian netting statute.

13–5 (c) The following countries (amongst others) might not permit default netting on bankruptcy except in the case of connexity:

> Greece (no insolvency set-off)

Luxembourg (no insolvency set-off)
Portugal (no insolvency set-off)
Spain (no insolvency set-off)

The exception in (e) below might apply in some or all of these countries.

(d) For the rest of the world, there are four main groups: **13–6**

1. About 70 jurisdictions likely to adopt traditional English attitudes
    which favour netting, e.g. India, Malaysia, numerous island states
    and many countries in Africa. But South Africa has no insolvency
    set-off and New Zealand has a special insolvency law which des-
    troys the general netting predictability in that country which is
    otherwise available under the ordinary insolvency regime.
2. Nearly 70 jurisdictions based on Napoleonic bankruptcy law—
    mainly former Belgian, French, Portuguese and Spanish jurisdic-
    tions. This group tends to be inimical to netting because of a prohi-
    bition on insolvency set-off, e.g. in most of Latin America and in
    North African countries. But Panama has insolvency set-off.
3. A smaller number of jurisdictions based on Dutch, German, Aus-
    trian or Swiss bankruptcy law, e.g. Indonesia, Poland (unless
    recently altered), Czech and Slovak Republics and probably Thai-
    land. This group tends to favour netting.
4. A number of countries with no or very limited bankruptcy laws,
    e.g.:
    – Islamic countries, such as Kuwait, Qatar and Saudi Arabia, so
      that the position on netting is unclear.
    – former Soviet republics with new bankruptcy laws. Most of these
      laws are too skeletal to deal with set-off or netting, e.g. Russia,
      Ukraine and Kazakhstan.
    – China, although the Bankruptcy Act contemplates insolvency set-
      off.
    Again, the position in refusing countries as regards executory con-
    tracts may be saved by the exception in (e) below.

(e) In those countries which are listed as preventing default netting by   **13–7**
    reason of the fact that they do not have insolvency set-off, netting may
    be permitted if the contracts are executory contracts, e.g. foreign
    exchange contracts or interest swap agreements, and it is possible for a
    solvent counterparty, pursuant to an express clause, to terminate or
    rescind contracts on the insolvency of the counterparty, even if they are
    profitable to the counterparty. In such a case all that is necessary is the
    ability to rescind on the insolvency and it is not necessary that insol-
    vency set-off should also be permitted. See para 10–13.

CHAPTER 14

OUTLINES OF SET-OFF AND NETTING AGREEMENTS

14–1 This chapter contains an outline of a foreign exchange netting agreement, a full form of set-off clause and a note on group account pooling.

Outline of Foreign Exchange Master Netting Agreement

1. **Single agreements** All foreign exchange contracts between the parties are governed by this master agreement. All contracts are to be treated as a single indivisible agreement governed by this agreement.

2. **Confirmations** The parties will confirm contracts in writing (including electronic reproduction) immediately after they are entered into and not later than a specified cut-off time. Form and content of confirmations.

3. **Settlement netting** All reciprocal deliveries deliverable by one party to the other on the same value date and in the same currency will be netted as soon as the relevant contract is entered into. Only the balance will be deliverable by the relevant party on the value date. This netting will be effected between the matched pairs of branch offices specified in the schedule. This clause applies even if the parties do not record the netting in their books or confirmations.

4. **Termination events** The following events relating to either party: non-payment under a contract; non-performance of other obligations; insolvency events; repudiations; warranty untrue; merger without consent; cross-default; creditor attachments. Include guarantors and subsidiaries in appropriate events.

5. **Close-out** If a termination event occurs, the other party may cancel all existing contracts or suspend its delivery obligations.

6. **Net termination sums** If a party cancels under clause 5, that party will:

    (a) calculate the cost of acquiring each cancelled currency obligation at current market rates for delivery on the original value date (or, if past, the date of the close-out), in return for an agreed reference currency. Discount that cost back from future value dates to the close-out date at market interest rates (discounting procedures vary). Add interest at market rates to overdue deliveries. Set-off the resulting reciprocal sums. Only the net sum is payable either way;

(b) the performing party may change the reference currency to the currency of the non-performing party's insolvency jurisdiction;

(c) the parties agree that the calculation of the net termination sum is a reasonable pre-estimate of losses suffered and is not a penalty.

7. **Force majeure** If a party is prevented or hindered by force majeure, or it becomes illegal or impossible to deliver or receive a currency, then either party may require a close-out in accordance with clauses 5 and 6.

8. **General** Contractual set-off of debts; representations and warranties; telephone recordings as evidence; notices; payments by wire transfers in immediately available same day funds; default interest; enforcement costs; currency indemnity; parties act as principals (no agency); no assignments; waivers; remedies cumulative; severability; counterparts; time of essence; jurisdiction, governing law, waiver of sovereign immunity.

Main points on contracts to set off bank loan against customer deposit

This is a check-list of the main points on contracts to set off a bank loan   **14-2** against a customer deposit.

1. Insolvency set-off available in customer's jurisdiction?

2. Mutuality (two debtor-creditors, both personally liable and beneficially entitled). All jurisdictions require this.

3. Loan must mature before deposit.

4. Availability of set-off against interveners, e.g. attaching creditor, assignees? Insert contractual right of set-off. Prohibit assignments of deposit, undisclosed agency, by customer. Warranties as to sole unencumbered ownership by customer of deposit. In England, a contractual set-off is effective against an intervener if both claims were incurred before notice of the intervener.

5. Set-off available in customer's rehabilitation and composition proceedings? Ability to accelerate loan and set-off prior to any postponement of maturity of the loan by creditor voting? The risk can be covered by appropriate drafting in England: see para 6–43.

6. Set-off of different foreign currencies? Convert loan and deposit into common currency for solvent set-off. Convert currency of deposit into currency of customer's main jurisdiction for purposes of insolvency set-off so that currencies coincide. On insolvency, creditor claims are usually compulsorily converted into local currency of the place of the insolvency proceedings.

7. Original payment in of deposit not a preferential payment by customer?

8. If claim against customer is a claim for reimbursement of bank which has issued a letter of credit or guarantee for the customer, the letter of credit or guarantee should require the beneficiary to claim against the bank first before submitting a proof in the customer's insolvency: para 6–17.

Set-off clause

14–3   The following is a full form of set-off clause for a loan agreement.

"The bank may set off each matured obligation owing by the company to the bank against any obligation owing by the bank to the company (whether or not matured), even if the obligations are owing at different places. If the obligations are in different currencies, the bank may convert either at a market rate determined by the bank. If the amount of an obligation is unascertained, the bank may in good faith estimate its amount and set off in respect of the estimate, and the relevant party will account to the other for any shortfall when the amount is ascertained."

Group account pooling

14–4   Where it is desired to net credit and debit bank balances between companies in the same group, the necessary mutuality should be created by cross-guarantees given by each company in the group, coupled with a contractual right to set off the guarantee liability owed to the bank by a company in respect of another company's debit balance, against a credit balance owed by the bank to the first company.

For contracts to set-off, see para 7–23 *et seq.*

PART IV

SWAPS AND DERIVATIVES

CHAPTER 15

SWAPS AND DERIVATIVES: GENERAL PRINCIPLES

Introduction

Derivative products is a generic term used to describe futures, options, **15–1** swaps and various other similar transactions. Apart from interest swaps, most derivative contracts are contracts for differences – the difference between the agreed future price of an asset on a future date and the actual market price on that date.

The jargon is confusing (because it is non-legal and imprecise), the varieties of transaction are very numerous and the contracts themselves often complex in their detail. The tax, stamp duty and regulatory aspects are labyrinthine. But the transactions themselves are relatively simple in outline.

Futures contracts

Meaning of futures contracts

A futures contract is a contract under which one party agrees to deliver to **15–2** the other party on a specified future date (the "maturity date") a specified asset at a price (the "strike price") agreed at the time of the contract and payable on the maturity date. The term "forward contract" is often used in relation to private contracts not transacted through an organised exchange.

The asset may be a commodity or currency or a debt or equity security (or a number or basket of securities), or a deposit of money by way of loan, or any other category of property.

The effect is to guarantee or "hedge" the price. The hedging party protects himself against a loss but also loses the chance to make a profit.

Futures are usually performed ("settled") by the payment of the difference between the strike price and the market price on the fixed future date, and not by physical delivery and payment in full on that date. Hence they are called "derivatives" because settlement is not by actual full performance

---

of the sale or deposit contract but rather by a difference payment derived from an actual asset and an actual price. The contract is based on or related to or derived from an ordinary commercial contract.

A "spot" contract is one which is to be performed, generally, within two days, i.e. the shortest practicable time to arrange settlement.

Examples are given below.

Commodity futures

15–3   In March Joe sells grain to Bill for 100 for delivery in September. Joe does so to fix the price of his grain crop in advance. If in September the market value is 90, Joe makes a profit of 10 because he gets 100 from Bill when the market price is 90. If in September the market value is 110, Joe has made a loss of 10, because he could have sold his grain crop for 110, instead of 100. But at least Joe did not take the risk of a loss. Joe has sold a grain future, a commodity future. He has guaranteed his grain price, i.e. hedged it.

In a derivatives contract, the parties do not actually contract to deliver grain and pay for it, but only to pay or receive the difference between the contract price and the market price on the maturity date. The transaction is "cash-settled" without physical delivery and is not a contract for the sale of grain. Joe has still hedged his grain price, because he can sell his grain at the market price and receive from Bill any shortfall between the market price and the contract price. But, in return for the certainty of guaranteeing the price and hence not making a loss, Joe has foregone the potential profit.

Commodity futures may also relate to oil, gold, copper or aluminium or any other commodity.

Currency futures

15–4   In March Joe in Britain sells goods to a buyer in the United States in return for $100 for payment in September. Joe sells Bill the $100 for £50 sterling, for delivery in September when Joe expects to receive the $100 from his US buyer, so as to be sure that the $100 will be worth £50 and that he does not make a loss on the sale of goods due to currency fluctuations. If in September the $100 are worth £45, Joe has ensured that he does not suffer the loss of £5. But if it is worth £55 he has made a loss of £5. Joe has bought a sterling future, or sold a dollar future. He has guaranteed his price, i.e. hedged it.

In a derivatives contract, Joe and Bill do not actually contract to deliver the gross amounts of the two currencies, but only to pay or receive the net difference between the contract price and the market price. The transaction is a contract for differences ("cash-settled") and is not an exchange of gross currency amounts.

Interest futures

In March, Joe agrees to borrow 100 from Bill, the borrowing to be made in   **15–5**
September, for a year at an interest rate of 10 per cent p.a. Joe agrees to do so because he will need the loan in September and wishes to fix the interest rate in advance. In September the market interest rate is 12 per cent, so Joe avoids an extra expense of 2. If the rate in September had been 8 per cent, Joe would have saved 2 because he could have borrowed at 8 per cent in the market. Joe has guaranteed his maximum cost of borrowing, i.e. hedged it but at the expense of losing the benefit of downturns in interest rates. In the jargon, Joe has "sold" an interest rate future even though this is strictly a borrowing contract, not a sale contract. If he had agreed to lend, he would have "bought" an interest rate future. He might have wished to lend because he expected to receive 100 in September and wished to guarantee the interest rate.

In the derivatives market, this is a contract for differences, i.e. Joe does not actually borrow the 100, but only pays or receives the difference between the contract interest rate and the market interest rate in September calculated over the agreed period and on the agreed amount of the loan. Joe is still protected against rises in interest rates, but does not benefit if interest rates fall.

Stock index futures

In March Joe agrees to sell the stocks comprised in a stock market index for   **15–6**
100, delivery in September. The stock index is made up of a sample basket of shares listed on the exchange. Joe wishes to do so because he has a portfolio of stocks which are roughly the same as those used for the stock exchange index and thinks their value will go down. If in September, the index is 90, Joe has made a profit of 10. If the value is 110, Joe has lost 10 because he could have waited and sold for 110, instead of the agreed price of 100. Joe has sold a stock exchange index future. He has guaranteed the value of his portfolio, i.e. hedged it.

In a derivatives contract, Joe does not agree actually to sell the stocks, but only to pay or receive the difference in price. The transaction is "cash-settled" without physical delivery of the stocks against payment of the full price.

15–7   Stock index futures are used for hedging and portfolio management. Examples are:

- An investor wishes to invest 100 in shares. He could borrow 100 and buy the shares in which case he will incur interest on the borrowing and transaction costs on the shares. Instead he could buy a stock index future and avoid these costs.

- An investor with a portfolio of equities included in a stock exchange index of top shares (such as the London FT-SE 100 Index) might choose to buy a put option on the FT-SE 100 Index from a financial institution to protect himself against the value of his portfolio falling. When the value of his portfolio decreases, there is an increase in the value of his option. Unless the portfolio matches identically the shares constituting the FT-SE 100 Index, the hedge would be imperfect. Nevertheless the put, if of a sufficient size, offers a degree of protection.

- A fund manager holding for investors a particular mix of debt and equity investments may decide to increase the debt investments and decrease the equity investments in the portfolio, e.g. because he thinks that equities will decline in value. By selling stock index futures and buying long-term interest rate futures, the fund manager can replicate the performance of an altered portfolio without incurring the expense and disruption of selling any of the underlying investments.

Indexes based on the value of a basket of the shares of the largest companies on the leading stock exchange in the world are available, e.g. S&P 500 (equity shares of 500 US companies) the FT-SE 100 (100 UK companies), DAX (30 German companies), Nikkei 225 (225 Japanese companies) etc.

Options

15–8   A **call option** is the right (but not an obligation) to acquire an asset in the future at an price (the strike price) fixed when the option is entered into.

A **put option** is the right (but not the obligation) to sell an asset in the future at a price (the strike price) fixed when the option is entered into.

The person who is given the option is typically called the "buyer" of the option and the person who grants him the option is called the "writer" or "seller". These terms are non-legal vernacular. Thus the buyer of an option is the "buyer" whether or not he has the option to buy or sell under the contract.

An option is "in the money" (i.e. profitable) if, in the case of a put option, the strike price exceeds the market price. Thus if the strike or contract price of a currency option is £50 for $100, the option is in the money if the market price on the exercise date is £45. Conversely, if the strike price is less than the market price, the option is "out-of-the money" (i.e. loss-making). In such a case the option-holder will not exercise the option but let it lapse.

Options may be classified according to how they are exercised, i.e. the dates on which the option-holder can call for settlement and convert the option into a firm contract. A "European" option is exercisable only on a fixed future date by reference to prices on that date. An "American" option is exercisable on any day over the agreed fixed period.

> **Example** In March Joe agrees that he will have the option to sell grain for 100 (the strike price) for delivery and payment in September. For this he pays a premium of 5. If in September the market price is 90, Joe would exercise his option to sell, and would thus make a profit of 10, less the premium of 5. The option is in the money. If the market price is 110 in September, Joe would not exercise the option but let it lapse. He has lost his premium of 5 but could sell his grain for 110 and so make a net profit of 5.
>
> The same applies to options to sell currency, or borrow money (an interest option) or to sell stocks comprised in a stock exchange index.

Again, the exercise of the option does not in a derivatives contract result **15–9** in an actual obligation to sell or buy the asset against the full price, but rather results in a contract to pay the difference between the strike price and the market price on the exercise date.

The maximum loss that the buyer of an option can suffer is the loss of his premium. Unlike a futures contract, he is not committed to deliver but has merely the option to do so. Conversely, the seller of the option has an unlimited risk because the buyer can, by exercising his option, insist on performance. Hence speculators can expose themselves to risks far greater than a wager, where the money at risk is just the sum wagered.

Options are an inexpensive way of investing. For example, an investor who expects a rise in securities or commodities price can buy a call option for the assets for a premium which will usually be much less than the cost of financing the purchase of the assets themselves. In addition, if the investor bought the assets, he would be exposed to an unlimited drop in their value. In the case of an option, he loses only the premium.

The party which may have to deliver the asset under an option can hedge his risk either by buying the asset at the inception of the transaction (although often in the case of financial institutions he will already hold the asset, e.g. securities) or by entering into a reverse transaction with a third party.

Interest swaps and other interest contracts

Interest swaps

15–10   An interest swap is a contract whereby each party agrees to make periodic payments to the other equal to interest on agreed principal sums and where the interest is calculated on a different basis.

> **Example** Joe and Bill have each borrowed 100 from third party lenders. Joe's loan bears floating rate interest at LIBOR plus 1 per cent, and Bill's loan (which is a eurobond issue) bears fixed interest at 10 per cent. Under the interest swap contract, Bill pays Joe periodic amounts equal to the floating rate interest on 100. Joe pays Bill periodic amounts equal to the fixed rate interest on 100, plus an extra amount representing Bill's profit.

> The usual reason for transaction is that Bill is a bank of high credit-standing which can borrow at a fixed rate, e.g. by an issue of eurobonds, while Joe which is a little-known industrial company which cannot borrow cheaply (or at all) in the eurobond market.

> **Example** Joe can issue bonds at 12 per cent but Bill is a Triple-A bank which can issue them at 10 per cent. So Joe borrows a floating rate bank loan at LIBOR plus 2 per cent and Bill issues bonds at 10 per cent. Bill agrees to pay Joe amounts equal to floating interest so that Joe can pay his lender. Joe pays Bill amounts equal to the fixed rate so that Bill can pay the bondholders. But, for this privilege, Bill charges Joe 1 per cent so that Joe pays Bill 11 per cent. The effect is that Joe is paying a fixed rate of 11 per cent (instead of the 12 per cent Joe would have had to pay on a eurobond issue made by Joe), and Bill is paying floating rate interest of LIBOR (instead of LIBOR plus 1 per cent). The result is that the interest benefit is shared. Bill's position is protected so long as the floating rate payable by Bill does not exceed the fixed rate plus the 1 per cent profit and so long as Joe does not become insolvent.
>   Note that the payments are not actual interest, but amounts equal to interest calculated on the same notional principal amount. The lenders to Joe and Bill are not affected. Joe and Bill must pay the lenders actual interest on their respective loans, regardless of whether the other party makes its swap payments. Thus if Joe becomes insolvent, Bill must still pay his bondholders 10 per cent, even though Bill is no longer receiving swap payments from Joe.

Often a bank is interposed as an intermediary between the swapping par-   **15–11**
ties.

Example If Joe and Bill are both industrial borrowers, although Bill is
much larger and more well known company which can issue eurobonds,
then a bank may be interposed between the two parties. Joe pays floating
to the bank which pays floating to Bill. Bill pays fixed to the bank which
pays fixed to Joe. In this way, both Joe and Bill rely on the credit of the
bank, not each other, since the bank's obligations to pay are not
conditional on receiving. For this credit protection, the bank takes a turn
or spread, by paying less than it receives.

There are numerous variations of the simple interest swap. For example,
an investor may buy a fixed rate bond and swap the fixed rate for floating
rate from a bank. The bank may take security over the bond to secure the
investor's obligations to pay amounts equal to the fixed rate.

A party may be granted an option to enter into an interest swap – a
"swaption".

The same principle can be applied to commodities or any other asset.   **15–12**
Thus an oil producer, fearing a drop in oil prices, may agree to pay to a
dealer the floating market price of 100 barrels of oil periodically and the
dealer, in return, agrees to pay the oil producer an agreed fixed price for 100
barrels of oil. In this way, the producer guarantees the price of oil which it
receives. It simply pays the dealer the market price it receives for the oil on
sale to the agreed market and receives a fixed price from the dealer.

A bank may acquire fixed rate bonds and grant an investor a sub-participation in the bonds. The investor deposits an amount equal to the bonds
with the bank on terms that the bank will pay the investor amounts equal to
principal and interest when received by the bank from the issuer. However
the bank pays amounts equal to floating rate to the investor instead of the
fixed rate.

Interest caps, floors and collars

Interest cap Under an interest cap, one party agrees, in return for a fee, to   **15–13**
pay the other party amounts equal to interest above a specified rate on a
notional principal amount.

Example Joe issues floating rate notes of 100 and wishes to be sure that
the interest rate will not be more than 10 per cent. In return for a fee Bill
agrees to pay Joe amounts equal to interest on 100 in excess of 10 per cent

so that if the rate goes up to 11 per cent, Bill will pay Joe 1 per cent on 100 during the period of the excess.

15–14   **Interest floor** Under an interest floor, one party agrees, in return for a fee, to pay the other amounts equal to interest below a specified rate on a notional principal amount.

Example Joe invests in floating rate notes of 100 and wishes to be sure that the interest rate will not be less than 5 per cent. Bill agrees to pay Joe amounts equal to interest on 100 to the extent it is below 5 per cent during the period it is below 5 per cent.

15–15   **Interest collar** Under an interest collar, one party agrees, in return for a fee, to pay the other amounts equal to interest above a specified rate on a notional principal amount over an agreed period, and the other pays the first party amounts equal to interest below a specified rate.

Example Bill pays Joe if rates go over 10 per cent, but Joe pays Bill if rates are less than 5 per cent.

15–16   **Caps and floors in other markets** The same principle can be applied to other assets, e.g. commodities, such as grain or oil or securities. The dealer agrees to pay the investor according to whether the market value goes above the agreed cap price or below the agreed floor price.

Currency interest rate swaps

15–17   An interest rate swap may be combined with a currency swap.

Example Joe in the United Kingdom has issued debentures of £100 at a fixed rate. Bill in the United States has borrowed a bank loan of $150 at a floating rate. Both loans mature in five years. The loans are made simultaneously and immediately. Joe sells his £100 to Bill at the current market rate and receives $150. They agree to reverse the transaction at the end of five years at the same exchange rate, regardless of the market rate. Joe pays periodic amounts equal to floating rate on the dollar sum of $150 to Bill. Bill pays Joe periodic amounts equal to the fixed rate on the sterling sum of £100. The commercial effect is that Joe in the UK has converted his sterling fixed rate borrowing into a floating rate dollar loan. Joe wanted the dollar loan without having to enter the US market which might be expensive. Bill similarly has a sterling fixed rate loan without having to enter the UK domestic sterling market. Both parties remain liable to pay their lenders the original currency and interest, regardless of whether their counterparty pays the swap payments.

Derivatives markets

Exchanges, OTC and primary markets

Broadly there are three principal markets for derivative products: **15–18**

— organised securities and commodities exchanges, including the specialised futures and options markets;

— the "over-the counter" ("OTC") markets, namely, private transactions;

— the new issues markets for primary offerings of debt securities, as, for example, commodity – or equity-linked bonds, notes or warrants. Primary offerings of commodity and equity-linked bonds, notes and warrants are normally hedged with OTC or exchange-traded instruments.

Primary offerings

These are issues of debt securities, often listed, in the bond market which   **15–19** carry a derivative feature. Examples of such instruments are:

— Index-linked bonds, where the interest or redemption amount is calculated by reference to the movements in a specified index, e.g. a stock index or a commodity index.

— Warrants attached to bonds or issued on their own and which are linked to an index, a single security or a basket of securities or to a commodity index. These provide for cash settlement (payment of differences) by the issuer by reference to levels of an index or prices of an equity or debt security or a basket of such securities or, in the case of single security or basket warrants, physical delivery of a security or basket of securities. A warrant is essentially an option, but the term "warrant" is normally used in the context of a primary offering. Although the holder accepts the credit risk that the issuer will fail to perform, the value of the warrant itself is not related to the value of the issuer, but rather the external index.

It is somewhat more difficult to warrant prospectus information about the asset on which the warrant is based – this is usually not information within the issuer's direct knowledge.

The issuer often protects itself against its liability on the bonds or warrants by hedging contracts in the OTC or exchange markets. It is then necessary to ensure that the calculation of the relevant index level or security prices and any market disruption events and adjustments in the bonds or warrants match the underlying hedging transaction.

Exchange-traded derivatives

15–20   Derivatives in the form of futures and options are traded on numerous exchanges around the world, including specialised futures and options exchanges such as the London International Financial Futures and Options Exchange (LIFFE), the *Marché à Terme International de France* (MATIF) and the Chicago Mercantile Exchange (CME). Exchanges are usually constituted by companies which are ultimately owned by their members or by financial institutions.

Typically all contracts with the exchange must be between members and the exchange. The members are traders whose credit-standing, competence and integrity have been approved by the exchange. Outside investors must contract with a member who then enters into an identical contract with the exchange.

Exchange-traded derivatives are much less flexible than OTC derivatives since they can only be traded in standard trading amounts or "lots" and settled at set maturity dates, for example, on LIFFE only in March, June, September and December in each year.

15–21   The advantages of exchanges are:

-   The terms of contracts and size of lots are standardised, leaving only the prices and transaction costs to be settled each time. Hence liquidity is increased since the contract is more easily saleable and the exchange facilitates a market.

-   The clearing-house may administer the matching and settlement of transactions.

-   The counterparty credit risk is minimised, since under the rules of the exchange the clearing house becomes the counterparty of each party to the original trade. In other words each trade concluded on the relevant exchange is replaced by two trades, one between one party to the original trade and the clearing house and a mirror trade between the clearing house and the other party to the original trade. Traders do not have to make a credit assessment of counterparties since the clearing-house takes the risk from each trader. It is impracticable for traders to make credit assessments of counterparties when deals are done quickly. The exchange's risk is mitigated by security.

- Since all trades between a trader and the clearing-house are mutual, the clearing-house can potentially net the contracts on the insolvency of the trader, thereby reducing exposures: see para 12–12.

- Usually, each member of the exchange has to provide "margin" (i.e. collateral) to the clearing house to the extent that its contracts are out-of-the-money. The contracts are regularly "marked-to-market" (i.e. valued at current market prices) to determine the margin required. Therefore, in theory at least, the clearing house is never exposed to the credit risk of its members. The solvency of the clearing company may be further protected by initial capital reserves and by guarantees granted by its members.

- Contracts of a trader can be easily closed out (assuming sufficient liquidity in the relevant contract) by simply entering into a reverse trade. Since the counterparty is the clearing house in each case, the original and reverse trades are then netted: see para 15–23. In contrast the close-out of an OTC transaction generally requires counterparty consent, which may not always be forthcoming at an acceptable price.

Other functions of exchanges include the possibility that, if a contract is to be physically settled, the exchange can assign the delivery notice to a seller member on a random basis, and the fact that the exchange can maintain market statistics, e.g. as to volumes.

Documentation of swaps and derivatives

Master agreements

In OTC markets, contracts may be tailored to the occasion, but usually parties use standard master agreements covering all transactions between the parties. Each individual transaction is documented by an exchange of confirmations, i.e. written memoranda recording the details of the transaction.   **15–22**

Standard forms have been developed by the International Swap Dealers Association, the British Bankers Association, the Foreign Exchange Committee of New York, the French Banking Association and many others.

The advantages of standard master agreements include (1) the terms have been considered in depth and so are more likely to be legally safe and sophisticated; (2) saving of time and expense compared to documenting each transaction separately; and (3) a master agreement can improve the efficacy of netting and may have received the approval of regulators for this purpose. Contract standardisation is essential in fast-moving markets with huge volumes.

Main terms of master agreements

15–23   The following is a summary list of the main terms in options, futures and interest swap master contracts. Terms appearing only in options and futures contracts, and not interest swap contracts, are asterisked.

> **Master agreement** All individual trades are governed by the master agreement, either automatically or by express incorporation via the confirmations.
>
> **Exercise** Whether multiple exercise possible. Exercise procedure (telephone, writing, etc.). Automatic exercise (if in the money). Exercise days and cut-off times prior to settlement.
>
> **Confirmations** Oral transactions are intended to be immediately binding contracts. Parties must exchange confirmations after each trade. Form and content of confirmations. Time for exchange. Matching of confirmations and procedure if unmatched.
>
> **Payments and settlement** On business days. Netting of settlements. Whether cash settled or physical delivery.
>
> **Tax grossing-up** Each party to gross-up for compulsory tax deductions. Affected party may initiate a voluntary close-out for subsequently imposed taxes.
>
> **Voluntary close-out** A close-out is a cancellation of a futures contract prior to its maturity upon payment of the loss or gain. Sometimes the close-out is effected by the hedger entering into a reverse contract. Express rights of premature close-out are unusual in the OTC markets.
>
> **Example** In March Joe agrees to sell Bill $100 for £50 for delivery in September. In August the price of $100 for delivery in September is £45. Joe then enters into a reverse contract with Bill to sell £45 (the current market price) for $100 for delivery in September. Hence in September Joe pays $100 and receives $100, receives £50 and pays £45. He makes a profit of £5. The effect of the close-out is to fix his profit at £5 in August. If he had waited until September, his $100 may have been worth £55 in which case, by selling at £50 he would have made a loss. In practice, many contracts on exchanges are closed-out in advance in this way.

15–24   **Market disruption** Market disruption can make it difficult or impossible to obtain a price, or at least a fair price, on a valuation date for a forward or option contract on an index, equity share or bond. This is a significant risk for users of the market.

A market disruption clause generally provides that, upon the occurrence of the specified events, the determination of the relevant exercise price of the underlying securities or level of the index will be postponed until the event ceases to exist. Market disruption clauses traditionally cover an inability to obtain the relevant price of the securities or relevant level of the index as a result of suspension or a material limitation on trading in the relevant markets. Some market disruption clauses extend to situations where the relevant price or level has moved excessively either up or down or where liquidity has been impaired for some reason other than an imposed suspension or limitation on trading, i.e. extraordinary events so that the market does not reflect true values.

In the case of physically settled transactions, the agreement distinguishes two types of disruption event: market disruption and settlement disruption. Market disruption occurs, e.g. where a seller is unable to purchase shares in the market to satisfy a call option because the exchange on which the shares are traded has closed unexpectedly. Settlement disruption occurs, for example, where the seller of a call holds the shares it intends to use to cover the call in a clearing system which is shut down because of a systems failure.

Discontinuation or modification of an index The contract may deal with   15–25
discontinuation or modification of an index (e.g. by the inclusion of additional shares) and the events which should trigger these provisions, and specifies who should make the relevant adjustments, e.g. a calculation agent.

Corrections to an index If a correction to an index is announced following a determination and pay-out on an index option, the seller may be obliged to pay or receive extra as a result of the original error.

Adjustments and extraordinary events In the case of single share and bas-   15–26
ket share options, the documentation commonly includes provisions adjusting the strike price or the number of options (or, perhaps, the number of shares represented by a single option) in the event of certain changes affecting the underlying equities. Broadly speaking, the adjustment provisions are designed to give to the buyer any benefits it would have received had it held the underlying equities directly. Adjustments are usually to be made if the shares are sub-divided or consolidated or if shareholders are given benefits, for instance, by a bonus or rights issue or capital redemption. The adjustment provisions will either include a complicated formula outlining the adjustments to be made or, more commonly in the OTC market, give a discretion to a calculation agent to make such adjustments as are necessary to preserve the economic equiva-

lent of the options prior to the relevant adjustment event. The latter generic approach is sometimes adopted for documentation intended to cover shares from markets in various jurisdictions. A formula approach might be favoured where the shares are limited to one jurisdiction. Another approach, where there is an exchange-traded option on the same security or basket as the relevant OTC option, is to link the adjustments provision to adjustments made by the relevant exchange.

Transactions related to shares may be closed out if certain extraordinary events occur in relation to the shares, e.g. the issuer merges, or is taken over or its assets are nationalised, or the issuer goes into liquidation.

These adjustments are not dissimilar to anti-dilution and other protective clauses in convertible bond issues which are summarised in another work in this series on international financial law.

15–27   **Representations and warranties** These are in the usual form, e.g. status, powers, authorisations, no conflict with laws or contracts, official consents, legal validity, no default, no material litigation, and tax representations by each party as to current non-deductibility of tax from payments provided the payee has the stated tax status.

Undertakings Typically these are very limited, e.g. as merely an obligation to maintain official consents and authorisations and to comply with material laws. There are usually no loan agreement covenants, e.g. no negative pledge, no prohibitions on disposals or change of business and no financial ratios. The contract is essentially not a credit contract, is usually much shorter term and does not involve gross amounts, only differences.

15–28   **Termination for illegality** If a party's obligations become illegal, that party may initiate a close-out. All transactions are cancelled and the parties account to each other (after netting) for losses and gains, calculated in a similar way to a default close-out. Loan agreement illegality clauses are reviewed in another work in this series.

15–29   **Events of default** These are the usual events, e.g. non-payment or non-delivery; non-compliance; misrepresentation; cross-default (sometimes limited to transactions of the same type); insolvency events; merger without assumption of trades by an acceptable entity; creditor's enforcement; and extension to guarantors, parties providing security and (sometimes) other group companies. There is a general discussion of events of default in another work in this series.

Close-outs If an event of default occurs, the innocent party can suspend performance and can cancel all existing transactions and the defaulting party must pay (a) amounts already due and unpaid and (b) any extra cost to the innocent party of replacing the contracts in the market. The agreement may simply provide a broad indemnity against losses or alternatively endeavour to fix the losses by a formula in the form of a liquidated damages clause (especially in the case of foreign exchange contracts), e.g. by reference to (an average of, say, at least three) market quotations for replacement contracts. Many contracts provide that the defaulting party is to be credited with profits on the contracts in his favour. The reciprocal amounts due either way are then netted or set off so as to produce a single balance due from one party to the other. For close-out or default netting, see chapter 10 *et seq.*

Force majeure   15–30

Calculation agent One of the parties or an independent third party will make any calculations provided by the agreement. Calculations are to be final in the absence of manifest error. The agent's liability is limited by a conventional exculpation clause.

Miscellaneous Notices; telephone tape-recordings to serve as evidence; default interest; currency indemnity; enforcement costs; set-off; assignments; waivers; remedies cumulative; time of essence.

Law and forum Governing law; jurisdiction; waiver of immunity.

Validity of oral contracts

Contracts are often made orally by dealers over the telephone. The question   15–31
may arise as to whether a binding contract arises at the time the transaction is agreed orally by the dealers or only subsequently either when telex or fax confirmations are exchanged or when more formal documentation is signed by the parties.

This depends on normal contractual principles. For example, a binding oral contract will usually arise at the time a transaction is concluded by dealers on the telephone, assuming that there is sufficient agreement at that time on all the essential terms of the transaction and they intended that there would be a contract (as is usually the case and is usually presumed). A subsequent telex or fax confirmation of the deal simply evidences the oral agreement, although it could vary or supplement the original terms. Any variation or supplement would have to be agreed by each party in order to form part of the contract. In the absence of agreement, the contract remains as it stood prior to the attempted variation or supplement.

Confirmations

15–32   Most ordinary trades in the OTC markets or on the exchanges are sub-sequently evidenced by an exchange of confirmations between the dealers which record the details of the transactions. Obviously this is highly desirable to evidence the terms of the contract if there should be a dispute. Guarantees often have to be in writing. The conflict of laws position is reviewed in another book in this series on international financial law.

The international tendency is to dispense with formalities in commercial contracts. No writing is required for those transactions under English or Dutch law. In 1994, New York abolished the writing requirement in certain cases.

15–33   Tape recordings are often used to evidence the contract. The Court of Appeal in *The Italia Express*, *The Financial Times*, February 12, 1992 laid down applicable principles: broadly, these require the recording party to notify the other party that conversations are being taped.

As mentioned, ideally transactions should be carried out under the umbrella of a master agreement. If not, the parties must supplement their initial oral agreement on the bare terms of the transaction with a full set of representations and warranties, undertakings, default and early termination and other provisions to provide adequate credit and tax protection to each party.

The Bank of England's London Code of Conduct for the wholesale money markets (including off-exchange options and futures on foreign exchange, forward rate agreements, interest rate and currency swaps) set out requirements for expeditious confirmations and documentation.

Capacity

15–34   Some specialised bodies may not have capacity to enter into derivatives transactions. Attention should in particular be paid to the powers of statutory corporations, building societies and similar savings institutions, insurance companies, municipalities, and international organisations.

Regulation of derivatives

Purpose of regulatory regimes

15–35   Regulatory regimes contain rules as to (1) the authorisation of entities which deal in derivative products so as to monitor their solvency, competence and honesty, (2) the investors to whom these products may be sold so as to protect the non-sophisticated (retail) public, (3) the fair conduct of business by traders, e.g. rules against market-rigging, false markets, misleading statements, negligent advice and inadequate documentation, and (4) the level of solvency of traders, e.g. the amount of capital which authorised institutions must maintain against exposures on derivative contracts so as to protect the state (and investors) against systemic risk. An ancillary objective is often to control speculation. Because derivatives span traditional markets, there is sometimes overlap between supervisors or no supervision at all.

As regards supervision of the solvency of participants, the prime risk is that counterparties will become insolvent and not perform, thereby potentially affecting the solvency of the innocent party. The markets on which derivatives are based, e.g. securities and commodities markets, are prone to sudden and volatile price movements so that the value of derivatives contracts can change very quickly. A change in a primary market could affect a much wider range of dealers who have entered into derivatives related to that market. Hence the impact of primary market volatility could have a ripple effect.

Since the regulatory regime is developing rapidly it is not proposed to deal with the topic in any detail as any summary is likely to be almost immediately out-of-date.

Securities regulation generally is described in another work in this series on international financial law.

United Kingdom

Off-exchange options and futures on foreign exchange, forward rate agreements, interest rate and currency swaps, caps, collars and floors entered into between listed institutions or between a listed institution and a wholesale counterparty generally fall within s 43 of the Financial Services Act 1986 ("FSA") and therefore outside regulation under the FSA 1986. Instead they fall within the regulation by the Bank of England of the wholesale money markets and are subject to the Bank of England's London Code of Conduct. **15–36**

However, s 43 of the FSA only applies to certain limited types of "contracts for differences" including transactions relating to fluctuations in interest and currency rates and does not apply to equity-linked or commodity-linked transactions. Accordingly, these types of transaction are subject to FSA regulation including the relevant rules of the self-regulating organisations, e.g. the Securities and Futures Authority. Generally speaking, the more onerous provisions of the rules are disapplied where, as will usually be the case, dealings are only with sophisticated institutions as opposed to private or individual customers.

United States

15–37   The detail is complex. Broadly, the US Commodities Exchange Act prohibits, subject to certain exceptions, the trading of futures contracts and certain types of option contract outside certain designated exchanges (which are regulated by the Commodity Futures Trading Commission – the CFTC). The exceptions are essential to the survival of a viable OTC market in the United States, and they generally exempt dealings between sophisticated investors, subject to conditions.

Derivatives related to securities, e.g. stock index options, may be caught by the US securities legislation – notably the Securities Act 1933 (requiring registration of offers and sales of securities), the Securities and Exchange Act of 1934 (requiring registration of broker-dealers in securities and imposing anti-fraud sanctions) and the Investment Company Act of 1940 (regulating investment companies). The application of these statutes, which are administered by the SEC, to derivatives, the question of whether the SEC or the CTFC regulate which derivatives, and the question of whether interest swaps are regulated at all, is very detailed and fast-changing. Exemptions are usually available for private dealings in wholesale markets between sophisticated institutions, subject to conditions.

A contract with a US institution or having a US contact should contain suitable "private placement" representations in connection with OTC equity and fixed income options with a view to mitigating possible liability under the US Securities Act of 1933.

In the United States, state law may apply to derivatives transactions, including state "blue sky" securities laws and state banking laws.

Other countries

15–38   Elaborate regulatory regimes exist in other countries. These adopt similar basic principles, e.g. Canada and France.

Capital adequacy

15–39   Banks operating in the London market are subject to both Bank of England and EU requirements. Non-bank financial institutions which are members of a self-regulatory organisation will be subject to their SRO's rules regarding capital adequacy. The question of whether parties may treat mutual trades as netted for capital adequacy purposes is the subject of current and pending central bank guidelines and EC directives.

Miscellaneous

Taxation

The tax treatment of derivative products is outside the scope of this work. **15–40**
However, among the issues which should be considered are: withholding
tax, capital gains tax, stamp duty, VAT, eligibility of option premiums for
relief, timing of payments and receipts when an income treatment applies,
and the timing of disposals when a capital gains treatment applies.

Gaming

Contracts for differences and swaps may be deemed to be gaming or wager-   **15–41**
ing contracts which are void under gaming laws, e.g. the British Gaming Act
1845 as amended. These were originally intended to protect individuals and
to control speculators. Often the position depends upon whether the parties
truly intended a commercial sale or borrowing contract as opposed to a contract for differences and, if it is a contract for differences, whether at least
one party had a legitimate commercial interest to protect, e.g. hedging, and
is not merely speculating.

Many states have introduced exceptions to gaming laws in order to facilitate markets and to remove the threat of nullity if either there is a satisfactory alternative system of protection or the contracts are entered into
between sophisticated institutions who do not need the protection of gaming legislation.

In Britain, s 63 of the Financial Services Act 1986 exempts certain contracts relating to investments (which include most options, futures and contracts for differences) entered into by either party by way of business, since
those dealing in investments will usually be subject to the Act's supervision
and regulation of dealers.

Other countries which have exemptions, notably for contracts on
exchanges, include: Belgium (1934, 1939), France (1885 legislation exempting futures contracts extended to derivatives 1985 and see para 11–13 for
changes in 1993), Germany (Stock Exchange Act 1896 as amended in
1989), the Netherlands (1986).

The conflict of laws position is reviewed in another work in this series.

Insurance

Whether derivatives contracts might constitute insurance business requiring   **15–42**
an authorisation is a matter for investigation. Some contracts are literally
similar to insurance because one party pays a premium in return for the

agreement of the other party to pay on a future event which may or may not occur. Derivatives trading does not feel like insurance, although the distinctions are not easy to draw when faced with usual black-letter statutory definitions of insurance. In Britain, insurance business does not require authorisation if it is carried on solely in the course of, and for the purpose of, banking business – because banks are supervised separately. Evidently US insurance regulators do not in the main consider this business to be insurance business.

Margin

15–43   Derivative transactions may be supported by security. The main exchanges commonly require two forms of security, known as "margin", in the form of securities or cash or bank letters of credit. Initial margin must be provided at the inception of the transaction. Variation margin must be provided if market rates on the transaction would cause a loss to the investor if the transaction were closed out immediately. Valuing a transaction according to fluctuations in market rates is known as "marking to market". Margin usually has to be provided on very short notice, and sometimes several times in the day if prices are falling rapidly. A discussion of collateral constituted by investment securities and cash is to be found in another work (on the comparative law of security) in this series on international financial law. For set-off clauses, see paras 7–23 *et seq* and para 14–3.

SELECT BIBLIOGRAPHY

Articles from the journals are not listed. The main English journals on international finance include *International Financial Law Review* (Euromoney), *Journal of International Banking Law* (ESC Publishing Ltd/Sweet & Maxwell), and *Butterworths Journal of International Banking and Financial Law*. Bibliographies referring to the article literature may be found in many of the works on the domestic law of a jurisdiction and this is not intended to be a comprehensive bibliography.

1. Title finance

Tom Clark	*Leasing Finance* (2nd ed) Euromoney
Norton, Gillespie, Rice (eds)	*Corporate Finance Guide* (1990-) Matthew Bender
Judith Mabry	*International Securities Lending* (1992) MacMillan
Howard Rosen (ed)	*Leasing Law in the European Union* (Euromoney) 1994

2. Securitisations

David Bonsall (ed)	*Securitisation* (1990) Butterworths
Eilis Ferran	*Mortgage Securitisation: Legal Aspects* (1992) Butterworths
Tamar Frankel	*Securitisation – Structured Financing, Financial Asset Pools and Asset-Backed Securities* (1991) 2 vols, Little Brown & Co
Henderson & Scott	*Securitisation* (1988) Woodhead-Faulkner
Helena Morrissey	*International Securitisation* (1992) IFR Publishing
Norton & Spellman (eds)	*Asset Securitisation – International Financial and Legal Perspectives* (1991) Blackwell

Schwarcz S	*Structured Finance – A Guide to the Fundamentals of Asset Securitisation* (1990) PLI
Stone, Zissu, Lederman (eds)	*Asset Securitisation: Theory and Practice in Europe* (1991) Euromoney

3. Set-off and netting

Rory Derham	*Set-off* (1987) Oxford
Sheelagh McCracken	*The Banker's Remedy of Set-off* (1993) Butterworths
Francis Neate (ed)	*Using Set-off as Security* (1990) Graham & Trotman
Philip Wood	*English & International Set-off* (1989) Sweet & Maxwell

4. Swaps and derivatives

Paul Goris	*The Legal Aspect of Swaps* (1994) Graham & Trotman
Price and Henderson	*Currency and Interest Rate Swaps* (2nd ed 1988) Butterworths

LIST OF RESEARCH TOPICS

This list contains topics which could be considered for a research thesis or a shorter article. The topics relate to the areas covered by this book. Research topics in relation to the areas covered by other books in this series on international financial law will be found in the volume concerned.

The selection is based on relative originality and usefulness. Topics which have already been extensively covered by the legal literature are not included. In many cases there is an existing literature on the listed topics, but further work is considered worthwhile to develop what has already been achieved or to explore a new approach. If the chosen titles do not appeal, it is hoped that they will be suggestive of those which do. Some of the titles are no more than pointers which would have to be developed into a proper topic. The author would be very glad to receive a copy of any essays which may be written and which are derived from this list. See the address after the Preface.

Title finance

- Title finance and security interests: international survey
- False wealth: recharacterisation of title finance as a security interest: comparative law
- Recharacterisation of financial leasing and hire purchase as security interests: comparative law
- Liabilities of title finance creditors (financial lessors, vendors, etc.)
- Sale and repurchase as an alternative to security interests: comparative law
- Stock borrowing: comparative survey
- Financial leasing and insolvency
- Title finance and corporate rehabilitation proceedings
- International comparison of liabilities of mortgagees and title financiers
- Title finance in groups of jurisdictions (for these and other groups, see the listings in *Comparative Financial Law* in this series):
  - Title finance in common law jurisdictions
  - Title finance in Germanic jurisdictions

- – Title finance in Scandinavian jurisdictions
- – Title finance in Franco-Latin jurisdictions
- – Title finance in emerging (former communist) jurisdictions
- – Title finance in Islamic jurisdictions
- Comparative history of law of title finance
- Taxation of title financiers
- Priorities of title finance compared to priorities of security interests
- Title finance and accessories (aircraft engines, spare parts, additions to investment securities, etc.)
- Financial leases and the rights of sub-lessees
- International conventions and title finance
- Conflict of laws and title finance
- Judicial jurisdiction over title finance

Set-off and netting

- Legal theory of insolvency set-off
- Insolvency set-off as a security interest
- Why no insolvency set-off in Franco-Latin legal systems?
- Set-off and corporate rehabilitation proceedings
- Discriminatory and non-discriminatory netting laws
- Netting against unincorporated trust funds
- Characterisation of financial trading contracts: foreign exchange, swaps and derivatives (see para 10–9 *et seq*)
- Insolvency set-off and insolvency preferential transfers
- Comparative history of insolvency set-off from classical Rome to 1900
- Comparative law of set-off against assignees, attaching creditors and other interveners
- Foreign exchange clearing-houses

Derivatives

- Master agreements for swaps, derivatives and foreign exchange: international survey of the main forms
- Regulation of derivatives
- Use of derivatives in eurobond and other capital markets
- Derivatives and clearing-houses

INDEX

All references are to paragraph number

Accounting,
  recharacterisation, 2–7
  securitisations, 4–5
Africa. *See also* **Liberia; Nigeria; South Africa; Zambia; Zimbabwe**
  insolvency set-off, attitude to, 6–8, 6–9
  netting, 13–6
Aircraft, finance lease of,
  aircraft, meaning of, 3–11
  conditions precedent to grant of, 3–9
  corporate covenants, 3–16
  delivery, 3–13
  documentation, 3–9
  engines, temporary replacement and pooling, 3–20
  exclusion of lessor liability, 3–14
  generally, 1–7, 3–9
  guarantees, 3–5
  indemnity, 3–22
  inspection, 3–16
  insurance, 3–21
  lawful and safe operation, 3–16
  lease period, 3–11
  lessee representations, 3–10
  maintenance, 3–19
  miscellaneous, 3–24
  operational covenants, 3–16
  premature termination, 3–14
  quiet enjoyment, 3–12
  redelivery, 3–23
  rent, 3–15
    payment of, 3–15
  requisition for hire, 3–22
  sub-leasing, 3–18
  termination, 3–23
  title and registration, 3–17
  total loss, 3–21
  transferability, 3–24
  warranties, 3–10

Argentina,
  current account set-off, 6–10
  independent set-off, 7–5
  insolvency set-off, 6–9
Asia and Pacific. *See* **Australia; China; Hong Kong; India; Japan; Korea; Malaysia; New Zealand; Pakistan; Singapore; Sri Lanka; Thailand**
Assignments,
  set-off. *See* **Set-off**
Australia. *See also* **English-based countries**
  netting,
    company arrangement and, 10–23
    default netting, 13–3
    voluntary administration and, 10–23
  set-off,
    contracts against, 7–35, 7–37
    current account set-off and special purpose payments, 7–18
    independent set-off, 7–1, 7–2, 7–3
    insolvency set-off,
      attitude to, 6–8, 10–21
      mandatory, 6–34, 7–18, 7–35
    transaction set-off, 7–20
Austria,
  default netting, 10–20
  executory contracts, rescission of, 10–20
  netting,
    default netting, 10–20, 13–3, 13–6
    legislation, 11–1, 11–2
  security, attitude to, 2–3
  set-off,
    current account set-off, 7–15
    independent set-off, 7–4, 7–8

England—*cont.*
  set-off—*cont.*
    assignments,
      part of debt, of, 8–28 to 8–29
      proceeds, of, 8–31
      successive, 8–30
    conflict of laws. *See* Set-off
    contracts against, 7–35
    contractual set-off against
      interveners, 8–15
    current account set-off, 7–15
      contracts against, 7–17
        special purpose payments,
          7–18
      global set-off between branches,
        8–4
      midnight rule, 7–14
      without notice, 7–16
    debtor cross-claims ineligible for
      set-off,
      foreign immune creditors, 7–40
      time-barred cross-claims, 7–39
    equitable set-off, 7–19, 7–20
    floating charge and, 8–32
    fund set-off, 7–30 to 7–32
    independent set-off, 7–2
      generally, 7–1, 7–2, 7–3
      interveners, against, 8–17, 8–19,
        8–20
      judicial independent set-off, 7–8
      maturity of debt, 7–8, 7–10
      midnight rule, 7–8
      retroactivity, 7–6
      self-help independent set-off, 7–8
    insolvency set-off,
      acquisition of debts in suspect
        period, 6–12, 6–38, 12–22
      involuntary, 6–40
      administration order and, 6–43
      attitude to, 6–8, 10–17, 10–21
      collaterally secured debts, 6–24
      contingent debts, 6–16
      contingent reimbursement
        liabilities owed by insolvent,
        6–18
      debts owing by insolvent,
        contingent debts, 6–16
        discounting, 6–14
        provability, 6–13
      debts owing to insolvent,
        executory contracts, 6–32
        foreign currency debts, 6–33

England—*cont.*
  set-off—*cont.*
    insolvency set-off—*cont.*
      debts owing to insolvent—*cont.*
        secured claims, 6–31
        unliquidated debts, 6–30
        unmatured credits, 6–29
      executory contracts, 6–25, 6–26,
        6–32, 10–17, 10–18
      foreign currency debts, 6–20,
        6–33, 12–28
      mandatory, 6–34, 7–18, 10–17,
        10–22, 11–3
      preferential debts, 6–22
      return of property of estate, 6–41
      secured claims, 6–31
      secured debts, 6–23
      subordinated debts, 6–21, 6–35
      unliquidated debts, 6–30
      unmatured credits, 6–29
    insulated claims, 7–33, 8–25
    interveners. *See also* assignments,
      supra
      assignments of part of debt, 8–28
        to 8–29
      contractual set-off against, 8–16
      independent set-off against,
        8–17, 8–19, 8–20
      intervener rule, 8–9
      netting, 12–6
      transaction set-off against, 8–13
    midnight rule, 7–8, 7–14
    money and property claims, 6–46
      tests of whether money held in
        trust, 6–50
    multicurrency set-off, 7–42, 7–43
    mutuality doctrine, 8–2
    retainer set-off, 7–30 to 7–32
    self-help, 7–43
    solvent set-off, 7–20
    tracing claims, 6–53
    transaction set-off. *See* equitable
      set-off, *supra*
  title retention, 2–3
  undisclosed principal, 8–16
  warranty liability, 1–25
    correspondence with description,
      1–25
    fitness for purpose, 1–25
    implied terms, 1–25
    quality, 1–25

English-based countries. *See also*
    Britain; England
floating charges. *See* **Floating charges**
set-off,
    conflict of laws. *See* **Set-off**
    contractual set-off, 8–15
    current account set-off, 7–18
    independent set-off, 7–2
        interveners, against, 8–19, 8–20
    insolvency set-off,
        mandatory, 6–1, 6–34, 7–18
        suspect period, build-up of set-
            offs in, 6–38
    interveners,
        contractual set-off against, 8–15
        independent set-off against,
            8–19, 8–20
        intervener rule, 8–9
    solvent, 6–1
    time-barred cross-claims, 7–39
    transaction set-off, 7–20
title financing, 1–17
    nemo dat quod non habet, 1–17
    priorities, floating charge, 1–16
Environmental liability,
    generally, 1–28
Exchange controls,
    netting, 12–31
Exchanges. *See* **Derivatives**

Factoring,
    generally, 1–4, 1–15, 2–3
    with recourse, 1–4, 2–3
False wealth doctrine,
    generally, 1–1
    recharacterisation and, 2–2 to 2–5
Far East. *See* **Asia and Pacific**
Finance leasing,
    accounting, 2–7
    aircraft. *See* **Aircraft**
    authorisation as bank, 3–2
    capital adequacy, 3–2
    default, remedies for, 1–26
    equipment trust, 1–7, 1–13
    frustration of contract, 1–28
    generally, 1–7, 3–1
    guarantees, 3–5 to 3–6
    insolvency and, 1–7

Finance leasing—*cont.*
    leveraged leases, 3–4
    manufacturers warranties, 3–3
    operating/true lease distinguished,
        1–7
    recharacterisation, 2–7
    regulation of leasing businesses, 3–2
    remedies for default, 1–26
    residual value, 1–15
    risks, 2–7
    sub-leasing,
        aircraft lease, 3–18
        assignments, 3–7
        freeze on possession of head lease,
            3–8
        possession rights, 3–7
        termination of, 3–7
    tax advantages, 1–7
    warranty liability, 1–25
        manufacturers warranties, 3–3
Financial statements,
    purpose of, 2–7
Finland. *See also* **Scandinavia**
    independent set-off, 7–4
    insolvency set-off,
        attitude to, 6–8, 10–21
        discounting, 6–14
Flawed assets,
    generally, 8–16
    set-off distinguished, 6–5
Floating charges,
    generally, 1–6, 8–32
    priority, 1–16, 2–1, 4–15
    retention of title, 1–16
    set-off and, 8–32
    vesting of title, 1–16
Forfaiting,
    generally, 1–4, 2–3
France,
    derivatives regulation, 15–38
    executory contracts, rescission of,
        10–20, 11–4
    fiduciary assignment, 8–32
    fonds commun de créances (FCC),
        5–22
    fund sponsor, 5–22
    gaming laws, 12–30
    insolvency,
        contract cancellation, 2–11, 11–4

Preferences—*cont.*
  netting,
    compensating contracts, 12–26
    generally, 12–25
    payments to counterparty, 12–27
    settlement netting, 10–7
  prepayments, 10–7 to 10–8
  securitisations, 5–5
Prepayments,
  bonds, 4–12
  preferences, 10–7 to 10–8
  receivables, 4–11
  recharacterisation, 2–11
  suspect period, in, 10–7, 11–12
Priorities,
  floating charges, 1–16, 2–1
  mortgages, 1–17, 2–1
  publicity and, 2–2
  purchase money security interest,
    1–16
  retention of title and, 1–16
Product liability,
  generally, 1–28
Publicity,
  false wealth, 2–2 to 2–5
  priorities and, 2–2
  secret security, 2–2 to 2–5

Qatar. *See also* Middle East
  netting, 13–6
Quebec. *See* Canada

Recharacterisation,
  accounting, 2–7
  capital adequacy, 2–8
  contractual restrictions, 2–10
  false wealth, 2–2 to 2–5
  form, not substance, 2–3
  generally, 1–1, 1–11, 2–1
  insolvency, cancellation on, 2–11
  licensing of credit institutions, 2–11
  moneylending laws, 2–6
  mortgages, 2–1
  prepayment rights, 2–11
  secret security, 2–2 to 2–5
  securitisations, 5–3 to 5–4
  stamp duties, 2–11
  substance, not form,
    publicity required, 2–4

Recharacterisation—*cont.*
  substance, not form—*cont.*
    transaction prohibited, 2–5
  taxation and, 2–9, 2–11
  usury laws, 2–6
Rehabilitation,
  netting and, 10–23 to 10–24
  proceedings, 1–18
    insolvency set-off, 6–42 to 6–45
  statutes, 10–23, 10–24
Republic of Ireland,
  current account set-off, 7–15
  examinership, 1–18
    netting and, 10–23
    sub-leases and, 3–8
  insolvency set-off, 6–8
Residual value,
  generally, 1–15
Retention of title,
  aggregation clause, 1–3
  conditional sale, 1–3
  continued retention clause, 1–3
  current account clause, 1–3
  floating charges, 1–16
  generally, 1–3, 2–3, 2–5
  object of, 1–3
  priority and, 1–16
  repossessions under, bankruptcy
    freezes on, 1–18
  resale proceeds clause, 1–3
Russia,
  insolvency set-off, 6–8
  netting, 13–6

Sale and leaseback,
  generally, 1–9
Sale and repurchase,
  generally, 1–5, 2–3
Saudi Arabia,
  insolvency set-off, 6–8
  netting, 13–6
Scandinavia. *See also* Denmark;
    Finland; Norway; Sweden
  set-off,
    contractual set-off, 8–15
    independent set-off, 8–20, 8–21
    insolvency set-off,
      acquisition of debts in suspect
        period, 6–39
      involuntary, 6–40